NEWFOUNDLAND

AND ITS UNTRODDEN WAYS

BY

J. G. MILLAIS, F.Z.S.

AUTHOR OF "A BREATH FROM THE VELDT," "BRITISH DEER AND THEIR HORNS"
"THE WILD-FOWLER IN SCOTLAND," "THE NATURAL HISTORY OF
THE BRITISH SURFACE-FEEDING DUCKS," "THE MAMMALS
OF GREAT BRITAIN AND IRELAND," ETC.

WITH ILLUSTRATIONS BY

THE AUTHOR

AND FROM PHOTOGRAPHS

LONGMANS, GREEN AND CO.
39 PATERNOSTER ROW, LONDON
NEW YORK, BOMBAY, AND CALCUTTA
1907

Copyright © 2005 by Boulder Publications Ltd.

Library and Archives Canada Cataloguing in Publication

Millais, John Guille, 1865-1931

    Newfoundland and its Untrodden Ways / John G. Millais.

Reprint. Originally published London: Longmans, Green and Co., 1907.

Reprinted: New York: Arno Press, 1967.

hardcover ISBN 0-9738501-2-4
softcover ISBN 0-9738501-0-8

1. Millais, John Guille, 1865-1931—Travel—Newfoundland and Labrador.
2. Caribou hunting—Newfoundland and Labrador. 3. Micmac Indians
—Newfoundland and Labrador—History. 4. Beothuk Indians—History.
5. Whaling—Newfoundland and Labrador. 6. Newfoundland and
Labrador—Description and travel. I. Title.

SK152.N4M64 2005   917.1804'2'092   C2005-905516-2

5 4 3 2 1

Printed in Canada

Boulder Publications Ltd.
11 Boulder Lane
Portugal Cove-St. Philip's
Newfoundland & Labrador
Canada A1H 2K1

CONTENTS

CHAPTER I

INTO THE TERRA-NOVA COUNTRY

CHAPTER II

CARIBOU HUNTING NEAR LAKE ST. JOHN

CHAPTER III

BEGINNING OF THE MIGRATION AT MILLAIS'S LAKE

CHAPTER IV

EXPEDITION INTO NEW GROUND UP THE GANDER RIVER

CONTENTS

CONTENTS

LIST OF ILLUSTRATIONS

LIST OF ILLUSTRATIONS

MAPS

FOREWORD

Since the time of earliest discovery, Newfoundland has enthralled visitors with her wild beauty and abundance. From the first aboriginal adventurers, and through the dramas of European settlement, her riches have been chronicled, prized and fought for. For centuries, Newfoundland lay at the heart of illustrious mercantile ventures, whose wealth accumulated thousands of miles to the east. From her great schools of fish and flotillas of whales poured the makings of dynasties, and her value to the administrators of European industry was as indisputable as it was irreplaceable.

It was Newfoundland's fulsome sea that aroused and fed the passions of survival and commerce; but the great interior wilderness was to also play its part in creating her mystique, and in luring men of adventure and capacity to her shores. A vast landscape virtually unexplored by Europeans until the turn of the twentieth century, the interior of Newfoundland had for millennia been home to scattered bands of native North Americans, most recently the Beothuck and Mi'kmaq peoples. Their cultures were sustained by hunter-gatherer strategies, rhythmically entrained to the island's seasonal ebb and flow of abundance. They took advantage of both coastal and inland resources, forsaking and embracing each world in a pattern tied to natural cycles. Along the coast they sought a diversity of natural foods, but inland it was largely the great herds of Woodland Caribou (*Rangifer tarandus terrae-novae*) that they sought and depended upon.

However, Newfoundland's wild abundance was not only important to native peoples and men of commerce. Men of science and adventure came to observe and record, and to test themselves hunting the land and fishing the inland waters. Naturalists Joseph Banks and John James Audubon visited, as did geologists Alexander Murray and James Patrick Howley. While each of these men came with a specific purpose, a different company of men eventually made their appearance: hunter-naturalists, whose main goal was to pursue the game animals and sport fishes that teemed within the interior. Of these, few have left us with lasting testimonials to their impressions, and fewer still provided such detailed observations as James Guille Millais.

Millais' work, *Newfoundland and Its Untrodden Ways*, here reprinted a full century after its first appearance, is both a classic work of its period and an irreplaceable commentary in our understanding of our island's recent past and our culture's unique signature.

Millais made several trips to Newfoundland between 1902 and 1906. The son of renowned painter Sir John Everett Millais, he was himself an artist, to which may also be added hunter, naturalist and author. He was a particularly keen observer of people, and his treatise on Newfoundland is in many ways as much a commentary on the native and European settler cultures as it is on the wildlife and hunting experiences he had while here. His obvious fondness and understanding of the rough and able rural Newfoundlander is palpable in the text, as is his desire to clear up the ignorance and misconceptions concerning Newfoundland that prevailed in Great Britain and elsewhere.

His admiration for the vitality and endurance of the men who went afield with him, and for those who made their living from the land and sea, is clear in his writing. Their quiet and unassuming dignity, and extraordinary capacity to live from nature, obviously impressed him. Still, his is no whitewash fantasy – no infatuated caricature. He identifies some of the idiosyncracies that, in his view, delayed progress in Newfoundland, and which stemmed from a collective personality and perspective of her citizenry. These observations are of value to all of us who wish for our little nation's greatness.

The fondness his Newfoundland companions developed for him, and their expressed desire to travel with him on future expeditions, attests to the favorable impression that Millais, in turn, had on them. Traveling together for weeks at a time in the interior country, or on whaling ships along the south coast, offered his companions the opportunity to judge him as a man, and Millais obviously passed the test.

Still, it is the chronicle of his glorious days hunting caribou and recording the drama of Newfoundland's interior wilderness that best reflects the heart of Millais' great work. Famed as a hunter-tourist destination, Newfoundland was known for her large herds of Woodland Caribou, and it was in pursuit of these animals that Millais directed his greatest energies. Traveling up the great waterways of eastern and southern Newfoundland, Millais made his way deep into the interior and saw land that, despite four centuries of European settlement, had been viewed by no more than a handful of white men. Paddling and hauling canoes up great rivers, including the Terra Nova, Long Harbour, North-West Gander and Baie D'Est, Millais moved deep into the heart of Newfoundland's southern wilderness. He traversed the waters of Bay D'Espoir, Long Pond, Pipestone Lake and Newfoundland Dog Pond; and east into the Middle Ridge country, across Little Gull, Jubilee, Eastern Meelpaeg and Terra Nova lakes. Immersed in this wild beauty, Millais endured rain, mosquitoes, heat and snow, in pursuit of great caribou trophies and memorable hunting experiences.

Hundreds of arduous miles were covered on foot under the burden of heavy packs; but through it all one has the sense of a man in his element, reveling in the physical and emotional challenge of wilderness hunting. Fatigue was the measure of endurance, and endurance the measure of passionate pursuit.

But Millais was more than a hunter, and *Newfoundland and Its Untrodden Ways* is more than a hunting tale. The text offers valuable insight into the abundance and quality of Newfoundland caribou a century ago, and provides detailed descriptions of landscapes then undisturbed, but now increasingly altered by human intrusion and development. It offers the naturalist and scientist of today a rare study of a species' past. It inspires wonder for the animals themselves and for the land they inhabit, and it implores us to safeguard their existence. The images of caribou emerging ghost-like from the forest, wading through the clear shallows of meandering streams, or swimming the dark waters of great lakes must surely call to each of us. To see them as Millais did – the great stags raking their antlers to a polished bronze on junipers, or charging across the golden wetlands in pursuit of rivals or mates, their heads festooned with rags of bloodied velvet – this fires our imagination and makes us long to share the experience. Such visions inspire wonder for creatures other than ourselves, and from such inspiration comes an enhanced understanding of the connectedness of life itself.

No one could read Millais' work without wishing to visit

Newfoundland's wild places and to experience the wondrous stags that so symbolize the barren lands of this country. To see them rise from the crimson barrens, their black faces and white neck manes offsetting the great curved antlers – branching like tongues of fire and massive in their golden beams – is to behold wild beauty in its purest form. In their power and unspoken wildness they simply belong here and to this place.

On these barrens, Millais understood that man and beast are inseparable. In wild places everywhere the story is whispered, but in Newfoundland it seems to be proclaimed. Millais, like so many other visitors, felt this power and offered its voice in a unique and lasting tribute.

Shane Mahoney, 2005

Note: Reproductions of all colour plates, painted by Millais, are located after the appendix.

INTRODUCTION

THIS volume is a hunter's book dealing mainly with the natural history and the chase of the wild animals and birds of Newfoundland; but in addition to this I have endeavoured to set forth all that goes to make up the daily life of the people of that island and the Micmac Indians, purposely refraining from saying much on social life or of the various phases of Newfoundland politics. Rather have I tried to enter into the life of the true Newfoundlander—the man of the outports—who throughout the year follows a variety of dangerous callings which build up characters of remarkable strength. Of the Micmacs I have made a special study, for their numbers, distribution, mode of life, trapping areas, and characteristics seem to be as little known as when Cormack wrote in 1822. The stories and conversations in this book are genuine, and not worked into the narrative for the sake of padding. I have only added such words and local phrases as served to make the tales consecutive and easily understood.

In no country have I experienced such enjoyable hunting as in Newfoundland. Game I have always found abundant when once the distant hunting-grounds were reached. The men I have employed were one and all the best of companions and good fellows. To have been able to make an exhaustive study of the wild animals of the country, I am deeply grateful to the Bond Government, who, with a broadmindedness one seldom encounters, have granted me the special privilege of a natural history licence. This has allowed me to make extensive journeys which could not otherwise have been undertaken. My thanks are due to Sir Robert Bond, Mr. W. D. Reid, the Hon. John Harvey, the Hon. Edgar Bowring, and Mr. Henry Blair, and especially to Judge Prowse, who has at all times done everything in his power to further the success of my journeys with maps and information. I am also indebted to Mr. Alfred Gathorne Hardy and Mr. John McGaw for the use of photographs, and to the latter for his able collaboration in the map of Central Newfoundland.

The centuries roll by, but our primal passions to chase and overcome the beasts of the field are just the same as when Fingal cried, "The desert is enough for me with all its woods and deer." In his mythological creed the Gael believed that the Spirits of the Dead found delight in pursuing aërial deer over the mountains of the silent land, as well as those of the earth. The poet Ossian, too, says: "The departed children of earth pursue deer formed of clouds, and bend their airy bow. They still love the sport of their youth, and mount the wind with joy." Spiritualists tell us that in the future state we shall continue to lead the lives we have lived here, but with greater joy and wider scope. If this is so, the pleasure of chasing herds of giant megaceros on the astral plane will be no little consolation in the Great Unknown.

J. G. MILLAIS.

HORSHAM, 1907.

"Shadows we are, and Shadows we Pursue"

NEWFOUNDLAND

AND ITS UNTRODDEN WAYS

CHAPTER I

INTO THE TERRA-NOVA COUNTRY

THE Indians say that when Manitou, the Great Spirit, was making the Continent of the New World, he found that he had much material left over in the shape of rocks, swamps, and useless trees. So he formed a big rubbish heap by casting it all into the sea to the north-east, and called it Wee-soc-kadao. Several years after, Cabot discovered and claimed the island for Great Britain, when it was called Newfoundland.

The world in general knows little of Newfoundland, and the average Englishman imagines it to be a little bit of a place somewhere near the North Pole, which, with two or three other colonies, could be safely stowed away behind the village pump. If he has been to school, he will have learnt that it is our oldest colonial possession, famous for codfish, caribou, and national debts. To him the island is inseparably connected with fogs, dogs, and bogs, just as he imagines Africa to be a "mass of lions mixed with sand."

Should he wish to be still further enlightened as to its size, he will find that one cannot watch seals in the Straits of Belle Isle and walk down to tea at St. John's on the same day ; in fact, it is one-sixth larger than Ireland, and has an area of 42,000 square miles. Moreover, it may be of interest to know that

A

the Newfoundlanders are not black or red, but are of a good old English stock, and that they wash themselves twice a day.

In reality Newfoundland is a most attractive place, with its thousands of lakes and pools ; picturesque streams teeming with salmon, trout, and ouananiche ; great open moors and marshes dotted with the ever restless herds of caribou. A wild sea-coast inhabited by thousands of sea-birds ; dense forests of varied and beautiful trees, all contribute to make the island one of the most delightful of all wild countries to the sportsman and the lover of Nature.

There is more than a little fascination, too, in knowing that here is land, within seven days of England,[1] a great part of whose interior has never been trodden by the white man, even by Government surveyors, and that you can plunge into this beautiful wilderness and feel all the delights of wandering at will through the recesses of an untrodden waste, where deer-stalking—and such deer too !—may be pursued. It is perfect, because you can do it all by yourself, and not trust to your guides for this part of the hunt, as the Newfoundlanders, though excellent fellows, are not well versed in the finer points of the art of venery.

Here in these forests and barrens with their natural sanctuaries the caribou are holding their own—one of the few instances where the purely wild game of Europe and America are not decreasing.

With the exception of some of the large animals, Newfoundland contains much the same fauna as Canada. The

---

[1] It is hoped that in two years we shall have a fast route from Ireland to Green Bay in three days. Messrs. Ochs have entered into a contract with the Newfoundland Government to build seventeen-knot steamers which are to run every week. The credit of inventing and the carrying through of this important scheme is entirely due to Mr. H. C. Thomson. After many difficulties and much hard work it is satisfaction to his many friends that Mr. Thomson may see his dreams of a quick-transit route realised,

black bear is still to be found there; wolves are very rare, and lynxes increasing. The principal animal, however, which is of interest to the hunter and naturalist is the woodland caribou (*Rangifer tarandus terræ-novæ*), which is still exceedingly abundant in spite of the persecution to which it is subjected. For its size, Newfoundland to-day contains more of these animals than any other part of the world; and, owing to the nutritive qualities of its super-excellent caribou moss, the deer grow to a great size and in some respects throw out finer horns than any other form of the reindeer in existence, if we except only those of British Columbia, Alaska, and Labrador.

In the autumn of 1900, my friend, Mr. F. C. Selous, the well-known hunter, being disappointed of what he saw of the annual Howley bombardment,[1] made an expedition into the centre of the island, more as a sort of preliminary canter for a future visit than in the hope of catching up the migrating caribou, for which he had arrived too late. He was told that no one could get any distance into the interior owing to the difficulty of carrying food, and that he would most certainly get "bogged" before he had gone far. But difficulties of this kind presented no obstacles to a man who has spent his life in overcoming them; so getting three men who were willing to follow him, he started off from Terra Nova in the middle of November. The tramp was assuredly a hard one, but it was not undertaken in vain.

He killed one nice stag, and found certain signs in the interior near St. John's Lake that convinced him of the

[1] When the September migration sets in, hundreds of camps are set up near the railway to intercept the deer. The sport, if it may so be called, is dangerous alike to man and beast, but there are many brave men in the island. At least four hundred face death annually at Howley, Patrick's Marsh, and the Gaff Topsails, and numerous accidents occur.

existence of a southern herd, whose presence was unsuspected by either sportsman or naturalist, and which never journeyed north in the spring. On this expedition went one Robert Saunders as packer, a thoroughly reliable man, whom he engaged to visit this ground the following autumn, if it were possible to ascend the Terra-Nova River with canoes. So in the September following, Mr. Selous again went to Newfoundland, and after some trouble reached St. John's Lake, where he had excellent sport, killing all his five stags (one of them a splendid forty-two pointer) in one week. He saw but few deer, as the migration out of these east-central forests had only just commenced, but told me he believed that if I could get farther into the country to the west, which was quite unknown, I should probably strike the main trails of a big southern herd. All of this reasoning proved to be quite correct. Mr. Selous kindly engaged Robert Saunders and Jack Wells for me, the two men who had travelled with him, and he spoke of them in the highest terms. Only those who have been a journey or two to distant lands know how important it is to have the very best men in an expedition of this sort; for there are a hundred occasions where just a little extra determination and just a little hard work are necessary to insure success.

I arrived at St. John's on August 23. Mr. Reid, of the Newfoundland Railways, came to meet me, and offered me every assistance in his power. Next day Mr. Withers, a friend I had met in the boat coming out, introduced me to Mr. T. Murphy, the President of the Marine and Fisheries Department, and from him I received a permit to collect for scientific purposes such specimens as I required—an unusual concession on the part of the Government, for which I was most grateful.

ENTRANCE TO ST. JOHN'S HARBOUR

THE HARBOUR FROM THE SOUTH

St. John's is a quiet old-world place, something between a Canadian town and a Norwegian fishing village. On one side of the beautiful harbour are endless cod-flakes and a few sealing vessels, and on the other is the main town, built on the side of a steep hill, where electric trams and lights add the one jarring note; but the whole atmosphere of the place is charming and without noise. They discourage the American spirit there, and the man who wants to hustle soon breaks his heart. Business men stroll down to their offices at ten o'clock, and have always time for a cigar and chat. Life is very much as it was fifty years ago, with the addition of a few innovations which the people have been powerless to prevent. At the summit of the hill are splendid churches, which seem to give a certain tone of distinction to the place, and at the back of these are the houses of the more affluent. Beyond this we find agricultural scenery amidst rolling hills, and still farther, but not too far for a walk, are dense fir woods of peace and beauty. St. John's is really a charming city viewed from a distant spot such as the verandah of Judge Prowse's house, and after several visits I was never tired of this landscape.

But to return to the city. The main thoroughfare is Water Street, where the traveller can obtain anything within reason. The shops are excellent and up-to-date, and the people extremely kind to strangers, especially when they come from the Old Country. The cabs are a feature of the place, and are drawn by wiry little Canadian horses. When you go up the steep hills you feel you ought to be prosecuted for cruelty to animals, and when you come down you wish you had never been born. You drop from the Cathedral to Water Street in one horrible swoop, scarcely reassured by the optimism of the Placentia Irishman who drives you, and who always makes a point of conversing at the most hair-raising corners. "Och! slip is it?" he says; "sure if she was goin' down the sides of hell itself, she'd never put a fut wrong at all, at all. Kim up." In proof of which confidence in his steed, Bucephalus is urged to greater exertions.

If you ask a policeman a simple question, he will not kill you with his club; and even the tramcars are not run for the express purpose of murdering absent-minded strangers as they are in New York. Life, in fact, is quite safe as long as you keep clear of the accommodation train and "hert pie." I have mentioned "hert pie" as a danger to the traveller, because at every meal you get "hert pie," and it is so horribly good that many helpings are sure to follow in rapid succession, to the ultimate ruin of one's digestion.

The daily papers are very funny, especially their items of local news, and—it need hardly be mentioned—a deadly enmity exists between the rival editors. Nevertheless they have several men in St. John's who have done and are still doing excellent press and magazine work on subjects relating to the people of Newfoundland, notably Mr. P. T. M'Grath, of the *Herald*, and Judge Prowse. The articles of these writers are always well-informed and accurate, and abound in the pathos and humour that go to make up the life of the men of the sea. The following items from the St. John's *Howler* are some specimens of another class of literature that daily meets the eye :—

LOCAL HAPPENINGS

Deer were plentiful at Topsail and Quidi-Vidi last week. Ananias P. Slechter of Providence, N.Y., shot a fine 72-pointer.

———

Last night the white steam car belonging to Mr. W. D. Speed ran into a New York drummer on Water Street. The car will have to go to Boston for repairs.

ROBERT SAUNDERS

In future rotten potatoes will not be taken in lieu of monthly subscriptions. Cape Spear farmers please note.

———

Happiness and woe are ever joined together in this Vale of Tears. With the announcement of his election to the constituency of Dirty Bay comes news of the bankruptcy (for the second time) of our esteemed townsman, Mr. Charles Sculpin. Sculpin has had a chequered career, but now that he has drifted into the harbour of peaceful affluence we trust that he will not forget his many long-suffering creditors. The life of Charles Sculpin may serve as a beacon light to the youth of this island, for, without education or the possession of those advantages which are supposed to conduce to success in life, he has reached a high pinnacle of fame, and now his foot is on the ladder he will not look back. There is some talk of making him Minister of Public Instruction.

———

Another example of low thieving from our news column of last night occurs in the pages of the *Terra-Nova Express* this morning. The incompetent ass who sits in the editorial chair of that dull rag will leap with joy when he learns that the item in question relating to the death of the Czar of Russia was quite untrue, and purposely inserted to expose his infamous pilferings.

———

News comes from the Labrador of the safety of the Painter-Glacier expedition which left St. John's on the 10th of this month. After a two days' stay in Battle Harbour, during which time they borrowed several boats and provisions from the missionaries of that place, the gallant explorers are returning in the *Virginia Lake*, and hope to arrive this evening. Forty-two new lakes, five rivers, and six new mountain ranges were noted and charted, and the members of the expedition speak in high terms of the admirable work achieved by Colonel Painter and Major-General Glacier. Arrangements for a lecture tour in the States are already in progress.

———

Miss Clementina Codflakes, who has been visiting friends in town this week, returned to her home at Pushthrough yesterday.

———

Despite the universal impressions to the contrary, the editor of this paper is always prepared to accept cash on subscriptions.

———

Owing to an unfortunate error, we referred in a recent issue to that admirable vocalist, Miss Birdie St. Hilaire, commonly known as "Sure-death Birdie," and now on a visit to the island, as a "bony" warbler, when it was obvious to the meanest intelligence that we meant "bonny." Miss Birdie weighs somewhere about seventeen stone, so she arrived at our office a bit flustered yesterday, and demanded an explanation of our ungallant remarks. We need hardly say that Miss Birdie is far from being "bony," and is a perfect lady in every respect.

My canoes, bed, boxes of stores, and waterproof sheet were all in readiness, so, leaving St. John's by the "accommodation" train at four in the evening, I was turned out at Terra-Nova Station in the darkness at five the next morning.

Close to the line was a wooden building, where a small boy of about eleven met me, rubbing his eyes. He said his name was "Mike," and that he was the stationmaster, his adopted father, one "Tim," being section man of this part of the line. Mike I found was a bit of a character, and I much enjoyed his chatter, and his views on the subject of Newfoundland in particular and life in general.

"You'd like to see my friends?" he said.

"Yes, certainly," I replied, wondering who his friends could be in such an out-of-the-world corner.

"Well, I'll bring them all ter breakfast with you," he remarked drowsily, folding his arms under the telegraphic instrument and composing himself for a few hours' sleep. Poor child, he wanted it; up six nights a week, and with a heavy weight of responsibility on his little shoulders, no wonder he was tired. We snatched forty winks when a cheery voice from the door, saying, "Glad ye've come," woke me to see for the first time Bob Saunders and the handsome face of Jack Wells looking over his shoulder.

It was nearly daylight by the time we had got all our kit down to the river bank, and started the kettle for break-

fast. Then the boxes were broken open, and we soon had
an excellent meal in preparation, whilst Jack Wells littered
the whole stock of supplies on the bank preparatory to sorting
it all carefully in bags for disposition in the two canoes.

It is necessary, perhaps, to say a word or two about my
guides. Robert Saunders is a sturdy little man of about 5 feet
6 inches; his face lined and beard grey, but there was also the
unmistakable appearance that showed the man of vigour and
energy in spite of its fifty-five years, which were all he would
acknowledge. His manner was straightforward and his eyes
possessed the honest and sincere look of absolute truth which
is always found in the best men accustomed to hardship and
the constant struggle with the forces of Nature. "Little Bob"
had led a hard life if any man ever had in Newfoundland. In a
country where toil in all weathers is the common lot, his life had
been one of exceptional self-sacrifice, and what he had passed
through was certainly beginning to tell on him. He had never
spared himself, nor considered that he was more than some
old pack-horse. Twenty years at the "ice fishing" (seal
hunting), and packing and hunting in the woods in winter
on wretched food, will try the strongest man when we consider
that they are constantly wet through and allow their wet
clothes to dry on their bodies. Yet he had survived it all
while many of his fellows had fallen on one side, and thanked
God daily that He was so good to him in giving him food
to eat and a little croft with a good wife down at Alexander
Bay. I liked Saunders very much at once, and still more so
when I got to know him and his single-hearted efforts to do
everything in his power to insure a pleasant time. Of a truth
he looked a bit shy at me one evening when I got out my
note-book to snatch one of his entertaining stories for future
digestion, and I hoped he wouldn't notice it. But after a bit

he evidently considered this no bar to our conversation round the fire, and rattled away when in the mood.

Jack Wells, too, was also a good fellow. He had a handsome, rather melancholy face, with a low, quiet way of talking that was very nice to listen to, and was both amiable and good-natured. I make a special point of this, because four days straight on end barking your shins and slipping off the greasy stones into the Terra-Nova would try the temper of an angel, and not once during those four days did I hear Saunders or Wells swear or complain that the work was beyond their powers, but took the discomfort to be the common lot of man. There is a saying that, to be uncomfortable without being unhappy, you must be either a philosopher or a woman with tight shoes. Yet neither Bob nor Jack were of this category.

After the detestable fog of St. John's it was a great delight to sit and sip one's tea in the pellucid clearness of an autumn morning, waking to the sun's warmth, "Incalescente sole aperuisset diem," as old Cæsar poetically describes the dawn of day. The grey mists were drifting off the river-lake, and showing up the green woods in the distance, when a splendid herring gull came sailing up along the shore and pitched within twenty yards of us. His arrival was the signal for the appearance of the "stationmaster," who with sundry outcries to his various friends was approaching our temporary camp. His "friends," I noticed, were all either four-footed or web-footed, for hurrying at his heels were two dingy-looking mongrels of undeterminable species, a billy and two nanny goats, a sheep, another gull, and far in the rear, endeavouring to keep pace over the logs of an abandoned saw-mill, three adipose ducks. Occasionally "Mike" would stop and call to his strange family in various ways, and they

Jack Wells

Little Mike

hurried along according to the peculiar progression of each. It was a strange and pretty sight, and still more so when the herring gull, uttering his familiar "Waw-waw-waw" of his species, rose, flew up to the boy, and, with outstretched wings, ran before him to our fireside.

"Well, I hope you've brought the entire menagerie, Mike," I said, as we offered to each some acceptable dainty.

"Oh yes," replied the boy, with a sigh, as he poured himself out a cup of tea. "They allus go with me everywhere, 'cept of course to trains. Trains is bad for birds. Goats and sheep can look after theirselves, but birds get kind of silly when ye pets 'em. Thar was Dan, a big gull like Jack thar (pointing to the grey bird), I had 'im fer three year, and he'd 'most come to bed wi' me, but his wing was cut, as I feared he'd go away altogether. But one day that blamed fool of a no account engine-man, Bill Straw, what can't drive for nuts, run over 'im 'ere in Turnover Station and cut his head off. I wudn't 'a' lost that bird fer ten dollars, an' Bill said he'd get me 'nother gull, but he never done it. Damn him," and little Mike sighed and expectorated reflectively.

"How do you get the gulls, Mike?" I inquired.

"Oh, there's plenty come to nest here, summer time, but they're hard to rear. 'Jack' thar, now, I took when he warn't no bigger than a chicken, and though he goes away winter for a few weeks, he allus comes back in the spring with the old grey and white fellers. I've had 'im three years now, and he's a splendid catch. Here, Jack, catch!" said the little fellow, flinging a piece of bacon rind high into the air. The sharp-eyed gull instantly floated aloft, and caught the piece dexterously as it fell. "Tom now thar," continued my visitor, "he can't fly, as he's kind o' crippled in one wing, but he's a great runner;" and to show his skill a piece of biscuit was hurled twenty yards away, to be instantly raced for, but Thomas, half running, half flying, proved an easy victor.

"They're great friends to a feller," said the little man reflectively, adding as an afterthought—"when he ain't at work."

Poor boy, they were about the only friends he had to talk to in all the comings and goings of the seasons, except when a passing hunter or fisherman came to beg an ounce of tobacco of the old section man. Mike helped us to stow the last of our packages aboard, and, wishing us good luck, we left behind the last trace of civilisation in his lonely little figure meditatively "chucking" rocks for the happy family to retrieve.

The morning was beautifully fine, with no wind, so we made good time with the canoes pushing along the river-lake for some miles before we emerged into the large Terra-Nova Lake, a fine sheet of water about five miles long and one and a half across. We landed on a shingly beach to readjust some of the stores that were not riding well, and here I saw the fresh track of a small bear, the first sign of the wild game, always an inspiriting sign to every hunter. At the west end of the lake, where the river comes in, we stopped and had dinner, and then on again up a dead stream for another ten miles or so until sunset. In some places I had to land whilst the men dragged the canoes, and here I always found some fairly fresh sign of caribou. By sunset we halted, and the men made a comfortable camp in a "droke" (belt) of spruce close to the water; and though wet to the waist they did not change their clothes, but lay down soaking as they were, and allowed the fire to steam the water out. Next day it was a case of walking up along the stones of the river bed, while Saunders and Jack dragged the canoes

ROUGH PLACES ON THE TERRA-NOVA

HAULING OVER THE SHALLOWS

through almost continuous rapids the whole day. To prevent the canoes and their contents from being upset the men were constantly in the water hauling and easing the boats, whilst on the slippery rocks they kept frequently slittering and falling up to their middle the whole day. It was coarse work, and of a kind that none save those inured to hardship could stand. "Jest dog's work," was Saunders' definition of the business.

About midday I sat down by the side of the river to await the coming of the boats. They were close at hand when I heard Saunders shout, and looking up stream saw a fair-sized caribou stag rushing through the shallows about 150 yards away. My rifle lay resting against a bush, and by the time I had seized it the chance was gone. After dinner the river bed became worse and worse, and the men had to spend all their time amongst very bad rocks, whilst in one part I had to take to the forest to get along. Newfoundland forest is not like that of any other country; it is principally composed of spruce and white pine, with a few larch, var, birch, dogwood, and maple scattered amongst them; and the trees, though not large, are placed so close together, and interspersed with so many fallen ones, that progress is excessively arduous. I was getting along pretty well when, chancing to stand on the top of a large fallen white pine, the bark suddenly gave way and I was precipitated over a high rock on to the ground. Natural instinct compels one to save one's face with the arm and whatever it holds. Unfortunately in this case the Mannlicher rifle was the interposing object, with the result that the stock snapped clean off close to the action. This was disgusting, to say the least of it, before one had fired a shot. I had no other rifle, and for the moment I doubted my capacity to mend the weapon. Saunders, however, was nothing if not a man of resource, and after a protracted search in his voluminous pockets he produced a screw nail about one inch long, and, with the aid of a tailor's needle straightened in the fire, we drilled a hole in the brittle walnut stock and made a very fair mend of the broken weapon. This was lashed with string until we killed a caribou stag, when a piece of raw hide sewn tightly round the narrow part of the stock made things as firm as ever. However, it gave me a lesson, and I shall not travel again without a spare rifle.

In the evening we reached the beautiful waterfall of the Terra-Nova, where, after a stiff portage straight up the hill and through the forest, we made camp again near the upper river. The early part of the next day was especially hard on the men. The stream was so swift and rocky that the canoes had to be dragged every inch of the way for the two miles that intervened before Ollygo Lake was reached. I, too, had no little difficulty in making way through the forest, for the deep water on the forest edge often forced me to take to the hillside.

Along this part of the stream I saw many fritillary butterflies, and at the entrance of Mollygojack Lake there was a fair number of birds. Belted kingfishers, goosanders, red-breast mergansers, Canada geese, and yellow-shank sandpipers were occasionally moved on the river; whilst on the lakes of Mollygojack and St. John's I noticed a good many dusky ducks (*Anas obscurus*), the northern form of our mallard. Grebes, probably Sclavonians, interested me also, great northern divers, buzzards, peregrine falcon, merlin, and for the first time the magnificent bald-headed eagle, or bird of Washington, made its appearance. In the woods we heard the rattle of and occasionally saw the beautiful golden-winged and three-toed woodpeckers, whilst in camp at night the horned eagle-owl serenaded us with his melancholy hoots. Twice I flushed these big birds in the daytime, and they flopped slowly away as if disturbed out of a siesta. Sometimes as I crept through the wood at dawn something would impel me to look up, and meet a pair of great golden eyes that surveyed the intruder with intense disapproval. The hawk-owl, too, was sometimes seen perched on a withered tree, from which point of vantage he searched the ground for voles. As yet we had not met that delightfully cheeky fellow, the Canadian wood jay, moose-bird, or whisky jack, as he is variously named; but of him more anon.

Mollygojack Lake is a fine large sheet of water, roughly speaking about twenty miles round, and the surrounding forests are a great summer house of the woodland caribou. It has one or two pretty little islands, where the great northern divers evidently breed (I saw two females with young ones close to them), and it took us till evening to reach the western end where we camped for the night. Here was plenty of fresh sign of caribou, but not too fresh, so we decided not to hunt but to move on next day to St. John's Lake, on which our hopes were centred, at the camp where Selous had killed his deer.

We made an early start the next day, August 28, up the eight or ten miles of lake-river which separates Mollygojack from St. John's Lake, and which was only difficult for short distances. Our midday dinner was taken on the river about half-way, when shortly after re-starting I saw something move behind a large rock on the left bank about 300 yards up stream. In another moment the head of a doe caribou appeared and again disappeared, so we rushed the canoe under the shelter of a projecting headland, and I landed. After leaving Saunders and signalling to Jack to keep out of sight,

I crawled up along the stones, and immediately saw the doe standing in nearly the same spot. She was still 250 yards away, so to make sure of our meat I took advantage of another miniature headland, and crawled on to make a closer acquaintance. There was little cover, but the caribou took no precautions for her safety, and allowed me to come within 80 yards without once raising her head for observation. A nice rock to shoot from presented itself at this corner, so, pressing the trigger, I had the satisfaction of seeing the deer drop dead in her tracks. On a fresh trip, with new men, it is always a satisfactory thing to kill the first animal at which you fire, as it gives confidence to your followers and creates a favourable impression, so I took as much care over the easy shot at that wretched doe as if I was firing at a fifty-pointer.

We had some fresh meat now, and after photographing the animal we cut it up, and then paddled away in high spirits for St. John's Lake, which we reached about five o'clock. We had made good progress, but desired to complete the whole distance to the end of the lake before nightfall, so pressed on. On the way up the lake we passed four more doe caribou gazing into the water, like some others of their sex, apparently lost in admiration of their loveliness as reflected by Nature's mirror. One old lady allowed us to go by within 15 yards, and seemed in nowise upset at our presence, as she had not got our wind. At last our temporary Ultima Thule hove in sight, the river mouth at the west end, and I immediately recognised the Indians' observation tree, which Selous had told me to look out for—a gnarled and bent old white pine, standing out in picturesque solitude from the forest of spruce. As we moved up to the landing-place a caribou doe was wading in the shallows about 300 yards away. She swam slowly across

A FINE OLD PINE, ST. JOHN'S LAKE

A MICMAC WIGWAM

the glassy river, and, after shaking herself like a great dog, wandered up into the timber right past the very spot where we were to make our home for a week.

There is little doubt that a family party of Micmacs came annually to this corner of the lake, and trapped during the winter. Next morning Saunders and I, poking about in the forest close at hand, came on their house, which had been used during the past season. It was a carefully constructed "tepee" of spruce poles, beautifully lined inside with birch bark and quite impervious to rain or snow. We saw here, too, a large hollowed pine which had been cut out for a trough, in which tanning had been made for curing caribou skins. Those skins had been then sewn together, and used as a covering for a canoe. Saunders assumed that these were some of the regular hunting Indians, which come all the way from the south coast in the late fall.

Later on in this work I give an account of the Micmacs, but a word or two about their predecessors may not be out of place. Recorded history enables us to go back as far only as the first appearance of European explorers, who visited the island about four hundred years ago. The "Red Indians," or Beothicks, were then the occupants of the soil, and they were said to resemble in every respect the indigenous tribes of North America, and were probably of the same stock as the Algonquins.

The Beothicks had straight black hair, high cheek bones, small black eyes, and a copper-coloured skin. In hunting and fishing modes they also resembled the natives of the neighbouring continent, and their weapons, wigwams, and domestic utensils were also similar. Ethnologists are not quite agreed as to the nature of their language, but it is generally accepted that they were probably a small branch of the warlike Algonquins, who at that time were the masters of the north-eastern continent of Canada.

Cabot landed on Newfoundland in 1497, and found the Beothicks à numerous and powerful race. Having practically no enemies, and being naturally ingenious and gentle mannered, he found them extremely friendly and anxious to show the white voyagers any hospitality. The rivers and seas of the country at that time swarmed with fish, and through the forests and barrens the countless herds of caribou roamed in comparative security. Consequently the Indians practised no agriculture, but lived a life of, to an Indian, great luxury, without the necessity of any form of toil. But after a short few years of peace the same old story was repeated here, as everywhere in the world, where the white man comes and wishes to make the country all his own. Quarrels arose between the whites and the reds, followed by the usual deeds of violence, and a bitter enmity that could only end in the ultimate extermination of one race or the other. As usual, too, the white man, with his superior brains and superior weapons of destruction, had the best of it. Yet the Beothicks held out through some three hundred years, during which time they were often treated with the greatest brutality, which was as frequently returned with equal savagery.

When the white men had at length exterminated two-thirds of the Indians, they became filled with a commendable spirit of conciliation, and from 1760 to 1823 many attempts were made to live on friendly terms with the men of the woods. But it was too late. Experience had taught them to hate the white man with a deadly hatred, and they now, after centuries of war, found it impossible to accept any advances of kindness. Broken and in despair the last of the Beothicks retreated to the shores of Red Indian Lake, where they perished slowly one by one till not a single member was left.

It is necessary to say a few words concerning the first writer upon the Beothicks. Captain Richard Whitbourne, of Exmouth, after having served as captain of his own ship against the Spanish Armada in 1588, made many voyages to Newfoundland for the purpose of fishing and establishing colonies there. He made his first voyage to that country in 1582, with the intention of trading with "the savage people" and killing whales. He says of it: "But this our intended Voyage was overthrown by the indiscretion of our captaine, and faint-heartedness of some Gentlemen of our Company. Whereupon we set sail from thence and bare into Trinity Harbour in Newfoundland: where we killed great store of Fish, Deere, Beares, Beavers, Seales, Otters, and such like, with abundance of sea-fowle: and so returning for England, we arrived safe at Southampton."[1]

On his second voyage in 1586 the gallant Captain had the command of a "worthy shipp, set forth by one Master Crooke of Southampton." He witnessed the taking possession of Newfoundland by Sir Humphrey Gilbert in the name of Queen Elizabeth. After this he made many interesting voyages to Newfoundland. One of the most striking passages in his book relates to his meeting and detention by the famous arch-pirate, Peter Easton, "whom I did persuade much to desist from his evil course." It is interesting to note that in 1608 one of Captain Whitbourne's ships was intercepted

[1] "A Discourse and Discovery of Newfoundland, with many reasons to prove how worthy and beneficiall a Plantation may be there made, after a far better manner than now it is—together with the laying open of certaine enormities and abuses committed by some that trade to that countrey, and the means laid down for reformation thereof." By Capt. Richard Whitbourne of Exmouth in the county of Devon. London, 1622. Republished in 1870 at Guildford by Mr. Thomas Whitbourne under the title of "Westward Hoe for the New-found-land."

by an "English erring Captaine (that went forth with Sir Walter Rawleigh)." The distinction between "an arch-pirate" and "an English erring Captaine" does not seem to be very clear.

Another point in this quaint book which he wrote upon his travels is of great interest to naturalists, for it refers to the Great Auk (*Alce impennis*), now, alas, extinct, but which formerly existed in great numbers on Funk Island, off the north-east coast of Newfoundland. These birds were always known as "Penguins" by the inhabitants, and I once met an old fisherman whose father possessed a stuffed specimen. He himself used to ride on the back of the bird as a little boy, little knowing that within his lifetime such things would be worth four and five hundred pounds.

"These penguins," says Captain Whitbourne, "are as bigge as geese, and flye not, for they have but a little short wing, and they multiply so infinitely upon a certaine flat island, that men drive them from thence upon a boord, into their boats by hundreds at a time: as if God had made the innocency of so poore a creature to become such an admirable instrument for the sustenation of man."

He thus describes the Beothicks and their habits:—

"For it is well knowne, that they are a very ingenious and subtill kinde of people so likewise are they tractable as hath beene well approved, when they have beene gently and politically dealt withal: also they are a people that will seek to revenge any wrongs done unto them or their woolves, as hath often appeared. For they marke their woolves in the eares with several markes, as is used here in England on sheepe, and other beasts, which hath been likewise approved: for the woolves in those parts are not so violent and devouring as woolves are in other countries. For no man that I ever

MARY MARCH

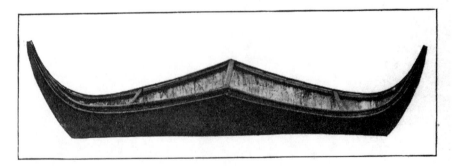

BEOTHICK CANOE

(*From the Model in the Edinburgh Museum*)

heard of, could say that any woolfe, leopard,[1] beare or any other beasts did ever set upon any man or boy in the New-found-land, although divers times some men have been by themselves in the woods, when they have suddenly come near unto them and those Beasts have presently upon sight of any Christian speedily run from them."

This close association of a friendly character between dogs and wolves has long been known in Newfoundland, where amongst early writers it seems to have been a matter of surprise. Writing in 1622, Captain Whitbourne says that the wolves frequently came down to the seashore when his men were labouring amongst the fish, and that on each occasion his mastiff dog ran to them. "The one began to fawne and play with the other, and so went together into the Woods, and continued with them, every of these times, nine or ten dayes and did return unto us without any hurt. Hereof I am in no way superstitious, yet is something strange to me that the wild beasts, being followed by a sterne Mastiff-dogge, should grow to familiaritie with him, seeing their natures are repugnant : surely much rather the people by our discreet and gentle usage, may bee brought to society being already naturally inclined thereunto."

Later he gives some particulars of utensils, weapons, canoes, &c., used by the Indians :—

"For it is well Knowne, that the Natives of those parts have great store of red Okar, wherewith they use to colour their bodies, Bowes, Arrowes and Cannowes, in a painting manner : which cannowes are their Boats, that they use to go to Sea in, which are built in shape like the Wherries on the River of Thames, with small timbers, no thicker nor

---

[1] This plainly refers to the existence of the Canada lynx (*Lynx Canadensis*) in the island at this date.

broader than hoopes: and instead boords, they use the barkes of Birch trees, which they sew very artificially and close together, and then overlay the seams with Turpentine, as Pitch is used on the Seams of Ships and Boats. And in like manner they use to sew the barkes of Spruise and Firre trees, round and deepe in proportion like a Brasse kettle, to boyle their meat in, as it hath been well approved by divers men: but most especially to my certaine knowledge, by three Mariners of a Ship of Tapson, in the county of Devon: which Ship riding there at anchor neere by mee, at the Harbour called Heartsease, on the North side of Trinity Bay, and being robbed in the night, by the Savages, of their apparell, and divers other provisions, did the next day seeke after them, and happen to come suddenly where they had set up three Tents, and were feasting, having three such Cannowes by them, and three pots made of such rinds of trees, standing each of them on three stones boyling, with twelve Fowles in each of them, every Fowl as big as a widgeon, and some so big as a Ducke: they had also many such pots, so sewed and fashioned like leather Buckets, that are used for quenching of fire, and those were full of the yolkes of Egges, that they had taken and boyled hard, and so dryed small as it had been powder Sugar, which the Savages used in their Broth, as sugar is often used in some meates. They had great store of the skins of Deers, Beavers, Beares, Seales, Otters, and divers other fine skins, which were excellent well dressed: as also great store of several sorts of flesh dryed, and by shooting off a Musket towards them, they all ran away naked, without any apparell, but onely some of them had their hats on their heads which were made of seale skinnes, in fashion like our hats, sewed handsomely, with narrow bands about them set round with fine white shells.   All their three Cannowes, their flesh, skins, yolkes of Egges, Targets, Bowes and Arrowes, and much fine Okar, and divers other things they tooke and brought away and shared it amongst those that tooke it, and they brought to me the best Cannowe. . . ."

Captain Whitbourne tells us that in 1622 the distribution of the Beothicks was over the north-west parts of the island, and on the east side as far south as Trinity Bay. Two hundred years later when Cormack wrote, the Indians had retired altogether from White Bay, Green Bay, and the east coast, but were still in the north and central parts.

Whitbourne states that in his time the ships did not fish in Trinity Bay, partly on account of the rocky ledges, but chiefly because "the savage people of that Countrey doe there inhabit : many of them secretly every year, come into Trinity Bay and Harbour, in the night-time, purposely to steal Sailes, Lines, Hatchets, Hooks, Knives and suchlike."

On page 2 Whitbourne says : "The naturall Inhabitants of the Countrey, as they are but few in number : so are they something rude and savage people : having neither knowledge of God, nor living under any kinde of civill government. In their habits customes and manners they resemble the Indians of the Continent, from whence (I suppose) they come : they live altogether in the North and West part of the Country, which is seldome frequented by the English : but the French and Biscaines (who resort thither yearly for the Whale fishing, and also for the cod fish) report them to be an ingenious and tractable people (being well used) they are ready to assist them with great labour and patience, in the killing, cutting and boyling of Whales and making the traine oyle, without expectation of other reward, than a little bread, or some such small hire."

Later Lieutenant John Cartwright, a brother of the famous Captain Cartwright of Labrador, was sent on an expedition up the Exploits River in 1768, and obtained a little information of the habits of the Red Indians.[1] Soon after this Captain Buchan went twice up the Exploits to Red Indian Lake, and on the first occasion had two of his marines killed.

In the winter of 1810 Captain Buchan forced an interview with the Beothicks on Red Indian Lake. Hostages were exchanged, but on the Captain retiring to bring up some presents which he had left at a depôt, the Indians became suspicious, fearing he had gone to obtain reinforcements with which to surround and capture them. In consequence they murdered the two white men that had remained in their hands and retired into the interior. Captain Buchan was mystified to find that the Indians had departed on his return, and the whole story was not made clear until 1828, when the particulars were explained by Shawnawdithit.

In the year 1828 there was a society in St. John's known as the Beothick Institution, whose business it was to communicate with and if possible civilise the Red Indians, as well as to ascertain the habits and history of that "unhappy race of people." The President was W. E. Cormack, who took a kindly interest in the fate of the Indians, and who became so interested in them that he undertook a journey to Red Indian Lake for the purpose of establishing communication with the Red men. On October 31, 1828, he entered the country at the north of the Exploits in company with three Indians—an Abenakie from Canada, a mountaineer from Labrador, and a Micmac from the south coast of Newfoundland. He took a north-westerly route to Hall's Bay,

[1] Report of the Beothicks, MS. by Lieutenant J. Cartwright, 1768.

which he reached in eight days, passing the country interior from New Bay, Badger Bay, and Seal Bay, a district well known as the summer resort of the Indians. On the fourth day he found traces of the savages in the shape of canoe-rests, spear-shafts, and rinded "vars,"—"This people using the inner part of the bark of that kind of tree for food." On the lakes near New Bay were the remains of winter *mamateeks* or wigwams, each intended to hold from six to twenty people. Close to these were oblong pits about four feet deep, designed to preserve stores, &c., some of them being lined with birch rind. In his report[1] Cormack mentions the peculiar vapour baths of which he also found traces at this place, and whose use was afterwards explained to him by Shawnawdithit. "The method used by the Beothicks to raise the steam, was by pouring water on large stones made very hot for the purpose, in the open air, by burning a quantity of wood around them ; after this process, the ashes were removed, and a hemispherical framework, closely covered with skins to exclude the external air, was fixed over the stones. The patient then crept in under the skins, taking with him a birch-rind bucket of water, and a small bark dish to dip it out, which, by pouring on the stones, enabled him to raise the steam at pleasure." Shawnawdithit explained that the steam bath was only used by old and rheumatic people.

After traversing the country on the high lands south of White Bay without finding further traces of the Indians, whom he had expected to encounter near the passes of the deer now in full migration, Cormack travelled to Red Indian

[1] Report of W. E. Cormack's Journey in Search of the Red Indians in New-foundland. Read before the Beothick Institution at St. John's, Newfoundland. Communicated by Mr. Cormack, Edinburgh. *New Phil. Journ.*, vol. xx., 1828–29, pp. 318–329.

Lake, but to his great disappointment, he found it had been deserted for some years by the Indians, "after being tormented by Europeans for the last eighteen years." After further search on the Exploits River, Cormack returned to the north on November 29 without having seen a single Red Indian. Amongst other interesting relics of these people which Cormack presented to the Beothick Institution was a vocabulary of the Beothick language, consisting of two hundred to three hundred words. This was supposed to have been given by Cormack to a Dr. Yates, but I have failed to trace the list, or the descendants of the recipient, which would go far to prove "the Beothicks to be a distinct tribe from any hitherto discovered in North America."

During his stay at Red Indian Lake, Cormack found many recent traces of the Beothicks which show their modes of life, treatment of the dead, methods of hunting deer, &c.

"One difference," he says, "between the Beothick wigwams and those of other Indians is, that in most of the former there are small hollows, like nests, dug in the earth around the fire-place, one for each person to sit in. These hollows are generally so close together, and also so close to the fire-place and to the sides of the wigwam, that I think it probable these people have been accustomed to sleep in a sitting position." He also found a large handsome birch-rind canoe, about 22 feet in length, comparatively new.[1] In its construction iron nails had been used, doubtless stolen from the white settlers.

John Hinx, a half-breed Micmac, who was present when

---

[1] I am enabled to give a photograph of the model of this curiously shaped canoe by the courtesy of the Director of the Royal Scottish Museum, Edinburgh. In form it is quite unlike the birch-bark canoes used by the Canadian tribes, being high raised at the bow and stern. The interior has sheets of birch rind. The exterior is of deal planking.

NEWFOUNDLAND CARIBOU.

Tarandus rangifer terrae-novae.

several of the old wigwam sites were unearthed, has told me that the floors of these abodes were sunk a foot or two beneath the ground, which was polished smooth and had turf seats. On this floor the family slept and kept their fire alight, one member always being deputed to keep watch. The lower part of the skin covering was raised from the ground, and all vegetation removed for a considerable distance, so that in case of surprise the Indians could bend low without fear of being seen or shot, and send a flight of arrows at any invader.

Their cleverness is shown by the way in which they constructed their retreat. A tunnel, sometimes 30 and 40 yards long, was burrowed from the wigwam into the woods, and by this means the Indians retired when the fight went against them. They used pots of iron and a few other simple utensils.

"Their wooden repositories for the dead," says Cormack, "are what are in the most perfect state of preservation. These are of different constructions, it would appear, according to the character or rank of the persons entombed. In one of them, which resembled a hut 10 feet by 8 or 9, and 4 or 5 feet high in the centre, floored with squared poles, the roof covered with rinds of trees, and in every way well seasoned against the weather inside, and the intrusion of wild beasts, there were two grown persons laid out at full length on the floor, the bodies wrapped round with deer-skins. One of these bodies appeared to have been placed here not longer ago than five or six years."

Cormack's most surprising discovery in one of these dead-houses was "a white deal affair, containing a skeleton neatly shrouded in white muslin. After a long pause of conjecture how such a thing existed here, the idea of *Mary*

March[1] occurred to one of the party, and the whole mystery was at once explained."

In the cemetery were deposited alongside the bodies two small wooden images of a man and a woman, doubtless meant to represent husband and wife, also a small doll, a pathetic emblem of Mary March's child which died two days after the capture of its mother; several small models of canoes, two small models of boats, an iron axe, a bow and quiver of arrows, birch-rind cooking utensils, and two fire-stones (radiated iron pyrites), from which the Beothicks produced fire by striking them together.

Another mode of sepulture described by Cormack was for the body of the deceased to be wrapped in birch rind, with his property placed on a sort of scaffold about 4½ feet from the ground, in a manner still employed by some of the Western American tribes. A third method was to bend the body together and enclose it in a kind of box laid on the ground, and a fourth to simply wrap

---

[1] Mary March, so called from the name of the month in which she was taken, was a Red Indian woman who was captured at Mary March's Brook, near Red Indian Lake, by an armed party of Newfoundlanders in March 1809. This was the immediate result of the Government's offer of a reward to any persons who would bring a Red Indian to them. Her husband was cruelly shot, "after nobly making several attempts, single-handed, to rescue her from the captors, in defiance of their fire-arms and fixed bayonets." The body of this red hero was found by Cormack resting beside his wife in one of the cemeteries at Red Indian Lake. The following winter, Captain Buchan was sent to the River Exploits, by order of the local government of Newfoundland, to take back this woman to the lake where she was captured, and if possible at the same time, to open friendly intercourse with her tribe. But she died on board Captain Buchan's vessel at the mouth of the river. Captain Buchan, however, took her body to the lake, and not meeting with any of her people, left it where they were afterwards most likely to meet with it. It appears the Indians were this winter encamped on the banks of the River Exploits, and observed Captain Buchan's party passing up the river on the ice. They retired from their encampment in consequence, and some weeks afterwards went by a circuitous route to the lake to ascertain what the party had been doing there. They found Mary March's body, and removed it from where Captain Buchan had left it to where it now lies, by the side of her husband.

The First Stag's Head (in Velvet)

A Good Stag

the body in birch rind and cover it with a heap of stones.

Cormack thus describes the long deer fences made by the Beothicks, and their method of killing the caribou: "On the north side of the lake, opposite the River Exploits, are the extremities of two deer fences, about half a mile apart, where they lead to the water. It is understood that they diverge many miles in north-westerly directions. The Red Indians make these fences to lead and scare the deer to the lake, during the periodical migration of these animals; the Indians being stationed looking out, when the deer get into the water to swim across, the lake being narrow at this end, they attack and kill the animals with spears out of their canoes. In this way they secure their winter provisions before the severity of that season sets in. . . . What arrests the attention most, while gliding down the stream (the Exploits), is the extent of the Indian fences to entrap the deer. They extend from the lake downwards, continuous on the banks of the river, at least thirty miles. There are openings left here and there in them, for the animals to go through and swim across the river, and at these places the Indians are stationed, and kill them in the water with spears, out of their canoes, as at the lake. Here, then, connecting these fences with those on the north-west side of the lake, is at least forty miles of country, easterly and westerly, prepared to intercept the deer that pass that way in their periodical migrations. It was melancholy to contemplate the gigantic, yet feeble, efforts of a whole primitive nation, in their anxiety to provide subsistence, forsaken and going to decay."

A Red Indian woman, named Shawnawdithit,[1] was living near the Exploits River with some white people at this

---

[1] Sometimes called *Shandithit*.

time, and through the interest of the Beothick Institution she was sent to St. John's.

Cormack kept this woman in his house all the winter of 1828, eliciting information from her and making notes, which have most unfortunately been lost. After leaving Cormack's house, Shawnawdithit went to reside with a merchant at Twillingate, where she lived for a few years. She never became a Christian, and at her death was buried in a log hut on the banks of the Exploits, where the woodpeckers and the passing deer are the only visitors. A portrait, albeit a very poor one, was taken of Mary March by Lady Hamilton, and is of interest as the only representation of a Beothick in existence. I am enabled to give it by the kindness of Mr. Albert Bradshaw.

CHAPTER II

CARIBOU HUNTING NEAR LAKE ST. JOHN

WITH such excellent sign of deer on all sides we made sure that it would not be long before we saw our first stag, but in this we were woefully disappointed. We stayed a week in Selous' camp, tramping miles every day up the river, through the forest, and on to the high ground, without seeing a single stag, and only one fresh track of a big fellow, and of him, I believe, I just caught a glimpse as he disappeared into a dense alder bed. Soon I became weary of thrashing around in this forest-bound country, and sighed for a place where I could wander about in the open and look for things with my telescope. Far to the north-west I could see with the glass an inviting-looking country where the white men had never been— so Saunders said, and Saunders had penetrated farther than any one in the swampy regions. So we decided to move on, as my guide said we could easily cut a road with the axe up to the high ground, and that we should be nearly sure in time to strike the main leads of the caribou that were known to journey south-west from the eastern forests. It sounded inviting, so we left the next morning, September 4, and paddled to the northern corner, where a brook came in. A disposition of the stores was soon made, and we started, carrying bed, waterproof sheet, and food for three days. This was enough for the present, for if things looked well Jack could keep coming back to the lake to fetch whatever we wanted. Saunders went in front with his axe and cut a path

for us to follow, but as we advanced to the higher ground
this became unnecessary owing to the presence of heavily
indented caribou leads, which got broader and more numerous
as we proceeded. Near the upper edge of the forest the
deer roads were so numerous and had been so well used
for years past that Saunders was in the highest spirits, for
these, he said, must be the main trails of which he had sus-
pected the existence somewhere in the neighbourhood. About
midday we emerged on to beautiful undulating high ground
covered with blueberries and a short bush called locally
"goudie." We had hardly done so when four caribou
does came to look at us. A little farther on, two others
came for a close inspection, and though we now wanted
meat badly (having eaten the best part of the doe I had
previously killed), I resisted the temptation to fire, as I
hoped to see a stag very soon.

Everything now looked so promising that I sent Jack
back to the boats to get more supplies, having determined
to make a standing camp here. Even if I waited a month,
I knew the stags were bound to come this way sooner or
later.

After a hurried meal, Saunders and I set off to find the
highest point above our camp, and soon selected a large
stone from whence a splendid view could be obtained for
three or four miles in any direction. Many of the main
trails led up from the woods below, and anything moving
out must be detected. Nor was there long to wait. Almost
as soon as I had got the glass out I spotted a doe and a
calf walking uphill, then another snow-white object on the
edge of the woods revealed another female, and a few minutes
later two more were to be seen moving slowly uphill about
a mile to the left. The glass was here of the greatest

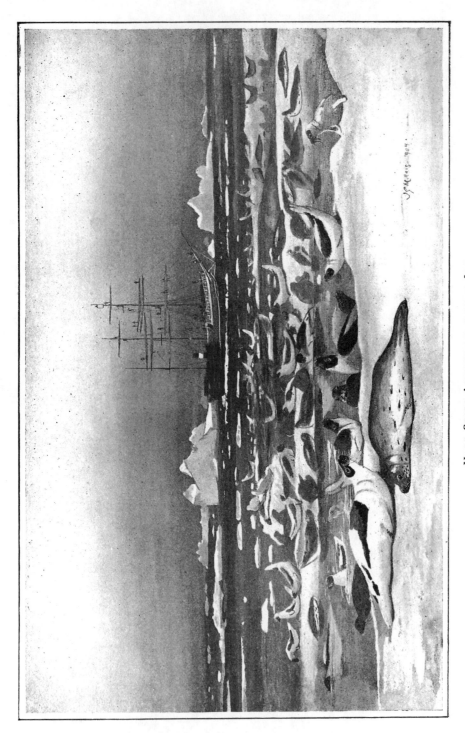

HARP SEALS ASSEMBLING ON THE ICE

(*From Millais's "The Mammals of Great Britain and Ireland"*)

assistance, for I counted no less than fifteen doe caribou coming out of the woods before my companion had seen one. The migration of the females had evidently just commenced, for they all passed uphill to the west, and then as I afterwards found, swung away to the south-west.

It was growing late, but was one of those perfect autumn evenings that tempt a man just to sit and enjoy the play of light and shade on distant hill and forest. Saunders talked away of his seal-hunting days, and I was quite happy enjoying the landscape, working the glass or watching the gaggles of Canadian geese that frequently passed us, for this country was evidently a great breeding-ground. In a little while it would be too dark to see, and there really seemed no chance of a stag showing up. It was too warm, and they were all up by this time in the forests, munching the moss that grows so luxuriantly within a few yards of their now well-worn beds.

"A' don't believe there's a blessed stag outside the woods in Newfun'lan'," said Saunders, yawning as he lay on his back chewing blueberries and, as he expressed it, "tired o' lookin'."

"Well," I replied, "I believe there's one anyhow, Bob," for at that moment I had caught in the glass the white stern of a deer feeding about a mile below in a little marsh. A small bit of horn stuck out at one side, though his head seemed half-hidden in a peat-hole. I kept the glass fixed, and in a minute he turned sideways and revealed the form and antlers of a caribou stag, and a big one too. At last! There he was, feeding right in the open and the wind perfect. Just the sight every hunter longs for! Leaving Saunders with the glass to watch events, I hurried down the hill and easily kept out of sight even in a stooping position

c

till within 400 yards of the beast. A momentary glimpse showed him to be still feeding, so I went on slowly in a crouching attitude till within 300 yards. Here I found it necessary to crawl for about 200 yards, and getting a large rock between myself and the deer found on peeping round the edge of a stone that I was within 90 yards. There was evidently no hurry, so I sat down and enjoyed my first view of one of the grandest beasts in existence feeding unconcernedly at a short distance.

During five minutes he only once raised his head, and then only to take a stupid and sleepy survey of his surroundings as the wet moss dropped out of the sides of his mouth. How splendid his long shovels and bays looked as he assumed a dignified attitude against the yellow sunset! But I could not leave him longer as the light was going fast, so getting a good sitting position against the rock, I put the white foresight on his heart and fired. Looking up, to my surprise I saw that the stag had never moved except to raise his head, and thinking that I must have missed, I fired again at once and saw four great feet kicking in the air.

He was dead as soon as I got up. Certainly not one of the best, but nevertheless as I afterwards learned, he carried a good head. The horns were still in the velvet, and the beast had evidently just come out for a quiet snack in an undisturbed place. He gave me the idea of an old animal going back slightly, as his tops were not up to the mark.

The usual rejoicings over the first trophy may be passed over, and seeing that the does (which always move a good fortnight before the stags) were only just beginning to travel, I knew it would not do to be too sanguine about getting another stag for some time. We were in for a long wait, especially as the glorious weather which we had experienced so far showed no signs of breaking. Every morning the sun rose in a cloudless sky, and every evening set in an ocean of flame. There had been a wet summer, so we were experiencing the consequent reaction. Saunders, who had never seen the like before, was nevertheless full of explanations and prognostications. Every evening he would minutely explain the particular position of certain clouds, and how they always foretold rain or snow in Newfoundland, but when the morning came and the sky was as brilliant as usual, he would be silent on the subject. Evening, however, always gave him renewed hope, and he would begin to prophesy again. For three weeks, during which Saunders repeatedly declared that he would die of sunstroke if the "tropical" heat continued, there was not a drop of rain, and Newfoundland experienced the driest season on record. About this time Saunders ceased being a weather-prophet and became somewhat sad. "Never before," said he, "were such things known. To come so far and see so few stags!" And I could see that his anxiety was chiefly because he feared I should be disappointed and wish to turn home. Nothing, however, was further from my thoughts. We had plenty of provisions, and I knew that as soon as the weather broke we should get stags.

"'I'm clean off my bearings,' as the 'Banks' captain said one day in a fog; 'accordin' to my kalkilations, we're fifty miles inside the Labrador woods,' and that's about the size of it jes' now," said my companion one day, as we seated ourselves after a fruitless tramp. "Sech a sight of deer and nar' a stag."

For four days we wandered over the high rocky barrens and "open" timber, hoping to meet a travelling stag. We made from ten to fifteen miles a day over fairly easy ground, difficulties only presenting themselves when we entered the wood trails,[1] which were sometimes "soft" going. Twice we nearly reached a large lake which we saw to the north-west, but to achieve this was rather more than we felt inclined to undertake as yet, until we had exhausted the intervening ground. The next stag we found involved rather an interesting follow-on chase, which I give from my diary.

September 8.—At daybreak, from the high ground above St. John's Lake, I spied eight does and three stags all coming along the high ridge above the New Lake. They were about two miles off, and were travelling and feeding at short intervals. One of the stags seemed to be a big beast with a fair head, so I determined to try and catch him before he reached the timber for which he seemed to be making, to lie up for the day. First we had to cross a wooded valley, and in this we disturbed two does, which fortunately moved off in a safe direction. Once on the ridge, and on the spot where we had seen the game, I spied again, and soon found the white sterns of the deer, which had fed on for about a mile. They were walking fast, and when a caribou is walking fast you have to run. Not more than a mile ahead of the animals was the opening of the forest, and so it was a case of who would get there first. The ground was perfectly flat and open, and so we had to run up-wind, keeping just inside the forest on the north side so as to gain cover. This made the travelling most arduous. To walk in the tangle of larch scrub, peat-holes, and fallen trees is hard enough work, but to

---

[1] Cormack, writing in 1822, speaking of the abundance of the deer paths, says : " One of the most striking features of the interior are the innumerable deer paths on the savannahs. They are narrow, and their directions as various as the winds, giving the whole country a chequered appearance. Of the millions of acres here, *there is no one spot exceeding a few superficial yards that is not bounded on all sides by deer paths.*" This is equally applicable to-day, but only of the interior.

"head" travelling caribou by running through such obstacles was almost beyond our strength. Three times we sank to earth utterly exhausted, and could only be revived by taking a look at the deer, which seemed to keep almost parallel to our route. There were only another few hundred yards more to fight through, and as it was a case of now or never, we made one final effort and arrived at a long point of small larch just as the first of the caribou, an old doe, came walking along. I think a fair chance would hardly have presented itself even then, had not a broad series of "leads" converged and led sharply to the right at this point, for the old lady, after stopping and carefully sniffing about to see if other deer had passed, determined to adopt this route, and so threw the game into our hands. I saw they would all come by nicely, so sat still and strove to quiet my heaving chest. The rifle performed strange parabolas in the air as I tried the sight tentatively on her shoulder. It seemed hopeless to shoot whilst in such a condition, yet the stag was due in a few seconds, and I must try and compose myself. One, two, six, eight big does filed slowly past at about a hundred yards, then after an interval came a small stag, then at a longer interval another stag about four years old, and then for a while nothing. Where on earth was the big fellow? Had he left them? I moved slightly forward to verify my suspicions, when the rolling horns and broad back of the warrantable beast came into view. How differently a big adult walks from a younger one! He seems indifferent to his safety, especially when in the company of others, and the Newfoundland expression of "soakin' along" seems to exactly express his solemn, lazy mode of progression. He did not seem inclined to stop, even when Saunders and I both whistled, so I had to take him as he walked. At the shot he "skipped," and I felt sure he was fatally hit. This, however, was not the case, but as he galloped across my front, looking quite happy, I fired again and knocked him head over heels with a bullet through the shoulders. The other deer now seemed to lose their heads, and ran around in the most stupid fashion. Even when we went up to the . fallen stag, they behaved altogether as no other deer do when frightened or suspicious. The stag was a fair-sized beast, but had rather a poor head, which I had mistaken for something better, seeing it only on the sky-line; a mistake all stalkers may make at times. Yet I wish now I had not killed him. Saw thirty-five deer to-day.

During the next few days I did nothing but explore and map the country, and make a few sketches of the new ground and lakes to the north-west. Sometimes we slept out at night, taking Jack to carry my bed, and making a shelter of spruce boughs. The men seemed quite merry and happy now, as long as they had a good fire of birch and plenty to eat. They had got over the idea that I wanted to shoot a big stag every day, and were now content to wait for the good ones when they should make their appearance. Altogether we had a very jolly time, and Little Bob told me stories of his early days which I was never tired of listening to.

Saunders' father had been the master of a little brigantine, which he had built himself down at Green's Pond, Bonavista Bay. With this little vessel he went every year to the seals, and did pretty well till one fatal spring when the boat got caught in the ice, and was driven ashore at Point o' Feather, Harbour Grace; but Saunders can tell his own story in briefer and more picturesque language than I, so I give it in his own words.

"A' got carried to the 'ice-huntin'' myself when a' was no more than seven and a half years old," said the old man, as he reflectively puffed at his twisted plug. "Most wonderful terbaccer this"—after which a long pause, only broken by sounds of suction.

"Well, go on, Bob," I said; "tell us all about it."

"What you got that book out for?"

"Oh, just to make some notes on seal-hunting."

"Oh," and the old man positively blushed. "Yer ain't goin' to put me in one of them books o' yours, are ye?"

"Well, what if I am? I shan't say anything nasty about you anyhow, unless you hurry up and get on about that time you got carried to the ice as a child."

After this threat the tale proceeded without a break, whilst Jack occasionally offered encouraging suggestions, such as, "You don't say!" "Well, well, Bob!" "Thet's what it is, now!"

"Ye know a' was brought up 'mongst seals and seal folk, and a' can't recollect no time when ma dad warn't goin' to the ice and ma mother warn't scared. Swoiles (seals) was much to us in the spring, for it meant 'bout what we lived on whether the seals drove down in the spring or not, and we struck 'em. So when a' was a little chap ma mother used to put me to bed and make me say prayers like this when swoiles was about: 'Lard God Almighty, send a swile fer daddy, an' send a swile fer mamma, and a swile fer Uncle Jim, an' wan fer Uncle Jim's wife, an' a swile fer little Tommy, an' one each fer Jarge an' Mary, an' a swile fer each of Cousin Will's family, not forgettin' a swile fer Aunt Jane what's a pore widder. An' oh, Lord, don't let de ice blow off shore when daddy's aboard, an' bring 'un safe to hum. Amen.' Then ma mother would call all over our relations to see a' 'adn't forgot none, an' if 'a hadn't remember 'em all she'd make me say de prayer all again.

"A' was a 'loose' (active) little kid, and used to help de men getting things aboard Bona'va Bay when my dad went to the sea, and one spring a' scooted up on deck and found de sea runnin' by and us far out in de bay. 'Good Lord,' said my dad, 'here's dat child, little Bob.' I said I'd gone to sleep in the cabin just before they was startin'. They couldn't put back, so a' got took. It was mighty cold, but a' didn't mind that, as the men were kind to me, and dad let me come on the ice one day, and I killed a seal. Ye know, sir, that when we gets to be young men in this country they don't think much of a chap unless he's bin to de ice. It's a sort o' test o' hardiness, and the girls think a heap of the young fellers that's bin once or twice to the swoile fishin' and come back free with their money. It's jest dog's work while it lasts, but somehow there's an excitement in it that sets young fellers kind o' restless in the spring; and 'fore they know, they're a-signing on wi' Joe Windsor or Sam Blandford. We sealers say, too, that man'll go for a swile where gold won't drag 'un. A' was but fifteen when old Sam asked me to go wi' him as cabin boy, and after that a' goes to the ice every spring for twenty-two years."

"Is that so!" interposed Jack, with a look of profound respect.

There was another long pause, but when a man's in the humour to talk it is best to do nothing but look interested. Presently Little Bob resumed:

"My first season wi' Sam we struck the 'harps' (Greenland seals), nor'-east of the Funks, and killed 4100 in a week.[1]

[1] This number was afterwards exactly corroborated by Captain Sam Blandford in a conversation I had with the "doyen" of the seal-hunters. A sealman takes a pride in remembering the statistics and returns of every hunt.

In those days if you killed two seals you had one of them, not like now, when you only take every fourth seal, and sometimes not that. We didn't form 'pans' (piles) of seals as they do now, but stuck pretty close to the vessel and hauled two seals a man. We never spent a night out on the ice, and allus went off wi' a piece o' fat pork, a few biscuits an' cakes. When times was good we'd take a few billets o' wood to make coffee, and eat the raw heart i' the young 'whitecoats.' Captains was kind to their men, and looked after them as fren's. We made a bit o' money then, and them was the good times o' sealing when men weren't treated worse than dogs as they are now," and Little Bob puffed fiercely at his pipe.

"Now it's full speed ahead up into the 'good' ice. Two hundred men in a foul tub not fit to carry thirty, an' a bully to thrash you out o' your bunk whether you're fit to go to the ice or no. They fling you out on the floe ice with a few billets of wood, and steams away a day to dump off another crowd, and like as not you've got to spend the night out wi' your clothes freezin' on you, for you're bound to fall in the cracks least once a night, however 'loose' you may be. Thar's no room below once the steam winch gets a-going and seals a-comin' aboard, so up comes the coal, and what with the grit and the blubber, two hundred men can't sleep very comfortable on the open decks in a mass of muck, wi' the cold freezin' your marrow."

"I wonder the men stand it, and they get crews year after year," I suggested.

"Ah, that's cos you don't know what the poverty o' Newfun'lan' is," returned the old man sadly. "There's boys goes once or twice to prove they're men, but the crews *don't consist o' them*. It's the poor, the very poor, and they just

have to go or starve.   It's this way.   Ye see there's lots
of poor fisher-folk all 'long the coast and islands that never
sees a dollar from one year end to another.

"'Fore they goes to cod fishin' in summer the merchants
give 'em grub to keep their families all summer while they're
away.   Fishin' goes on till October, and by December they've
got nothing, so has to go to the merchants again to get 'tick'
in provisions to last 'em through the winter.   Then to pay
this off they hev to go to the seals in the spring or they
won't get no more credit, as the merchants also own the
seal vessels.   Only the captains make any money at the
seals, and they're good fellers as a rule, but if they lose
a vessel or let their men 'break out,' as they do at times,
they're soon as poor as the rest o' us.   It 'ud make your
heart sore to see the way lots o' these islanders come aboard
the sealin' vessels in the spring—wi' pinched, half-starved
faces, and hardly 'nough clothes to stand a summer breeze.

"Yes, a've seen pretty rough times at the ice, 'specially
in the old sailin' vessel days.   One spring wi' dad, we were
out two and a half months without takin' a single 'whitecoat.'   We got caught in the ice, and a heavy gale came out
from the nor'-west, and none of us ever expected to see
Green's Pond no more.   We was twenty-two days smashin'
to an' fro in the ice, wi' all our boats gone and the bulwarks
stove in, but by-and-by dad got her nose to the gale, and
after lyin'-to five days and five nights the gale rounded,
and we got out and made Harbour Grace half full o' water.
It was rough a' can say, no sleep, in at de pumps all the
time.   Next year dad lost his vessel; got caught in the ice
and drove up in Point o' Feather, Harbour Grace.   So a'
shipped wi' Captain John Han for four or five springs.
Then a' went wi' Captain Sam Windsor for a spell; and

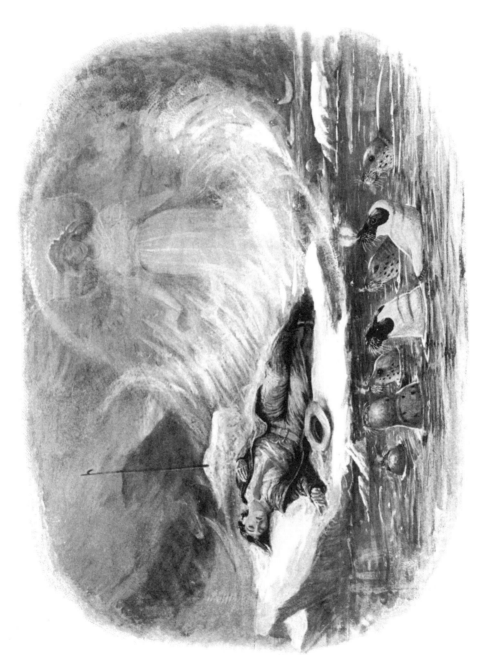

"Man'll goa fer swoile where gold won't drag 'un."

Newfoundland Proverb.

then wi' Captain Kane and Captain Green. A' also did two trips wi' young Bill Windsor.

"Most wonderful sealman was ole Captain Sam Windsor. The men on the east coast used to say that he could generally tell where the seals was 'fore he went out. Some twenty men, friends of mine, went one spring from Green Bay to Green's Pond, to get a berth wi' Captain Carter. The ship was about full, so only ten could sign on, and the others had to walk home again, feelin' sick and hungry. On the way home they saw ole Captain Sam Windsor standing at the door of his house, and he after askin' their business invited the whole lot in to breakfast. Then he says to 'em : 'Don't be downhearted, boys, for not gettin' a berth wi' Carter. The shore men hev bin haulin' whitecoats these two days in Green and White Bay. Green Bay is full o' swoile,[1] so hurry home and look on the "driven" ice, and you'll do better than goin' wi' Carter.' Each of those men killed about £60 apiece, and Carter got no seals.[2]

"First spring Bill Windsor, his son, had a steam vessel, a' went wi' him. She was called the *Vanguard,* and we got jammed in the ice off Belleville Island, near to the Grey Islands, on March 10. We couldn't move, so he sent me, bein' a 'loose' ice-man, over the ice to see if a' could get to the islands and hear news of the seals. It was moonlight, and a' travelled nine miles over pretty rotten stuff to the north island, and then nine miles more across the tickle[3] to the next. Then a' had to go six miles across

[1] The young Greenland seals only very rarely come as far south as this in the spring, and then only when driven in by an easterly gale.

[2] This is a perfectly true story, and well known to all dwellers in St. John's. The explanation is simple. Captain Windsor, as his nephew told me, perfectly understood the spring winds and the movements of the floe ice under exceptional circumstances.

[3] A strait between two islands.

the land 'fore a' met two young men. They told me that swoiles had been driving by into White Bay for seven days and seven nights. They themselves had hooked seventeen whitecoats out o' the slob (shore ice). One told me also Captain Toomey was anchored under the island, so I went straight back to my ship and was pretty well done up, as I hadn't had a bite to eat for twenty-four hours, and had fell in twice and was 'most froze. By-and-by Captain Bill comes to me, and asks me if a' would take a teller to Captain Toomey, as none of the other men liked to go. So after a few hours' sleep and a feed, a' starts again, and after a rare job delivers ma letter to Captain Toomey. 'Your Captain, Saunders,' says Toomey to me, 'is of the same mind as I am. Those seals that's bin passin' is only a patch o' the southern pack, the main body is away north in the Straits' (Belle Isle), so when I gets back to my ship, the Captain he up anchor and were off to the Straits and the Labrador, and we didn't take nar' a seal. When we come back to St. John's we finds all the other vessels had filled wi' seals up in White Bay. So it show's there's such a thing as being too clever," concluded the old man sententiously.

I thought he'd finished his seal talk for the time being, but Jack supplied a sequel by remarking, "Bob, sing us the song the sealmen used to make 'bout that trip."

"Oh, that's rot, that's nothing."

"Well, let's have a bit of it anyhow, Bob," I suggested. After some further persuasion the old hunter began to half sing and half recite the following lines in a cracked voice :—

"Come all you jolly Ice-men
That ploughs the ragin' Main,
I'll tell ye of the *Vanguard*,
Likewise our Captain's name.

His name is Captain Windsor,
Sailed out from Bonava's Bay,
In search of those young whitecoats
But still he got astray.

We steamed her down off Belleville
Our trials do begin

. . . . .

'Twas there we did get frozen in
For three long days or four,
We drift by the Grey Islands
And very near ashore.
'Twas here early next morning
Our Captain come on deck,
He says unto John William,
' Bob Saunders, you'll go get—
Bob Saunders, you'll go get, my boy,
And try to get on shore,
Or hear from Captain Toomey
On board the *Commodore.*'
We boarded Captain Toomey,
As you may understand,
A steamboat nigh three miles from us,
A frozen in the ' Jamb.'

A breakage from the Gull rock
It set the *Vanguard* free ;
She steamed into the harbour,
'Long with the other three.
Our people from the Island
These words I hear them say,
The Walrus and Paslusha
Driven in White Bay
Slipped in the spot of seals."

" A' don't remember no more," broke off Saunders, suddenly becoming modest, " but it's mostly rot 'bout myself ;" and he refused to speak further of his plucky act.

Hunting the Greenland seal from ships and hunting the same from the storm-swept coast of Newfoundland are two different matters. The chase in both cases is beset with sudden and dreadful dangers, seldom foreseen and often incapable of being warded off. In both, the advent of sudden storms may cause the grinding heavy mass to pack on the coast, and thence whirl it seawards again where it is dispersed in fragments with its human freight. The ships can often, and generally do, rescue their men when these untoward circumstances occur; but the lot of the poor coast hunter who snatches his precarious living from the outports is hardness itself, for when difficulties come he has but his own wits and bravery to help him. The wind that sweeps the ice in, bearing on its bosom the tempting whitecoat, may veer at any moment and drive the whole mass off shore again, and then only the watchfulness of the land look-outs and the ready resources of the men can save a disaster. It takes real and solid courage to make a good seal hunter; not the somewhat theatrical bravery of the soldier who leads a forlorn hope, but the dogged three o'clock in the morning article that takes things humbly and expects but little reward.

The true story of the Newfoundland ice-fields is not nor ever will be written, nor will the names of its many heroes be penned in the pages of an undying history, but in the minds of many to-day who have taken part in that annual strife with the forces of nature there live scores of instances of marvellous courage and unselfish devotion.

Down on the barren east coast they tell the story of Matilda Barworth and her half-witted son, born out of wed-lock. She loved the boy who grew almost to man's estate, and when he crept off in his quiet way after the others in the spring-time she used to watch in the dusk for his return, going with the other women of the village; for, in their universal charity, she had long since been forgiven.

One evening, as the men were returning, the wind veered suddenly, and in less than a minute there was a wide gap formed between the rocks on the shore and the pack. This little "tickle," as it is called, was not quite open water, but a space of slushy, fine fragments of ice on which none can run except the most experienced ice-men. In a few minutes most of the men, being skilled from their youth, ran across the dividing distance, which was every moment becoming broader. As the roll of the ocean caused the rotten ice to rise, they fell on their faces and lay flat, thus preventing a slip through. All passed safely over except Jim Barworth, whose courage seemed to have deserted him.

"Come, Jim, boy, try it now," cried his mother. "You can do it sure."

But Jim could not face it, and ran backwards and forwards in a panic. She kept calling to him again and again as an anxious hind calls her calf, but he would not come, and sank on the ice hiding his face in his hands. Suddenly the woman ran out on the rotten ice and would perhaps have crossed, had not a wave risen, formed a crack, into which she disappeared for ever. At that moment Jim looked up and sprang to his feet, for he loved his mother much. He gave but one glance round and rushed across the dreaded space with outstretched arms. But too late. The crack opened again, and in Death mother and son were not divided.

.   .   .   .

The weather still being brilliant, I revisited Selous' camp for two days, and then went down to the east end of the St. John's Lake for another two days, but in neither of these places did we see even a small stag, so returned again to my standing camp to the north-west of the lake.

Nearly all hunters have superstitions, and on September 15 I discovered that neither Bob nor Jack were above this pardonable weakness.

"A' dreamed o' Mrs. Bury last night," said Jack solemnly at breakfast-time.

"Then we're sure to kill a big stag to-day," echoed Saunders, with conviction.

Questioned as to the connection between this estimable lady (the wife of a storekeeper in Alexander Bay) and the monarch of the woods, Saunders at once gave the requisite explanation.

"Once de ole man Stroud had been hunting fer nigh a fortnight and nar a stag had he seen, till one night he seen Mrs. Bury, who's a lady o' persition down our bay, sitting on the top of a big stag and smilin' at 'un. Next day Stroud kills a great one. Again on the same trip one o' the packers, Dan Burton to name, he dreams he's bin a-talkin' to Mrs. Bury, and sure 'nough Stroud's party kills 'nother big stag. There's some connection 'tween the deer and dat lady, fer last year Johnny here sees her in his sleep, and next day Mister Selous kills the finest head I ever seen. We don't really think much on Mrs. Bury, but when she comes to us we're mighty glad."

The sun was sending great fiery shafts of light across the eastern sky and painting the emerald woods with crimson and gold as we stepped out of the forest on this particular morning. We thought ourselves out early, but a flock of Canadian geese rose clamorously from an upland marsh, and a pair of great northern divers were calling querulously from the clouds, showing that others had been up awhile before us. On a little lake up near the first spying place some dusky ducks were paddling along the edge and turning

SAUNDERS' WATERFALL, TERRA-NOVA RIVER

WHERE A STAG HAS CLEANED HIS HORNS

upside down in the familiar fashion of our own mallards. It was a glorious waking to life, and we sat for a while enjoying the crisp morning air and wondering if the stags ever intended to move.

"Think we'll take a walk round Island Pond to-day," said Saunders, suggesting a new ground, and to this I at once acquiesced, as my guide said that an old stag or two generally "summered" there in the stunted and isolated belts of spruce, often coming to the lake shore in the evening.

At noon we rested for our regular midday tea by a little stream, where were many larches recently scraped by a caribou stag.

"That feller's close about here somewhere," said Saunders, and so he was, for soon after commencing our stealthy walk round the isolated drokes, I suddenly looked to my left and saw the broad back and snowy neck of the game we sought for. We had surprised the deer within eighty yards, and he was feeding unconcernedly, so I ought not to have hurried as I did to take him "from the shoulder," as there was time to get into an easy position in which I could have made a certainty of the shot. Immediately the stag turned sideways I fired, the bullet going too high over his back. The deer at once galloped away from the cover a few yards and again stood. This time I hit him on the horn, which frightened him considerably and caused an instantaneous retreat to the woods. As he galloped away I pulled again, without effect, and yet again as he crossed a little sluit about a hundred and fifty yards away.

"You have him," said Jack; "I saw the hair fly from his side;" but I did not think so, seeing that the stag had, after the shot, galloped away easily, and then starting back with raised head and tail and extended "scut," leapt in the

D

air and took a few long. slinging steps to the rear. Then he gave one wild comprehensive survey of the landscape, kicked some stones into the air, and galloped away out of sight as hard as his legs would carry him.

We now ran forward, and on rounding a belt of forest saw my stag lying dead in the open. My last shot had taken him right through the heart. The head was a very ordinary specimen of that grown by the average Newfoundland caribou.

During the walk home it was terribly hot, and Saunders, having the head to carry, became thirsty, and most unwisely drank some water out of a stagnant pool. When we got to camp he complained of feeling ill, and could eat nothing. Unfortunately, too, the brandy had been left down at the boats on Lake St. John, so it was daybreak before Jack started to fetch the only medicine we possessed. By the evening Saunders was much better and ate some dinner, and next morning expressed himself as quite recovered and able to try the ground near the New Lake on which I had fixed some hopes.

At the east end of this lake, which was a large sheet of water some twenty-five miles round (and now named after me), is a broad open marsh. This space connected two great forests, and by all reasoning we assumed that many of the deer that would eventually come from the northern woods must cross this flat to reach the southern woods. It was directly in the line of migration nearly south-west, and so we decided to go down and examine the marsh, and, if there should be a good show of "leads" passing across it, to camp there for a week and let the deer come to us.

Jack came with us as usual now, for he was a sociable fellow and hated being left in camp by himself; and, as

J. G. Millais. 1903.

Walter Lewis Photo.

Millais's Lake from the East.

apart from other considerations, he had sharp eyes, I liked to have him with me.

A pleasant walk of five or six miles over the high ridge and then down through the timber for another two miles brought us to the eastern end of the New Lake. I did not go on to the shore, but stopped behind examining a splendid series of fresh caribou trails leading, as I had hoped they would, right across the marsh and round the lake edge. It was the very place to meet the deer, and I could put my camp in a "droke" of spruce close to the water's edge as long as the north wind, which had now started, continued to hold.

I sat down to rest well satisfied with the outlook, when Jack, who had gone to fill the kettle, suddenly came rushing back to me to say that a stag and a doe were at that moment swimming across the lake. Sure enough, there they were far out in the centre of the lake, and making for the southern shore about a mile to our left. There was no time to be lost, as caribou swim fast, so we got off at once, and fortunately found that the forest, which was new to us, was not so dense as usual, and that we could progress at a fair rate under cover. Looking over a high bank which concealed the point for which the deer were making, I saw the animals coming on fast about four hundred yards away, and heading straight for our position. Here I took the telescope from Saunders, who now expressed the opinion that the stag was a small one; and after bringing it to bear on the horned one, I was forced to a similar conclusion. The two deer now must have seen us, or changed their minds as to a landing place, for they suddenly turned to a right angle and gave me a good broadside view. The appearance of the deer with horns now presented a somewhat different aspect; it had upturned brow points like a red deer, and a thin grey neck utterly unlike that of any young stag.

"That's a doe," I said to Saunders, handing him the glass to take a look.

"Yes," replied my companion, "an' with the biggest horns I ever see in my life."

The two deer had now separated, the unhorned doe coming straight on and landing within a few yards of us before dashing into the forest, whilst the other one whose head I now coveted had turned east again, and was making for a gravel bank about half a mile on our back tracks. The wind being perfect, I easily headed the deer, and gave her a bullet immediately she landed on the shore. She carried unusually large horns of twelve points, and was evidently an old "yeld" doe.

As a rule caribou does have no horns to speak of, and as it was of scientific interest to know what proportion of females carried these cranial appendages, I kept a careful list of all the deer seen by myself during the trip, and what percentage of, in this case, the uglier sex, were so ornamented.

Number of female caribou seen, 306; made up of 1 with twelve points, 1 with eight points, 6 with four points, 40 with three points, (about) 120 with two points, 130 with no horns, or with only small knobby excrescences.

On our way home we noticed little sign of stags travelling; but on going up out of the forest we ran right up against a good beast, which I killed without any stalking, or in fact any incident that is worth recording. He simply stood and looked at me from about fifty yards, and I shot him from the shoulder. He had a pretty but not a large head of twenty-six points, and was evidently a young stag.

CARIBOU SWIMMING

(*From Photographs by* PARSONS)

On the night of September 17, Jack baked bread for three days, as we had decided on a three days' tramp to the east until the stags should show signs of moving past the New Lake to the north, whence I hoped to go by-and-by. As we left the wood close to our camp we came on the fresh sign of a black bear not an hour old.

"Shouldn't wonder if that cuss cleans out our camp while we're gone," murmured Saunders reflectively, as he examined it; then as we tramped along the old man indulged in a few reminiscences.

"A've know'd um do thet more'n once, and play funny wid de whole outfit. There was an Indian named Stephen lived down our bay a while back. He was just the best trapper in Newfun'lan', an' he told me wance when I was in, furrin' (trapping) wi' him, that one night he wakes up sudden cos de fire had gone out, and across the glow he sees a great black thing movin'.

"'Who's dere?' he call out, seizin' his gun. De feller don't answer. So he rips at 'un and finds he's killed a large black bear what's eatin' out of he's sugar-can. Stephen he kill more bears than any feller in Newfun'lan', and one fall he come to me and Jack's father and sed he'd shot the largest kind of a bear 'bout ten miles back, and sed too we could get all de fat and meat if we'd come. So he an' little Jack here, he warn't more than a child o' ten then, starts off, and late that evening we come to the carcase. I never seed such a bear as that, 9 feet long, if he was an inch, and I've seen as many bear in Newfun'lan' as any one but Stephen. We started for home next morning, little Jack here carryin' a load that made his nose bleed, but he wouldn't give up or say a word, the little varmint."

Jack looked shy and utterly uninterested as the old man continued.

"Stephen was married to the daughter of old Jim Baxter, himself half an Indian, and a man that had spent all his days reevin' through de woods, so o' course he warn't o' much account. People was mighty civil to Stephe as they was afraid of him, and thet's the way o' most. Yet he was a merry cuss, singin' and laughin' all de time and nothin' to scare a body till ye caught his eyes, and then folk was apt to feel cold. He tried to knife one young chap fer spillin' some coffee on his toes, an' he used to say straight that if he found any white man trappin' bear or huntin' deer too far from de Bay he'd shoot 'un dead. So most folk stop at home.

"He'd a great name as a hunter, and whiles used to take town's fellers to de woods, that is, them as didn't know 'un and was fools enough to go with 'un. Course those days they got nothin' cos Stephe 'ud tramp 'em all through de meshes and scare every mother's son o' deer so long as de grub lasted. One time he go out wi' a young 'un from St. John's, named Molony, for a fortnight, and when they come back that feller ain't seen so much as a deer's scut. So I ask Stephe, who liked me somehow, how 'twas.

"'What, *me* show Molony deer?' ses he sarcastic, 'while there's sugar and coffee and bacon. Oh no, no, no, that ain't Stephe." And the old man and Jack indulged in an amused chuckle.

I was interested in this queer character, so in response to my request for more "Stephe," Saunders continued.

"There was a loud blowin', bullyin' feller that kept a merchant store down Bonava' Bay, and made lots o' money by cheatin' us poor folk. His name was Stanley, an' he was powerful fond o' the gun. One fall he goes in wi' Stephe, and after a week o' seein' nothin' but drokes and meshes, he gets mad and cusses the Indian. Sed he'd lied to 'un, and that he'd be off for home right there at once and make things hot fer 'un. Stephe never sed a word at first, but jus' looks at 'un wi' his cold eyes, then he darts off, sayin' he'd show him deer for sure that day. They jus' walked and walked and walked, and by-and-by Stephe tells de feller to sit down and take a spell while he goes into the timber to light a fire and boil kettle. Presently the man from Bonava's Bay gets cold and hungry, and he goes to find Stephe and de kittle; but de Indian was far away by that time, and he didn't ever see 'un again—least not for some time."

"How did the man get out, Bob?"

"Well, if it hadn't bin that there was plenty blueberries that fall, and he had a box of matches, he certainly wouldn't a' seen Bonava's Bay agin, for he was clean lost. It took 'un three days 'fore he struck the Terra-Nova River, where some loggers picked 'un up famished and 'most crazy.

"When Stanley got back to de salt water, first man he met was Stephe, lookin' as sweet and pleasant as a day in June.

"'Ho, you damned rascal,' screamed the wanderer, 'I'm goin' now to de magistrate to have you arrested, and you'll be jailed sure fer two years.'

"'Very well,' says Stephe, 'an' as soon as I come out I shoot you dead very quick.' Stanley stood in the road for some time thinking about it all, and then—he walks home. Dey was all afraid to do anything to Stephe, but he didn't get many hunting parties after that trip."

I thought he had finished, but seeing my interest in the

character of this wild creature, he volunteered yet another excellent tale.

"Ever hear that old Newfun'lan' yarn o' Stephe and the two 'sports'? No? Well, ye know you can't lose an Indian even supposin' ye put him down blin'fold in the centre o' the island and tell him to make fer St. John's, and what's more, they don't like to be told they may be going faulty or there's apt to be trouble. Well, one fall, after he'd nearly killed de Bonava' man, Stephe takes in two townies to hunt. Disremember their names, but we'll call 'em Johnny and George. Johnny stays in camp one day, and Stephe goes off wi' George fer to find a deer. They reeves around all day now in de woods, now on de meshes, till by nightfall George gets uncomfortable and doesn't know where he is, and is precious sure the Indian don't know either, cos our woods is tough, as you know. By-and-by Stephe sits down to light a fire.

"'Guess we're lost,' ses George.

"'Oh no,' says Stephe, lookin' up, kind o' sour. 'Indian not lost. Indian *never* lost; Camp and Johnny lost.'"

"That's good, Bob! Where's Stephe now?" I said.

"Dead. Dead six winters ago. De woods and—er—other things done fer him, as it does fer all of us in time. He was haulin' a deer 'long de ice o' George's Pond when he slip up and cracked his skull. He got home to de Bay, but died a few weeks after. A' seen 'un just 'fore he goes, an' he say to me, 'Saunders, whisky's bad fer haulin' deer.'"

CHAPTER III

BEGINNING OF THE MIGRATION AT MILLAIS'S LAKE

"WHAT's this French shore question," I said to Bob one evening.

"There ain't no French shore question—least not in Newfun'lan'," said Little Bob, with a certain tinge of sarcasm. "We heard tell that in your papers they're allus talkin' about the French shore, and what right the Frenchies have thar'. But, sure 'nough, didn't these Frenchies make them villages, and work the land after the Government let them settle there. Yes, right enough. Well, those Frenchies hev been settled there that long, I guess neither English nor French Government's goin' to turn 'em out, and what's more, no Newfun'lan'er grudges them their luck, though they hev got the only bit of coast that isn't worked out and fished to death."[1]

"How's that, Saunders?"

"Lobsters, jest lobsters. They fishes lobsters, and makes a good thing of it, though they are growing a bit scarce now. Up there along the French shore the youngsters is born web-footed, and the old folk watch the ebb-tide. Yet it takes more brains to catch an old gran'pa lobster than a cod, one of those old fellows with seaweed on his back and a pair of nippers that could bite yer head off. He's brains, I tell you, and it needs brainy men like those

---

[1] Since this was written, the French shore question has been settled by the payment of a large sum on the part of the English Government. All the French settlers have now left.

Frenchies to catch them. One summer I went lobster catchin' along by de Grey Islands, and we done pretty poor till the spearin' came on."

"How do you spear lobsters?" I remarked, for this method of taking the crustacean was new to me.

"Well, 'long 'bout the month of August the lobsters cast their shells, and is sort o' soft and fleshy 'bout the back so's ye can drive a spear into 'un. We used to go out early in the day 'long the coast, to where there was caves with the sea washin' up into them. Round about the mouth of these caves we'd cast half a boatload of cod's insides or rotten herrings, always being careful to heave the bait where we cud see clean bottom. Then we lay by fer half-an-hour, an' the fun 'ud begin soon as the tide was sufficient ebb to reach bottom with our long spears. Great sport it was, too, and none too easy stickin' them lobsters as they grabbed the pieces of fish and made off. I liked that kind of fishing fine, and made a good pack of money at it too, fer we'd get as many as fifty to a hundred in a morning sometimes. Anyhow, those Frenchies is all right if you leave 'em alone, an' I know that if they was Newfun'lan' Englishmen they wouldn't turn out after they made the place too."

During the next few days "we reeved aroun' considerable" (as Saunders graphically expressed it), seeing a fair number of does and two big stags, both of which showed up in the timber for a minute, and disappeared as soon as I ran to head them. As there was now every sign that the larger deer had commenced to travel, I moved the camp ten miles over the two ridges, and descended into the valley by Millais's Lake, where I had settled to watch the open barrens at the east end.

I have already stated this barren forms a connecting

Happiness!

link between the northern and southern forest, and as it
lies immediately in the centre of the main deer leads of the
southern herd, I felt sure that I should soon be rewarded
by the sight of more good stags than we had encountered
during the first four weeks of spying and timber tramping.
There is no doubt that if you want to get really good heads
in Newfoundland, the only way is to sit still when the deer
are on the move. This is, of course, not the highest class
of sport, but it is interesting for a few days, and during the
week that we spent by the lake I thoroughly enjoyed my
stay, and saw more caribou than previously.

We waited all the 20th and 21st without seeing anything
worth shooting, and on the 22nd, after spying the barren
from daybreak till nine o'clock, I got a fit of restlessness, and
so determined to take a walk on high ground towards the
Gander. To reach this high ground it was first necessary
to cross the little river flowing at the north-east corner, and
then, after an uphill mile of dense woods, it was all plain
sailing. We tried to cross the river near the lake, and
found this impossible, afterwards holding right across the
open barren to effect a passage higher up. This was an
unfortunate manoeuvre, and one that almost cost us a fine
stag as subsequent events proved. One should not walk
about on the ground where deer are expected to cross.
Half a mile up the country the river was still impossible,
and, so as not to waste further time, I decided to go up
and work the ridge to the south-east. As we crossed the
barren I kept looking round (a habit one gets into when
expecting game to appear from any quarter); and suddenly
saw three does come out of the north woods, dash across
the river, and begin to traverse the open marsh. We had
hardly got out of sight when three more came suddenly into

view behind us, and all six presently worked on to the main lead straight up the southern woods and disappeared. This episode caused a few minutes' delay, then once more we rose and resumed our journey; but on giving a final glance back at the now distant river, I saw something moving on the edge of the north woods, close to the water. This brownish-grey thing resolved itself into a doe when the glass was fixed upon it, but there was something else in the field of my telescope. It was at first a shadowy grey spot, which, as I kept the glass upon it, grew lighter and lighter as it neared the edge of the woods, and eventually became white as a patch of snow.

"A stag, and a big one too," said Saunders and Jack simultaneously.

The grand old fellow came out of the forest with slow and dignified steps. He stood a moment haughtily surveying the open prospect before him, the sun shining on his splendid horns. Without hesitation he took the river, and, landing on the near bank, proceeded to shake a halo of sparkling water from his hide. Then off he set to cross the marsh, so I deemed it time to be going to meet him.

A sharp run of four or five hundred yards took us to "The Island," as we had christened a small clump of larch and spruce in the middle of the barren. Here I left my companions, and proceeded alone to crawl out on to the marsh towards a certain stone, within easy shot of the lead I felt sure the stag would traverse. Raising myself slightly, I had the satisfaction of seeing the pair coming quickly along. The doe well in front, looking uneasily from side to side, the stag following with steady footfall, but apparently indifferent to danger. They were all right, that was certain, because the wind was blowing straight from them to myself,

AFTER A LONG SHOT

and they must pass broadside on within a hundred yards. With the quiet satisfaction of a man who has got what is vulgarly called a "soft thing," I was just arranging a nice clump of moss under my left arm when there was a sharp whistle from "The Island," and I knew at once that something had gone wrong.

Rising up, there were the two caribou racing away back to the river at full gallop. There was nothing left but to sit down and try the stag before he should be completely out of shot. The third bullet struck him on the left horn and materially added to his fears, whilst the fourth just passed his shoulder as he swung slightly to one side. Seeing that he was about to turn quite broadside I kept the last cartridge in the magazine for such a contingency, and to my relief he not only did so, but slowed down to a walk as if about to stop.

The stag was now a good 300 yards away, but having a good position and a fine light I pressed the trigger slowly, feeling the shot was a good one. A loud crack and an instantaneous start on the part of the deer showed that the bullet had struck him. Nevertheless he went off again at full gallop, falling twice into bogs, from which he extricated himself with wonderful strength and skill, and then, with a final effort, he made at full speed for the river, tripped over a low bank, turned a complete somersault, and fell dead.

It was a moment of great exultation such as every hunter experiences after making a long shot that is successful. Saunders had seen the stag fall, and rushed out of "The Island" waving his hat and shouting with glee. Our quarry was a fine stag with a good Roman nose, such as only old stags (of all species) possess; but his horns were completely buried in the moss, so we had to dig them out for fear of a breakage. Jack set to work, and soon unearthed to view the antlers of a typical caribou, not an extraordinary one, but a fine well-developed head of thirty points, with good strong brows and bays. The horns were rather longer than the average, and the whole what Saunders described as a fine head. We sat long discussing the incidents of the capture, photographing, and skinning the head and neck whilst Jack appropriated the thick rolls of fat lying across the buttocks. This deer was the fattest I have ever seen when skinning any specimen of the *cervidæ*; a good three inches of fat lay all over the thighs, and there was also a thick layer all over the lower parts.

Next day, 23rd September, the equinoctial gales commenced from the west, and the wind increased till the 25th, when it blew almost a hurricane. It was my custom to rise at daybreak, the men getting up half-an-hour earlier to make the fire and boil the kettle for our morning meal. On the morning of the 24th, and when Saunders and Jack had finished their breakfast, they went out to spy the marsh from an open about 30 yards from the camp while I sat and sipped my tea. My boots lay at some distance, and I was just feeling pretty comfortable, thinking how much more delightful camp was than crouching under the lee of a wet bush, for it was still "blowing smoke," when Jack rushed in to say that a great stag had just crossed the river, and was even now traversing the marsh. There was no time to do more than pull on my boots and to fly out on the barren, up across the wind so as to head the beast, for I knew he would make for one of two passes.

"A shocking set o' harns," said Saunders, taking the glass from his eye as I dashed by him, but I did not do

more than glance at the beast, which was walking quickly
along in the grey dawn. In a few minutes Jack and I had
reached the edge of the hill forest up into which the stag
would presently pass, when to my extreme disgust the gale
came rushing in a mighty wave over the trees and driving
our wind straight towards the now rapidly approaching animal.
There was not a moment in which to make a fresh disposition. It was one of those occasions when action decisive and
immediate was imperative ; consequently I ran with all my
might to come within view of the main lead up the hill, so
that even if the stag bolted I should at any rate get a running
shot. But this was not to be, and I lost the finest horned
stag I had till then ever seen. As I ran along the wood edge,
and was still about 250 yards from him, I suddenly saw him
throw up his mighty antlered head and spring into the air,
as a caribou stag generally does when he gets the wind. A
frightened deer will usually halt a moment or two and give
you time for a shot, but this fellow seemed to know something about men, and at once made off down wind as hard
as his legs could carry him. He was in the worst kind of
hummocky ground, and I fired three hopeless shots at his
retreating form before he jerked round the edge of the
forest arm, and disappeared for ever. Then I went home
miserable.

On the way back I met Saunders, who, with the kindest
intentions, endeavoured to cheer me by saying that this stag
carried the finest horns he had ever seen in his life. He,
moreover, asked permission to take my rifle and follow the
stag as he felt sure I had hit him. I was equally certain that
I had not touched the beast, and should indeed have been
surprised if I had ; but Saunders, who cherished an altogether
unwarrantable view of my shooting powers, considered it

impossible that I had missed him, and so begged for leave to take up the spoor.

" I can take some tea and go two days, and then I will come up wi' him, if he don't go hard ground," said the old fellow.

" But what about stags in the meantime, Bob," I suggested, as we had only one rifle. This proved unanswerable, so we returned to camp to wait for another monarch of the woods.

During the day several deer passed the marsh, but it was not till the evening that the sight of another snowy neck and waving horns of a stag coming along the lake side changed the tenour of our thoughts. It was growing dusk, so I could not see the antlers very well, particularly as he kept close along a belt of trees that fringed the marsh. I ran and took up "the position favourable," as Monsieur Alphonse would say. With the stag was a doe who carried large horns with eight points, an unusual number. She came along in front of her lord and master, looking suspiciously from side to side as she took each step. I thought she would see me as I lay out on the bare moss not 100 yards away, but she went by quietly, and as the stag came on I gave him a shot that looked like a settler. He did not fall, however, but stood again at 200 yards, so I fired again and dropped him quite dead; the bullet piercing the kidneys, an instantly fatal shot.

He had nice brows, and was a fair beast, but not such a head as I would have shot had the light been sufficiently good to properly distinguish the animal. But one has to take one's chance sometimes. The first royal I ever shot in Scotland was killed at 200 yards in a failing light, when I could not do more than see he was a large beast.

CANADA GEESE

YELLOWSHANKS

WHAT YOU CAN DO IF THERE IS A BIG STONE TO HIDE BEHIND
AND THE WIND IS FAVOURABLE

It was rough at night, and snowing a little, so after dinner, when pipes were glowing, the conversation naturally turned on winter hunting and adventures in the snow. The men told me of rough times they had experienced when they went in to get the winter meat.

"A' mind a time," said Saunders, "when a' was 'most crazy. 'Twas once when ole man Stroud, the two Arnolds, and young Baxter come in wi' me to hunt our winter meat, and young Baxter Stroud, a boy o' seventeen, he got lost in de snow. Ole man Stroud sends Baxter out wi' me, and tell me to be perticler careful wi' 'un cos he ain't no good at findin' way, but I never think he'd stray the way he done. Third day out a' sees three deer, and goes fer 'em. They moved over a ridge, so I ran on, cut 'un off, and after puttin' three guns at 'em, kills one, and paunches 'un. By-and-by a' goes to look fer Baxter, but he ain't whar a'd left 'un, so I specs he'd gone to camp. When a' come in the ole man Stroud says kind o' sharp, 'Where's Baxter?' and a' looks round and sees he ain't thar. A' feels kind o' sick fer a minute, fer it's now snowing hard, and cold fit to freeze a body to death, but a' couldn't say a word even when de ole man say he won't see his boy again. We all starts off by-and-by to look fer tracks o' Baxter, fer the snow had stopped, and the moon had come out. Stroud he wants to go to the place where a' had left the boy, but a' knew well enough tracks was all covered by this time, and that Baxter would make fer the old camp which we'd left in de morning. 'Bout daybreak we come to a place where our ponies had broke through de ice morning before, and as we stops to look we hear a faint call from a droke o' spruce close by —a' runs up, and there lies Baxter 'most froze. We lights

E

a big fire, and brings him round, but we was only just in time."

"Tell Mr. Millais o' that time you had after ole Noah," here interposed Jack. To this Saunders immediately raised objections, and it was only after more leading questions, and many pauses, that the old man told his tale. His reluctance was, of course, because it involved no little credit to himself. But at last we got him fairly under weigh.

"Noah Dimot is an ole feller 'bout seventy years. He's allus lived down our Bay 's far as a' can remember, and whenever he go into de woods he got lost. Thar's some folk, d'ye know, can't fin' thar way around even if thar was finger-posts all de time, and ole Noah 'e was allus that kind. His folk shouldn't 'a' allowed him round without a string. He was terrible fond o' the gun, and thet was how we had the greatest hunt I ever knew. Ole Noah 'e gone out one winter towards a lake, four or five miles from de Bay, to look for rabbits. Some men at a lumber camp, 'bout three mile out, see 'un going out. Next evenin' one of those men's sittin' by de fire smokin', like to we, asks if any of 'em seen Noah goin' home, fer he'd promised to leave a rabbit. No, none of 'em had seen um, so they look in each other's faces, and that night one o' them comes down to the Bay to see if Noah's home. O' course, Noah had got lost as usual, and de whole o' de men in the Bay were out that night lookin' for Noah wi' birch bark torches.

"It was lucky there was no fresh snow, for if there had been, that would hev bin the end o' Noah Dimot. Early in the morning a' finds Noah's track, and follows it all the next day. There was three other men wi' me, and Noah's son, Sandy. We'd never a bite to eat, and snow was

"He wus jes' like thet old Rip."

threatening, though it didn't come, and a' hed to haul off to send two o' the men back for some grub. Then when the men come they was dead beat, so a' went on all through de night wi' Sandy. 'Twas most surprisin' the distance that ole man travelled—the further he went each day, the faster he goes towards evenin'. Sometimes we found where he'd made great springs like a scared rabbit, and a' see by-and-by a' warn't followin' no sensible man, but one just crazy wi' fear. It was curious to see how he'd crossed three lumber roads an' took no notice, he'd gone just straight ahead and reeved through the thickest places. Towards morning a' see we's goin' to have weather. Soon there comes a slight ruffle o' snow, and a' thought 'twas all up, for a' would hardly see trail. When daylight came a' was tired, and Sandy, though younger than me, says he can't go no further, or we'd be dead too, as we got no more grub; but just then a' finds where ole man had lay down and slept, and he ain't got up and gone on more'n an hour. So a' says to Sandy to cheer up, fer de ole man must be 'bout wore out, and must drop soon.

"'Twarn't long before we come to the edge o' the forest, an' lookin' across de mesh a' seen de old man Noah walkin' along slowly, slowly, an' usin' a long pole fer a walkin' stick. Down our Bay, sir, we've got a picter of an old Yankee feller called Rip van Winkle, an' when a' looks up and seen de ole man Noah, wi' bent back and snow-white hair and beard, dodderin' 'long, and resting on his long stick, wi' his clothes all tore to rags, a' thinks it's just old Rip came to Newfun'lan'. When we come up to 'un, we seen he ain't got no hat, and his clothes was most tore to rags, and a' tell you he looked wild. 'E didn't know his son Sandy at all, but when a'd give 'im a sup o' brandy, and told 'im a' was Saunders, 'e knowed me at once, and said quite merry, 'All right now, boys, a' ain't got lost; see de ole woman again, boys.'

"A' needn't tell you de trouble we had to get back, as we'd no grub but only brandy; but a' made a great fire, and was just startin' by myself for a lumber camp some twenty miles back, when the boys, who'd trailed us, came up, an' we got de ole man back to the Bay after takin' a good spell. Ole Noah was sixty-seven when 'e got lost like that, an' 'e was four days and four nights without food or fire, so don't tell me some old 'uns ain't tough, for there most young 'uns would a' gone under. Ole Noah 'e's seventy-three now, but 'e don't do no more rabbit 'untin'."

It was blowing a full gale all the 25th, but I decided to stop one more day, in the hope of seeing something out of the ordinary. In this I was not disappointed, for though I did not kill an extraordinary head this trip, I got that evening a stag with first-rate antlers, and quite the best I obtained. His capture was almost too easy, for the wind was perfect, and he was just "soakin'" along, smelling where some deer had passed, and not caring for anything in the world. I had been spying and watching all day, and had just gone a few steps to the camp to get a warm up, when a whistle from Jack recalled me.

"There's a great feller just come out on that little barren between the two 'drokes,'" said Jack, pointing to an open space about a mile away. "He's heading for the main woods, and I know his head's big, for I put the glass on it."

With this assurance I at once "made tracks," and in ten minutes was creeping over a stony knoll to see if the stag was still heading for the same road. For a few

L'Allegro

The beginning of the pack

Il Penseroso

The end of the pack

minutes I could see nothing, but on raising myself I saw his broad chocolate-coloured back about 100 yards off. He was coming along all right. I lay perfectly still, and allowed him to come mooning along to within ten yards, for I was curious to see how near he would approach. At this distance I could see his big nose, twitching as it scented the spoor of enticing females, and I was so near that I could see his eye " catch " mine as I peeked at him from behind the stone. In an instant his head flew up, and so did my arms with the rifle. I pulled the trigger almost before the weapon touched my shoulder, and immediately the great beast was kicking on his back with a bullet through the neck.

"Ye didn't need no bullet for that 'un. Ye cud a' cut 'un down wid de axe," said a voice behind me. It certainly shows how easily a stag may be obtained *sometimes*.

The head was a large one, with unusually fine double shovels in front and big bays, with many points. I do not think points are of the greatest importance in a good caribou head, and few would agree how many points this deer carried. Newfoundlanders count every knob and excrescence, but, following the old Scotch powder-horn test, which I think a very fair one, it had thirty-five tines. This was much the best head I secured, but not the largest. The deer was an old stag, evidently going back, for the tops were poor and almost pointless.

Having now obtained all the heads we could carry, I decided to leave next day for our standing camp above St. John's Lake, and, in a weak moment, said I could carry the three caribou heads we had just killed, so as to save the men an extra journey. Saunders and Wells each toted about 80 lbs., whilst my load went about 60 lbs., and never

in my life was I so glad to get rid of anything as that
burden when at last we reached our main camp. Skulls
and horns are awkward things to carry, even when you
are accustomed to packing, but, to an amateur in the
business like myself, they seemed at times almost unendur-
able. Yet, after a good dinner and a smoke, I carried them
on through the timber for another two miles to St. John's
Lake, where our canoes were, and paid for it with a sleep-
less night.

Our journey up the Terra-Nova and through the two
lakes had been comparatively easy and swift, owing to the
beautiful weather and absence of wind. Now, however, we
were to experience cold and to face half a gale. We started
early on the 27th to pass the St. John's Lake, where, by
the way, I saw a beautiful caribou stag moving along the
western shore; but, ere reaching the farther end, it began
to blow, and knocked up such a jabble that we were nearly
swamped; one wave nearly filled us, and Saunders and I
had to paddle with all our might to reach the shallows in
safety. Then we had to unload everything to get the water
out, and had hardly started again when another wave came
over the side of the little boat. After another bale out, we
had to advance with the greatest caution, and then could only
make slow progress against the increasing wind. Saunders
thought at one time we should have to camp for the day,
but by steady paddling we managed to keep on till the
last headland of the lake was passed, and the river which
joins the lake with Mollygojack came into view. There I went
ashore, and walked for a few miles till the men caught me
up in the canoes. It was easy water between the two lakes,
and we had only to unload twice in passing "rattles," as
they called the strong rapids, so we made good progress,

He Surveys you with a Look of Intense Disapproval

and by the afternoon reached the point on the Mollygojack where we had camped coming up.

Saunders was anxious to stop at this point, as he wanted to show me, if possible, the track of an extraordinary caribou stag that haunted this place for several seasons. Dan Burton, Stroud, Saunders, Wells, and Mr. Selous had all seen the track of this wonderful stag, and it was unanimously agreed that nothing like it had ever been seen before by any of them. The spoor was said to be almost as large as that of a moose, so naturally I was most anxious to see it.

When we arrived at the point, the low state of the lake prevented the heavily-laden canoe from getting near the shore, so Saunders, who wore seal-boots, kindly offered to carry me on his back. It was a well-meant offer, but entirely disastrous. Saunders was a little man and I somewhat large, whilst the bottom of the lake was of slippery mud. The shifting of weight from the boat to the biped also caused a loss of balance, so over the old man's head I dived into three feet of water and two of mud. It was comical but cold, and when Saunders had skilfully retrieved me by the seat of the trousers, we all three sat on the shore and had a good laugh whilst I changed into dry clothes.

Almost at once we found the track of the great stag; he had been here not many hours before, as his numerous footprints plainly showed. I certainly never believed a caribou could have made such a track, and went at once for my camera to take a picture. The measurement across the hoof prints was $7\frac{3}{4}$ inches, just the span of my outstretched hand. The fellow who made this spoor must indeed have been a Goliath amongst his species, and I regretted that I had to hurry on to Canada, where Indian guides were waiting, or I should certainly have spent a week in this place in the hope of seeing the "muckle hart." That night we slept at the end of Mollygojack, and next day the troubles of the men commenced in earnest.

I will not enter into details of all the rough work which my guides had to undergo during the next four days. In 1901 the river had been lower than it had been known previously, and its passage difficult, but in 1902 it was 50 per cent. worse. The river bed was nearly dry save for a rough and stony channel, down which it was impossible to "run" the canoes for fear of staving them in. What was a "rattle" when we came up was now nothing but a series of jagged points of stone with a swift stream running between them. When such were encountered, it was a case of unloading the whole of the stuff, carrying the canoes for a hundred yards, packing the goods and repacking them again. This had to be repeated at intervals dozens of times each day, and the work was extremely arduous and trying to the temper, but not once did I hear my men swear or show themselves put out. I know I was dog-tired myself each night, for, though I did not go into the water as they did, I assisted to the best of my ability in all the "portages," and that was pretty heavy work in itself.

But everything comes to an end in time, and we at last arrived at the easy water near Penson's Brook, and our troubles came to an end. Here I saw some nice trout rising, and, getting out my rod, I took fourteen trout, char, and ouananiche (land-locked salmon), the latter being still in good condition and delicious eating.

Next day, after a night of pouring rain, we passed the Terra-Nova Lake after a hard paddle against a head wind, and on a fine evening saw the end of our journey in the shape of the Terra-Nova Station and the trestle bridge.

A small figure was standing on the shore throwing stones into the river, and shouting various nondescript calls as we approached, and I presently saw it was our friend Mike amusing his lonely little self in the only way that was possible.

After our first greetings, he said, "What you bin gone so long for? There's a pile o' telegraphin' 'bout you. They think you're lost down in St. John's. But I see you got a heap o' deer."

"Where's Jack and Tom?" I said, running my eye over the menagerie which frolicked around the little man.

"A 'sport' went and shot 'em while you was gone," said Mike, turning away.

"The beast!" was Jack's remark, which entirely echoed our feelings.

Thus ends one of the pleasantest short journeys I have undertaken—thirty-six days of the best of sport, and the very best of companions. I had enjoyed myself immensely, and returned refreshed in mind and body.

All of us who are big-game hunters go to a new country hoping to find animals abundant and good heads occasional, and in Newfoundland I had encountered these conditions to the full.

After paying off my two guides, we sat round the camp fire at night waiting for the accommodation train to arrive. We did not talk much, but I know Saunders was thinking deeply, and wanted to say something nice. At last the old chap began, and we all three felt uncomfortable.

"D'you know, sir, that Providence is mighty good to us, whiles. Two years ago in the fall, I was 'bout on the rocks, and not knowing where to turn for a few dollars which I wanted particular. Just then I thought I'd struck a lucky, for Mr. Watson, in St. John's, who's bin a good fren' to me, gets me to go hunt wid an American who's coming from Port-an-basque, fer de American tells me where to meet him.   When a' gets to Port-an-basque, a' waits **three** days, but de American 'e don't come.   A' feels mighty sick at that time a' can tell you, but just when a'm wondering how I can get back to de Bay, a' meets a Bonava's man a' knows, and he says he'll frank me's far's Howley, where a' can shoot two deer, and that'll pay to take us home.   Well, we goes to Howley, and first day a' shoot a big stag wi' a forty-pint head, which a' sells to a doctor of St. John's fer fifteen dollars.   Then a' felt kind o' better.   Same day a' meets Mr. Selous, and he ask me to come up de country wi' him and Stroud.   Well, a' wasn't missin' de American particular by then. We has a rough time trampin' the meshes in November, and is too late fer de deer what's gone by, but Mr. Selous he like me, and a' like him, so he ask me to go in wi' him last fall.   That was good fer me, for though a' felt sick that American didn't come, now a'm glad he didn't, for a' know there's suthin better comin' my way.   And now Mr. Selous has sent me you."   And the old man got up silently and shook me by the hand.

It had been a mighty effort to put things quite in the way he wished, but I doubt if any born courtier could have expressed himself more delicately or with nicer feeling.

JACK STEERING HIS CANOE DOWN A SHALLOW

RESULTS OF THE FIRST TRIP

CHAPTER IV

EXPEDITION INTO NEW GROUND UP THE GANDER RIVER

"DERE's lots o' things in this world wot seems to strike us rough at the time, but which turns out the best in the end," was a frequent remark of my philosophical friend Little Bob; and with this he addressed me as I met him at the commencement of my second expedition, looking like a scared fox in the mundane wilds of Water Street. Towns were not to the liking of this man o' the woods, and we were discussing the disappointing fact that the steamer for North Labrador had departed on the previous day and would not be back for another month. It was disgusting, to say the least of it, as I had made my preparations carefully before leaving England, and meant if possible to add the barren-land caribou, of the north-eastern corner of America, to my collection of hunting trophies.

The loss of a month in the autumn means nothing in some countries, but in North Labrador winter closes down with a sudden snap about the beginning of October, and there you must remain with the Esquimaux till the next summer, if the last boat from the south fails to reach Nain and the north ports. As I had also hoped to hunt again in Newfoundland in the second season, it was clearly the best plan to make one good expedition in that delightful country, rather than to try and effect under pressure two shooting trips in the two countries both so wide apart.

Accordingly Bob Saunders and I retired to my lodgings, and flattened our noses on the map of Newfoundland.

Experienced hunters always say, "The first trip you go to a new country is for experience, the second you get what you want." This is very true, especially if the hunter himself is able to make deductions, if he does not mind travelling, and has, like the headmaster, the power of picking capable assistants. In the previous year I had learned something about the general habits of the woodland caribou, and became more and more convinced that during the month of September the big stags keep to themselves in various "putting up" spots situated near the unvisited lakes and rivers of central Newfoundland. When the railway was first made and opened, numbers of splendid stags came out of the north every September, and crossed the line between Bay of Islands and Howley on their autumnal migration. Nowadays, although almost as many deer come, they are chiefly does, so that men, who during these years of plenty were accustomed to go about and shoot these old stags like sheep in a pen, now grumble and say that the patriarchs are shot out. But this is not the case. The animals are not such fools as themselves. They have learnt by hard experience, and have protected themselves by hiding in peace and security in the untrodden forests of the interior, and only migrating in the late fall to the south coast barrens. There I believe they will continue to flourish for centuries to come unless another railway is made, which is not likely to occur.

The natural conditions, too, of the great sanctuary will in themselves keep this extent of country inviolate, for, in the first place, after the lower reaches of the rivers are passed, there is no timber worth cutting and likely to tempt the cupidity of man. Nor is it possible to reach the interior

SANDY BUTT AND FORTY-NINE POINT HEAD

except with expensive light-draught canoes, and these must be handled by experienced watermen who are not easily discouraged. The average Newfoundland guide likes to do things comfortably, both for himself and the sportsman who employs him, so he is quite content to take his man, or party, and sit about the leads of Howley, Goose Brook, the Gaff Topsails, or Patrick's Marsh. This involves no labour or fatigue, and so abundant are caribou, that three stags apiece may be killed at these places still. But rarely is a good head obtained in this manner. To shoot good heads the hunter must see many, and he can only do so by going far afield.

These at any rate were the conclusions we came to after carefully surveying the map of Newfoundland. Two rivers seemed to pierce to the very heart of the country, the Bay d'Est and the main branch of the Gander, the longest river in Newfoundland, whose source I afterwards discovered beyond the Partridgeberry Hills, about a hundred miles from the sea. We resolved therefore to adopt this last route, and to travel as far as we could haul the canoes.

The first thing to be done was to obtain, if possible, some information about the Gander, or the "Nor'-West" Gander as it is more generally called, and for this purpose I went to Mr. W. D. Reid, who on this and subsequent occasions kindly gave me every assistance in his power. It appeared that fifteen miles up the river was a lumber camp worked by the Newfoundland Timber Estates. This industry has mills at Glenwood, on the Newfoundland Railway, and its steamers ply the lake and haul the logs from both the rivers which flow into its waters. Mr. Crowe, the manager of this company, said that practically nothing was known of the main Gander, and that no one had been farther than twenty miles up the stream, for at this distance the workable timber ceased. As to the navigability of the river, neither he nor any one else knew anything, but it was thought that "steady" water existed for thirty-five miles to a point where there was a waterfall. Beyond this nothing was known, but as James Howley,[1] the geographer, with his two Indians, had reached a point over seventy miles up this river some time in the seventies, I hoped to be able to do the same, and, if the water held good to the Partridgeberry Hills, to portage across to Dog Lake and river system, and work south to Hermitage Bay on the south coast.

I stayed a week in St. John's with my friend Mr. Hesketh Prichard, who was bound for the Labrador. Waiting to start on an expedition is always tiresome, but our delay on this occasion was made pleasant through the acquaintance of Judge Prowse and other friends. The Judge is certainly one of the most interesting characters in the island, for he was born and educated there, and understands the people of his country as no other man does. He is a man of over seventy, but his vitality and energy are that of a schoolboy. He talked all the time, and I listened, which just suited us both, for one was never tired of listening to characteristic stories of the men of the sea and the woods; and he can tell his stories with a due appreciation of the humour and pathos of human life.

The life of a judge in Newfoundland, until he reaches the highest rank, is not one to be envied. He has both to try the case and get up evidence for the prosecution as the

---

[1] Mr. Howley, in a letter to Mr. Blair, said: "I should not recommend Mr. Millais trying this route. It is too difficult for canoe navigation owing to the scarcity of water in the Gander during the summer season. We were obliged to abandon our own canoes some twenty miles above the Gander Lake after nearly tearing them to pieces, and to proceed on foot the remainder of the journey."

procurator-fiscal has to do in Scotland. This involves many long and tedious journeys, often performed in the depth of winter to outlying camps and villages, where evidence is often well-nigh impossible to procure. This severe physical strain year after year had hardly left its mark on the genial old gentleman, who, though he has now retired, is as active as ever.

I think the reader would have laughed had he seen this Judge of the Supreme Court and myself hunting for the problematical snipe in the wood and marshes one October morning. The Judge, with his hat on the back of his head and a pair of bedroom slippers on his feet ("Ye get wet anyhow, my boy"), jumped over the streams and fences like a two-year-old, working a somewhat wild pointer, and so, whistling and prancing from marsh to marsh, he covered the country in a manner that quite astonished me. Nor shall I forget his charming disregard for appearances, so characteristic of the true sportsman, when he kindly came to see me off by the crowded Sunday train, bearing in one hand a bucket full of potatoes and in the other—whisper it not in the Fly-Fisher's Club, breathe it not in the gun-rooms in the north—a big bag of worms.

The Judge has told me many excellent stories which I hope he will some day himself give to the world, for his literary abilities are well known on both sides of the Atlantic, his *History of Newfoundland* being the standard work on the subject. He is just as fond of telling a good story against himself as in his favour. I must venture to narrate one little tale about him, which comes from his own pen, and which was common talk in the up-country camps of the interior.

" The inception of the railway in Newfoundland met with

great opposition. The merchants were specially hostile to
the new departure; one old business man used to stand on
the head of his wharf, and tell the people how 'a tall gate'
(tollgate) would be placed at the western entrance to St.
John's; every one with a horse and cart would have to pay
2s. 6d., and whenever the surveyor's tape was passed over
their land it was gone from them for ever. In consequence
of these stories the people were stirred into a state of frenzy
and madness. When the railway surveyors began their work
at Topsail, at least five hundred insane men and women
followed them about constantly insulting and threatening
them. I was sent out with a small body of police to talk
to the people, and explain all about the railway. For days
and days I sat on the hillside, and told them all about the
advantages of the new line. It was all in vain; I could not
overcome their dread of the new and dangerous enterprise.
At last one morning they made a murderous assault on the
surveyors, took all their instruments, and they had to run for
their lives. As soon as I had taken the deposition of these
frightened officials, I hurried back to where the crowd were
rejoicing over their victory. The leader in the assault on the
surveyors was a fisherman farmer called Charley Andrews.
We had some difficulty in carrying out his arrest. After he
had been conveyed to the city jail, I met him on one of my
usual rounds of inspection. 'Well, Charley,' I said, 'how
are you getting on?' 'I am all for the railway now,
Judge.' 'How has that change come over the spirit of
your dream?' said I. 'Well,' he answered, 'it was this
way. An English sailor chap got drunk and he were put
into my cell; when he wakes in the mornin' he says to me,
"Well, old chap, what in the name of heaven brought you
here?" I told 'un it were fer fightin' agen a railway.

A Man's Track—They find it

A Man's Track—About to go

A Man's Track—Off

A Man's Track—Settling Down to their long slinging Trot
The Suffragette Leads

"What an infernal old bloke you must be," he said, "to do the like o' that. Why, the railway is the poor man's road," and then that sailor chap he up and explained to me all about en, so I'se all for the railway.' 'But, Charley,' I said, 'did I not explain all this to you over and over again? Did I not tell you all the work it would give the people, how it would bring all the goods to your doors, and quick passages in and out to town?' He hung his head in confusion for some time. At last he took a sly glance up at me: 'Yes, Judge, *but we knowed you was paid for sayin' dem tings.*'"

On the morning of 7th September I found myself at Glenwood, a small wayside station in the east-central portion of Newfoundland, and here I met Little Bob Saunders, his friend Alexander Butt, commonly called "Sandy," and all the paraphernalia of canoes and provisions.

A word is perhaps necessary to introduce "Sandy" Butt, as he enters these pages for the first time. He was a strong, dark, loose-jointed fellow, standing about six feet high, whose face bore a chronic expression of supercilious amusement. Nearly everything in this world was to him something in the nature of a joke; whether it was building camp in the dark or nearly chopping his foot off with the axe, which he did one day, it was all the same to him, and a good subject for whistling. A twinkle never left his eyes, and, like most Newfoundlanders, he was hard-working and good-natured, and never swore, for which I was grateful to him. He came with me ostensibly as "cook," altogether a mistaken *raison d'être*, for after the first day on which he made some bread, I lived exclusively on wheatmeal biscuits. Sandy was not the least disconcerted at this insult to his calling, but only regarded his efforts at baking as another superb jest, and "something to make the boys laugh down the Bay." But he could handle a canoe, and for twenty-one days in cold water was pulling, hauling, and carefully raising his little boat over the rocks and through the stream, with endless endurance and patience.   This was just the sort of man I wanted.

It is only recently that Newfoundland has awakened to the fact that it possesses considerable mineral and forest wealth.   Until ten years ago it imported all the lumber it required.   Now it not only supplies its own local needs, but exports 50,000,000 feet annually.   Within the past three years Lord Northcliffe and his brothers have acquired 2000 square miles of the best timber land in the island in the neighbourhood of the Exploits, Red Indian, and Victoria Lakes.   Much opposition, chiefly due to political agitation, was at first brought against the grant, the wildest stories being circulated amongst the fishermen, such as the threat-ened destruction of ancient hunting privileges.   Now since the innovation is proving a success and stimulating labour and business, the coming of the Harmsworths is regarded as a blessing.   If we except a small area of country in the neighbourhood of Bay d'Espoir, there is only one other good timber district in the island, and that is the Gander country, till recently controlled by the Newfoundland Timber Estates, and now to be worked by an English syndicate, represented by Mr. Reed.

Newfoundland timber and spruce wood for pulp were booming, so little Glenwood presented a scene of unusual activity.   About two hundred and fifty men were employed at the mill; nearly all Newfoundlanders, with a sprinkling of Canadians, who from their older experience at the logging camps of Ottawa were in a sense regarded as superior.   I sat up late in the smoking-room of the little shanty hotel, listening to stories and "lumber" talk. All the men there, about fifteen, were Newfoundlanders, except one, a Canadian from Nova Scotia. He seemed a clever and rather bright youth, and had been evidently indulging his wit at the expense of what he considered the more slow men of the island. At any rate they had clubbed together to sit upon and snub him. An old Newfoundlander was expressing his views about circular saws, when the Canadian boy interrupted and contradicted him flatly. He then began to explain where the Newfoundlander was wrong, when five or six of the islanders attacked him and told him to "shut up or get." Up at Glenwood and other logging camps Newfoundlanders are fond of telling a story against themselves. It is generally given in some such form as the following, a Canadian being the spokesman.

"Say, boys, I'll tell you a funny dream I had last night. I dreamt I died and went to Hell, which wasn't fair anyway. Old man he met me at the gate, and said he'd jes' show me round. 'See, boy,' he ses, 'you'll notice we got to keep some sort of order down here's well's upstairs. Nations got to be separated jes' same, or else they be a fightin' all the time, an' I wouldn't hev no time to do my roastin'. Those black fellows over there's Spaniards. Them in that corner's Frenchies. That big crowd down yonder's trust magnates an' African millionaires ; those two fine fellows standin' there alone, 'cos they got here by mistake, those are Canadians.' Yet all those unfortunate people were a roastin' an' a sizzlin', and hevin' fearful times. Bimeby we comes to a lot of wretched-lookin' men fastened up to the roof with chains, and underneath them was a small fire of sticks with the smoke a comin' up.

" ' What's those ? ' I ses.

" ' Well—er,' ses the Devil, a rubbin' his chin, 'those is Newfoundlanders. They're too d—d green to burn, so I'm jes' dryin' them off a bit.' "

.   .   .   .

Mr. Whitman, the manager of the Glenwood mills, told me that the large steamer would be at my disposal next morning, so we obtained a trolly, and the men soon pushed the outfit down to the Gander Lake, about a mile and a half away. It was a delightfully hot autumn morning as we steamed slowly down the beautiful lake.

Gander Lake is one of the largest sheets of water in New-foundland, 33 miles long. Away to the north stands the fine mountain of Blue Hill, surrounded by dense woods, contain-ing the finest trees in the island. The lake was exceedingly low—so low in fact that even the flat-bottomed steamer had some difficulty in making her way into deep water.

"Suppose you know every stone in the lake," was my first remark to the captain.

"Yes, that's one of them," was the reply, as we simul-taneously measured our length on the deck of the steamer. A big rock had caught us when going full speed astern and created this slight diversion. It took about ten minutes of poling and shoving, with engines going full steam ahead, and then we were under weigh again. In four hours we reached the mouth of the North-West River, which debouches into the lake amid a crowd of beautifully-wooded islands, covered with timber, and intersected with channels. Here a Frenchman named Frank de la Barre came aboard, having received instructions to meet me and pilot us up through the islands on the following day.

Frank had been in the Newfoundland woods for fifteen

years, and when I shook hands and addressed him in his own language, a multitude of conflicting emotions seemed to sweep across his face. I suppose even my bad French called up a wave of happy memories of days gone by, for at first his expression was one of incredulity, passing to that of unrestrained delight. Then came such a rattle of the southern tongue that I had some difficulty in understanding him. For one dreadful moment I thought he was going to kiss me, so I merely backed away and gave some orders about getting our outfit into the ship's boats, for it was blowing too hard to paddle across the lake to a point where it was necessary to make our base for the start up the river on the following day.

We spent a comfortable night in the woods, and next morning just as we had all the outfit packed in two canoes, Frank de la Barre and his son turned up to guide us up stream. Our route lay through a winding channel in and out of dozens of small islands, past lovely backwaters which gave peeps like the Thames at Clieveden Woods. Over deep holes and "steadies" we paddled, having to get out and pull the canoes over many sandy bars which only held enough water to float them. In this way we progressed for a couple of hours, when the main stream of the Gander opened itself before us, and seeing that further pilotage was unnecessary I bid good-bye to Frank.

During the first day's journey we made excellent progress, although the stream was certainly more rapid than we had anticipated; in fact, it was only for short spells that we could get aboard and paddle. The whole river, about 200 yards broad, seemed to hold no deep pools or any excessive rapid. It was almost to its source for eighty miles one level "run" over a comparatively shallow bed. Consequently I soon went ashore and walked ahead of the canoes, which the men pulled the whole day. On each side was dense forest of good-sized birch, white pine, "haps" (poplars), "vars" (firs), and rowan, which stretched away in unbroken masses to the distant hill-crests, situated about five miles on each side of the river bed. Here and there stood up lonely old leafless giants, 80 to 100 feet high, the relics of bygone "timber" that had been burnt from forty to forty-five years ago. There seemed to be no fish, for fish do not care for shallow running rivers, and consequently there were no birds to enliven the scene; so we plodded away steadily till past nightfall, just reaching the woods opposite the lumber camp, where darkness had already fallen.

The next morning (10th September) a boat passed us, carrying the "boss" of the lumber camp down stream. To our question, he called out that there were no men above the lumber camp, nor was anything known of the river beyond the Great Gull River, about twenty miles up stream. This was satisfactory, for we now hoped to see deer at any moment. However, we plodded all day steadily on without seeing any sign of game, although about sunset I began to see some fresh tracks.

The following day we encountered a series of small rapids which took the men some time to negotiate, and here I saw the first birds, a flock of twelve old male goosanders, locally called "Gossets," diving and chasing trout in the roughest place. They were all moulting their "pinions" and unable to fly, but rushed up stream over the surface of the water at a surprising rate.

"Twilliks," too, were plentiful all along the river. The greater yellowshank (*Totanus melanoleucus*), locally known as "Twillik," is very common in all the Newfoundland rivers during the summer and autumn. It arrives in May and departs in October, after the breeding season. A regular winter visitor to America and the West Indies, it is there known as the "tell-tale," "tell-tale tattler," "winter yellow-leg," and "stone-snipe." The birds are commonly seen in Newfoundland singly or in small parties of four or five. They love to run about the stones, catching flies, or upon the boggy and sandy shores of the lakes, where their attitudes and movements much resemble our native greenshank. I have seen a party on feed sweeping their bills from side to side in the shallow water, after the manner of the avocet, and thus they obtain minute insects. When you approach a small flock they become very noisy, uttering a harsh note, something like the cry of the greenshank, but louder. If "cornered" in the angle of a lake or stream, they run anxiously to and fro, bobbing up and down with their bodies just like the redshank. In the British Isles it has only occurred once, namely at Scilly, in September 1906.

In the afternoon we came to a place where the sides of the river were broken, low-lying, and full of swamps covered with long grass and alder. So I kept a sharp look-out, sitting down constantly to spy ahead, and pausing to examine the broken leads where stags had been in the habit of breaking down from the forest to the river. I had come to the mouth of the Great Gull River, and the canoes had just caught me up, when, giving a glance across the stream, I saw the white stern of a deer feeding away round the corner of an island.

Saunders paddled me across the stream, and I landed on the marsh where the animal had disappeared. Walking rapidly up-wind, there was no sign of it, however, so we continued our way up a branch stream, commanding another island containing a dense alder thicket. I was about to turn back to the canoes when there was the sound like a stick cracking, and the next moment the top of a caribou stag's horn appeared above the bush about 130 yards away. The next moment it disappeared, though I could now see the line of the . animal's back. Another moment and the stag would be gone for ever, so I rested the Mannlicher on the top of Little Bob's head, and let go. The stag instantly plunged forward into view, showing at once that it was hard hit; I could now see the head and shoulders, so I fired again, and the beast, with a bullet in the neck, immediately fell dead.

Saunders soon brought the canoes round, and, crossing over the island, we examined our first prize, which proved to be a fair beast of about five years old. Sandy now joined us, and we lost no time in taking the best of the haunch meat, fat, and tongue, and in half-an-hour had continued our journey, feeling very happy, as every hunter does when his camp is well supplied with the food on which men alone can hunt.

Shortly after passing the park-like scenery on the banks of the Great Gull River, the river narrowed again, and fresh sign of deer—the tracks of big stags only—became more frequent. It was just getting dusk, and I was thinking of stopping to make camp for the night, when I heard the subdued roar of the waterfall about a mile ahead, so we resolved to press on in the dark, reaching a clump of timber close behind the fall itself, and at a spot where portaging would be easy on the following day.

Taken all round, this was about the most successful trip I ever made, but, just as there are always days in every hunter's life in which everything seems to go wrong and nothing is right, I instance the following as an example of

ROLLING FALLS.

how ill-luck and a bit of obstinacy may serve to upset what one fondly thinks are correct calculations. The following is copied from my diary:—

September 12.—Last night it rained in torrents, but the day broke clear and pellucid as a morning in Algiers. I was eating my breakfast when Little Bob, who had been to prospect the fall, came in to say that a short distance up was a beautiful open country on the right bank, and that, while he was looking in that direction, a young stag had come out and crossed the river, going south. It was evidently a pass, so, whilst the men were making a path to carry the outfit and canoes around the fall, I resolved to go and smoke my pipe and watch.

A series of rocky ledges jutted into the river on the south bank, and on this I lay down, as it commanded an extensive and beautiful view of the landscape—of the open, marshy country rising to the north, and the park-like country adjoining the river to the west. A dense wood of closely packed young spruces occupied the right bank of the river immediately opposite, and this was abruptly divided by a pebbly brook, up which I could plainly see for 500 yards, where it debouched from a broad marsh, a likely-looking spot indeed for game to haunt and to make passes, for they always choose the shortest and easiest routes from one open country to another.

It was pleasant to sit and watch the morning sunlight creeping along the tops of the forest trees, the dark green banks of spruce, the silvery birches, and over the yellow marshes. A belted kingfisher, with the sun glistening on his slate-blue back, came and contemplated the rushing waters within a few yards of where I lay, and two American goshawks soared overhead lazily, or chased one another in clumsy play. The heat of the day had not commenced, and the great grey curtain of midges were still a scattered mass of lethargic life, reposing on the river stones.

During the warm hours of the day black flies make life a burden to some people, especially to the natives, and to such an extent are their bites felt that many will not venture up the rivers in summer and early autumn. Personally I did not suffer much from their attentions, but I have seen men absolutely driven out of the country by them. In the evening sand-flies and mosquitoes are sometimes almost unbearable, the only relief being obtained by smoking continuously beside a good camp fire.

With regard to black flies and mosquitoes and their onslaughts on idle persons, a delightful homily with a beautiful moral is thus given by Captain Whitbourne (1622).

"Neither are there any Snakes, Toads, Serpents, or any other venomous Wormes that ever were known to hurt any man in that Country, but onely a very little nimble Fly (the least of all other Flies), which is called a Muskeito; those Flies seem to have a great power and authority upon all loytering and idle people that come to the New-found-land; for they have this property that, when they find any such lying lazily, or sleeping in the Woods, they will presently bee more nimble to seize upon them, than any Sargeant will bee to arrest a man for debt; neither will they leave stinging or sucking out the blood of such sluggards, until, like a Beadle, they bring him to his Master, where he should labour: in which time of loytering, those Flies will so brand such idle persons in their faces, that they may be known from others, as the Turks do their slaves."

Nothing moved, and there was no sound save the roar

ot the waterfall below, or the "clinking" of white-winged crossbills passing overhead.

I looked dreamily through the smoke of my pipe away up stream. All of a sudden some big animal burst from the timber about 500 yards up stream on the north bank. It turned sideways, and I saw that it was a large black bear. With that long, swinging stride so characteristic of the genus, she, for I am sure the beast was a female that had brought forth cubs this summer, advanced rapidly down the river, here about 100 yards broad. The head was held very low, and the legs struck me as being longer and more spindly in proportion to the body than those of other bears I have seen. Every now and then she raised her head, examining the character of the bushes, and once stopped and went up to a small tree, which I afterwards found to be a wild cherry, and clawed down a sprig or two which she munched as she continued the journey down stream.

All this time the bear was rapidly advancing nearer to me, and I had already chosen the best spot on the other side of the river where I should fire at her. I had a perfect position, my back comfortably tucked in the cranny of a ledge of rock and both legs firmly planted against the asperities of a slate slab. The distance would be just about 100 yards when she came opposite to me, and I was beginning to feel that there would be a certainty of an easy shot. But "the best laid schemes o' mice an' men gang oft agley." I looked up at the oncoming bear, and, to my intense disappointment, saw her suddenly leave the river shore and plunge into the forest. The bank was steep at this point, and it seemed a most unlikely place for a "lead" to exist; yet, as I afterwards found, there was one there which had been daily used by bears.

A slender hope now seized me, that the bear might work on through this belt of young spruce and cross the little brook coming down from the open barren. Accordingly, I kept a sharp look-out, and in a few minutes was rewarded by seeing a small willow tree violently agitated about 150 yards up the left bank of the stream. It now seemed possible that one might see and get a shot at the bear after all, though not an easy one, as she was likely to cross the brook, on which I could see her plainly. Hardly had I fixed myself into shooting position when she came swiftly down the bank, and at a quick walk entered the shallow stream. At this moment I fired, and saw the bear half flounder on to her side, but instantly recover and dash up the bank again out of sight. She was undoubtedly hard hit, for, had the shot missed, I should have seen the bullet strike the water above or below.

There was no hurry, for I expected the bear to run a hundred yards or so and fall dead, so I sat down with considerable satisfaction, lit another pipe, and awaited the coming of the men with the first portage loads. In about ten minutes Bob and Sandy appeared, staggering under a weight of provisions. The noise of the waterfall had drowned the sound of the shot, so that their astonishment was great when I told them that I thought I had killed a bear. Whilst explaining the whole story to Saunders and pointing out the spot where Mrs. Bruin had disappeared, suddenly another large bear appeared at the edge of the barren, about 500 yards away. It was evidently the mate of the pair, and he walked quietly down in the stream and started to cross into the timber where the wounded one had gone. The shot was nearly a hopeless one, owing to the distance and the fact that I had to stand up to see the object at all. The little bullet, however, went very near, and splashed the water all over Mr. Bear, who got a dreadful fright, and made off with all possible speed.

Bob Saunders and I now crossed the river, and found the spot where the wounded bear had entered the timber; indeed there was no mistaking it, for a trail of blood which looked as if it had been poured out of a tea-kettle led away into the densest bush. There was now a possibility of trouble, so I sent Bob back for the other Mannlicher. The young spruce trees were growing so closely together that in many places we had to crawl on our hands and knees, along the actual paths which the bears themselves had made. It was like hunting a flea in a box of matches. In the worst places, if one stood up, it was not possible to force a way ahead. Consequently we had to be careful, as the bear was probably not dead, and we should not see it at a greater distance than 5 or 6 feet. The blood trail itself showed a firm dark line on the bright yellow green moss, so we easily followed it for about 500 yards; then we came to a round knoll of soft wet moss, which plainly told its tale. The wounded bear had just been lying here, and we had moved her. There was the imprinted mark of her whole left flank and the bullet exit hole mark, where the blood had flowed freely. The poor beast was hit right through the lungs, and the bullet, a solid one with the nose well filled, had not sufficiently expanded. Immediately the bear had risen to run from us the blood had ceased to flow. I suppose that the cold wet moss must have staunched the wound, for the blood marks ceased. We threshed around for ten minutes or so, could find no further trail, for the soft paw of the plantigrade leaves no spoor on moss, and then sat down to deplore our ill-luck.

What would I not have given for a little Norwegian elk-hound at that moment. The bear may have gone a mile or two, or she may have been lying dead within a hundred yards of us; at any rate we were now incapable of following her, so reluctantly we fought our way back to the river, and tried to make as light of the loss as possible.

The black bear is still fairly numerous in the unfrequented parts of Newfoundland, but every year sees a diminution in their numbers owing to the attacks of the Indians. In 1822 Cormack describes them as abundant, and speaks of the numerous "bear-roads" which he found in all parts of the interior. Now such paths are rarely seen. Every year in the month of September the Indians repair to the high look-outs, and watch the open tracts of country covered with blueberry patches. Here they spy, stalk, and shoot the bears which come to feed at dawn and sunset. In this manner they kill from three to nine bears apiece, and few escape except those which live almost exclusively in the forests. In years when berries are scarce, many bears repair to the edge of the salt water and feed on caplin and fish refuse. Some-times they attack the farmers' sheep, and I know of one instance in which a bear swam a mile to an island in Fortune Bay, and killed twenty-five sheep in a single night. They are slow and poor swimmers, and the Esquimaux of Labrador go so far as to say that they cannot swim at all. But this is incorrect. About the end of April the black bear emerges from its winter retreat in some rocky cave or old tree stump, and commences to feed on roots and leaves of various trees. In May the female brings forth her two young ones, and tends them carefully until the autumn, when they shift for themselves. They keep closely to the woods until July, when

IN THE PLACE WHERE NO MAN COMES.

the berries are ripe, and feed on these until the middle of October. At the first frosts, however, they leave this food, which is now falling from the bushes, and go in search of the carcases of deer, scenting them from a great distance. In October, too, they ascend the rowan trees to a considerable height, breaking off the branches containing the fruit, and sliding down the trunk with the skill of an acrobat. I have seen several trees scored by the marks of their claws as they descended at top speed. The Indians have told me that when the bear is hungry he often grabs greedily at the rowan berries, and, losing his balance, falls with a thud to the ground. Whereupon he shouts with pain and mortification, and, finding that no bones are broken, sulkily ascends the tree again. John Hinx has seen a bear fall twice out of a high tree, and shot him as he was climbing the third time. Like the fox, they are exceedingly careful when approaching a carcase for the first time (as I shall presently describe), but after they have had a meal of it, will advance boldly upwind. A few are killed by the Indians in the "deadfall," but bears are so cunning in Newfoundland that they are not often captured in this fashion. Their mischievous habit of wrecking a camp or tilt is well known, and few travellers in the interior have not suffered from their unwelcome visits.

When the black bear enters a tilt or wigwam, it opens and scatters everything within, whilst it has a curious habit of never departing by the way of entry, preferring to scrape a hole in the side of the shelter by way of exit. Sometimes it tears the whole place to pieces out of pure wickedness.

Steve Bernard carried a sack of flour and all his stores and ammunition to his log tilt on Jubilee Lake in the autumn of 1902, and then repaired to the coast to see the priest. When he returned, the whole tilt, including fir logs weighing several hundred pounds, were scattered through the woods, and not a dollar's worth of the outfit remained. Two bears were the aggressors, and so cunning were they that the trapper completely failed to shoot or trap them. One man I know of, after losing all his stores, had his canoe bitten to pieces.

About the middle of November the black bear chooses a dry spot in which to hibernate. If the winter is mild, he comes out again for a short time, but the first heavy snowfall drives him again into his sleeping apartment, the entrance of which he closes carefully with moss and leaves. These retreats are but rarely found even by the Indians, who are always in the woods. A good skin is worth about £5, and the length seldom exceeds 6 feet. Joe Jeddore killed a large dog bear near Burnt Hill in 1901, which measured 7 feet 6 inches, and doubtless specimens even bigger than this have occurred in the island, but I can obtain no reliable records. In the autumn they are very fat, and the meat and grease are much appreciated, both by the red men and the white. If ordinary precautions are taken, these animals are not in the least dangerous, and the few accidents which have occurred were entirely due to carelessness on the part of the hunters. It is not safe, however, to fire at a bear when the animal is very close on a hillside above the shooter, because when receiving a mortal wound the bear always rushes blindly down hill, and then seizes with its teeth the first object that comes in its way. All bears do this. I once shot at a very big grizzly, and the first thing it did was to demolish a small tree standing near by. Charges by bears, described by youthful hunters with hair-raising sensationalism, are seldom charges at all, for the poor bear receiving the shot rushes madly *in any direction*, and in doing so, it may run on the top of you.

SIX HEADS KILLED ON THE GANDER, SEPTEMBER 1903

In the old records of Newfoundland we read that the white Polar bear was a regular winter visitor to the coast in the seventeenth century. Since then its appearance became rarer as time went on. Until 1825, a few were always found on the ice off White Bay by the spring sealers, and an odd one killed on the shore, but now it can only be recorded as very scarce. A Newfoundland lady, who was present at the following incident, has told me that twenty-five years ago the inhabitants of the village of Wittlebay were coming out of church one Sunday morning, when they were startled by seeing an immense Polar bear strolling down the hill close to the church door. There were no guns at hand, so four men bravely attacked it with axes and killed it. A dispute as to the possession of the hide arising, the skin was cut into four pieces, and may be seen in certain houses of the village to this day. *À propos* of this strange method of division, which has always been in force in Newfoundland, I am reminded of a true incident which occurred about eighty years ago in Fortune Bay, when the disgraceful practice of "wrecking" was by no means extinct. A barque which had been lured on to the rocks by false lights, placed there by some good Christian belonging to a certain village which shall be nameless, had on board a cottage piano, an instrument which neither of the boat's crews which claimed it had ever seen before. The matter was, however, eventually settled by its being sawn in two pieces, one party taking the treble and the other the bass.

Wrecking as a profitable industry ceased to flourish in Newfoundland about fifty years ago, "in the dear delightful days of Arcadian simplicity, when port wine was a shilling a bottle, and the colony had no debt." The Newfoundland Government had much difficulty in stamping it out, owing to the fact that the people of the south coast had indulged in

G

the nefarious practice for centuries, and could with difficulty be persuaded that they were doing anything that was not perfectly legitimate. Whatever came ashore as the flotsam and jetsam of the ocean was theirs by right, so they considered, and many cases of a shocking character were dealt with by Judge Prowse, who was sent to enforce the law.

"Seafaring people," he says, "look upon wrecks as their lawful prizes, gifts sent to them direct by Providence, and their views about these fatalities were characteristic. Mostly the vessels contained valuable cargoes, but occasionally it was otherwise. I heard an old Irishwoman declare about one 'wrack,' 'I don't know what God Almighty is thinking about, sending us a terrible bad fishery, and then an old Norwegian brig full of nothing but rocks.'

"In one instance I was sent to look after a very bad case of absolute piracy. The fishermen attacked the master and crew whilst their schooner was ashore, cut her masts, and forcibly took away all her gear and stores. I had to put up at the principal settler's house in this little cove. I well knew all were implicated in the wreck. They asked me to go in and see the mistress of the house, an old woman suffering from asthma. After I had told her of some remedies, she gasped out, 'Oh, why did they come so near the shore? Oh, why did they come so near the shore to timpt the poor peoples?'

"Wrecking cases always gave me capital sport, as they all happened in very out-of-the-way places, where there were very good grouse-moors. I once shot a whole covey of a dozen birds with the police, witnesses, and prisoners acting as beaters and markers. The grouse were scattered and rose in pairs. I had to swing round each time to shoot the second bird. The last killed was a very long shot, and it fell into a crevice of the rock; one of the prisoners, a long, slim fellow, was lowered down by the heels to recover it. All the accused and witnesses in the case were keen hunters. I knew right well that if I had made a bad shot, neither my legal acumen nor sound judgment would have won their appreciation half as much as straight shooting."[1]

But we have wandered away to the south coast, and must return to the Gander.

Looking up the river from the lower fall of the Gander was, I think, one of the most beautiful landscapes that I have seen in my expeditions in Newfoundland. The rocks in the foreground were of the most lovely colour, a rich blue grey. Over these poured masses of amber water of pellucid clearness. Little brooks and shining barrens peeping out from amidst the dark forest on the right bank, led the eye away up to distant hills of the most intense blue, whilst in the middle distance, away up the glistening river, were islands covered with the finest "haps" (poplars) in Newfoundland, every leaf a-quiver in the blazing sun. On the left bank the land rose in rugged and distorted shapes, and was all covered with a medley of golden birch and scarlet rowan, and trees standing clear against a brown mass of tall "vars," and spruces in whose depths the glints of sunlight mixed with the purple shadows. Yet all this heterogeneous mass of colour seemed to blend, for nature makes no mistake with her paints, whilst for once the composition of the picture was perfect and worthier of a more skilful brush than mine. "Rolling Falls" of the Gander is such a subject as only a great artist could do justice to.

About two miles up the river was another small waterfall, not so heavy as the lower one, but nevertheless neces-

[1] *Cornhill Magazine*, April 1904.

sitating a portage of the whole of the outfit. Here we saw some salmon jumping, which showed that the lower fall offered no bar to the progress of fish. After a hearty meal in the blazing sun, we resumed our journey up continuous "rattles" of water, through which the men made excellent progress, in spite of the fact that the rocks were covered with "slob," *i.e.* a green slimy weed.

We were now in quite virgin country, where the foot of the only two white men had ever trodden, once when Howley made his survey of the river with two Indians, some time in the seventies, and Mr. Willis in October 1901, and again when Mr. Willis went there on a prospecting trip. There was not a sign that Indians had ever been here; not an axe mark was seen on the trees above this, and we were far beyond the ken of the "White-Ends." The Indians, too, would never come here except for beaver, and of beaver there were none in the main stream. I experienced, therefore, the delight that every hunter feels in knowing that he has no neighbours except the deer and the bears, and that at any minute he may strike a new country, the veritable home of the mighty antlered monarchs, and such a sanctuary as the first travellers in the Rockies and South Africa discovered. In a minor form I did discover such a sportsman's paradise, for I do not suppose any previous traveller in Newfoundland ever cast his eyes on so many fine caribou stags in a short time, as I was fortunate enough to do during the next fortnight.

The bear incident was not the only unlucky event of this day, September 12. I must follow out its incidents with full confession to the setting of the sun. I had travelled on about a mile ahead of the boats, and was keeping a sharp look-out ahead, as well as on the many fresh tracks of big

PREPARING HEADS

BEAVER DAM ON THE UPPER GANDER

stags that were imprinted wherever there was sand betwixt the stones. About 4 P.M. I came to a broad sweep of the river, where a fine view expanded itself. Opposite to me was a large wooded island—"Twillik" Island the Indians call it—with shallows at its bend, and just a likely-looking crossing-place for stags. So I sat down and slapped continuously at the black flies and mosquitoes, which were very troublesome. Opposite was a backwater beyond the island. There was much grass, bog bean, and alder there, and a good place for a stag to "shove out," so I had more than one chance to see game. Half-an-hour went by, and the canoes had just reached me as I stood up to resume the journey, when, looking across the backwater, I saw a grand stag emerge from the woods and begin to feed without concern. I immediately sat down and got ready to fire. The distance seemed about 250 yards, for the beast looked large, and I felt I could hit him. First shot, a miss. The stag raised his head and looked about. I could not see where the bullet struck; took again a full sight, and fired. The stag stepped forward evidently untouched. I fired again —same result.

"What distance are you shootin' at?" said Bob hurriedly.

"Two hundred and fifty yards," I replied laconically.

"He's four hundred if he's a yard," replied Saunders.

"He's not," I said obstinately, and fired again without result. The stag now ran along the marsh looking for his "lead" in the forest. Presently he found it, and I let go the last cartridge in the magazine as he disappeared from view.

I stood up, feeling annoyed, as I was quite steady when making the shots. Immediately I came to my feet I saw that Bob was right, and that I had far under-estimated the distance. Across the river was at least two hundred yards, and from thence to the forest edge was as far again. I acknowledged my mistake, and humbled myself before Saunders, whose powers of judging distances over two hundred yards were usually at fault. This time, however, he had been quite right. The stag seemed to carry a very fine head, but then they always do when they get away.

We travelled on for a mile or two, and then camped for the night on a steep bank of larch, and the night closed in with heavy rain, which put a finishing touch to this unfortunate day.

CHAPTER V

A HUNTER'S PARADISE

THE next day being Sunday, we rested, and on Monday, 14th September, continued up stream, the men being greatly hampered by the shallowness of the water, the "slobby" rocks, and a somewhat tempestuous head-wind. Saunders fell in up to his neck four times during the morning, but the day was not cold, so we worked on five miles to the mouth of Migwell's Brook, a small stream that enters the Gander on the north bank about fifty miles from the lake.

I was about two miles ahead of the canoes, and sat behind a large rock. It was blowing half a gale, and the time being midday, I hardly expected to see game. As the wind swayed and rocked the forest at my back, one became accustomed to the crackle and brush of twig upon twig and bough against bough, but somehow more than once I could not help thinking that I heard dry wood "snapping" when there was a lull. The inner consciousness of doubt soon resolved itself into a certainty that some large animal was breaking down a tree close beside me, so I dropped my book, cocked the rifle, and looked over the high bank just as wild cherry was violently shaken almost in my face.

"Now, Mr. Bruin, I have you at last," I said to myself, in the excitement of the moment. But it was not a bear after all, but a great caribou stag, with horns evidently on the decline, staring me in the face at a distance of about six

yards. I have never been so near a wild deer before, and
he backed away from the cherry tree before deciding to
make a bolt of it. One moment we both stood still and
stared at one another, and having mutually decided that
our heads were unnecessary, he gave a plunge and was gone.
The stag had hardly vanished when a tinkle of falling stones
made me look to the left, and there I saw another good-sized
stag carrying about thirty points, walking leisurely along the
open stones away from me. He gave me one proud glance,
ran a few steps, and then settled to a walk, at which pace
he continued till lost to sight round a bend in the river.
He was a fine young stag of perhaps five years, but the tops
were unfinished, wherefore not deemed good enough in new
ground like this. I followed the track of this stag some
little distance, and it led me north to low sandy hills and
into a beautiful broken country, all leads, marshes, opens, and
clumps of spruces, just the place for "summering" stags.
I saw, too, five or six small larches newly "stripped," where
stags had cleaned their horns recently, so when the men
came up I decided to stop a day and hunt.

The sun was low as Saunders and I left the camp.
Glancing up the stream from the point of Migwell's Brook,
we at once noticed two young stags come from a lead on
the north bank, and across the river. Everything seemed
to show that we were now in a great stag country. The
does had all passed on out to the open marshes to the south,
and the old males would remain here solitary or in pairs for
at least another fortnight, before they, too, would follow,
and seek them in the open marshes of the high country.

We crept noiselessly up the sandy hills till we came to
a hillock rising higher than the rest. Here I ascended a
larch, and spied the surrounding country for a mile or two.

Much of it was very "blind," but towards the river there were many open spaces and little hills where game might be viewed. The sun was already setting when we decided to move on a little farther before returning, as a dip, fringed by large trees, hid the course of the brook, and many of the leads trended northwards along the waterside, always a favourite walk for deer. We had hardly rounded the first hillock when I perceived the white stern of a large stag on another little hill about one hundred yards away. The beast was feeding quietly, so I got out the telescope and examined him.

"He seems to have a lot of points, Bob," I said, "but horns look thin." At this moment the stag raised his noble head to chew the cud, and I had a good side view of it. That movement decided his fate. An instant later I sat with my back to a tree, and put two bullets into him. At the first he never winced, although a mortal blow, but on receiving the second he rolled over quite dead. As I rose to my feet a movement on another hillock to the right caught my eye, and immediately a second stag, nearly, but not quite so good as the first, stepped into full view. The glass was soon surveying his cranial ornaments, which, though carrying about thirty points, looked thin, whilst the "bays" were poor, so he was allowed to depart. He gave a "whoof" of terror as soon as I rose, and, erecting the hair of his scut, dashed off at full gallop. This was the third time on the same day that I had seen two stags together, which shows the disposition of the male caribou for society during his period of summer seclusion.

We now walked up to our first warrantable prize, which proved to carry a better head than I had at first thought. The horns were not heavy, but carried thirty-five points, and all set in those beautiful wild curves that go to make up a really good head. He had good double front shovels prettily interlocked, and very handsome wild "tops" to the horns, containing several extra straggly points, which add so much to the beauty of any head. At any rate I felt pleased with our first trophy, and it was with light hearts we returned to camp, where Bob at once set to work to skin, whilst Sandy prepared an excellent supper.

Next day Bob and I wandered far to the north, getting into some abominable ground, from which it took us some hours to extricate ourselves. The farther we went from the river and Migwell's Brook, the less sign of deer was noticeable, and the worse the timber became. Just as we left camp we saw two stags, but their heads were of no account, and in the evening two more crossed the river and came walking by the camp not more than fifty yards away. One of these was a regular old patriarch. His horns were narrowed to mere thin spires, and I believe he was partly deaf, for it was not till I had thrown two stones at him, and then warmed him up with a swan shot from my catapult, that he condescended to take any notice of me. Many of these stags which I now saw had probably never seen man before, for on several occasions, when the wind was right, one could take surprising liberties with them, without their seeming alarmed. Never in my life did I regret the loss of a camera so much as during the next fortnight. In the hurry of packing I had left it at the station at Glenwood, and it was not till I returned there that it came in for any use. During our absence Sandy said that a stag with a fair head walked by the camp between him and the river, a distance of fourteen yards. The unsuspecting animal had stopped a moment to observe our cook peeling potatoes, and had then resumed his journey down stream without altering his pace from a walk.

It may seem to the reader, if he only knows a little about big-game hunting, that to shoot such tame animals is almost devoid of sport, and in many cases he would be right in the case of the caribou. It is the other chances that produce the necessity of quick decision, with long and sometimes difficult shots, which make the chase of the caribou a fascinating one. The object of the hunter in new ground where game is abundant is naturally to secure the best heads, and an exceptional trophy may sometimes be obtained in the easiest manner. On the other hand, I had several times seen a stag rush out of the forest with a clatter of stones, scamper into the river as if in fun, stand a minute or two in the stream and drink, and then gallop or swim across to the farther bank, where he will only glance round for a second before disappearing for good up some lead. They are not frightened, but are perhaps in a hurry to reach some favourite feeding ground in a secluded glade back from the river. In such a case you may be five to eight hundred yards from the stag when you first view him, and have to strain every muscle to run that four or five hundred yards which brings you within a long shot. Then, temporarily blown, you must sit at once to take your shot, and have no time to hunt out a good position. The wind may be wrong, or the stag may just walk to the water's edge, drink for a second or two, and then turn again into the forest. During these few minutes, too, you must have your glass handy to see whether his head is good enough (and I do not know any deer whose horns are so difficult to judge in a short period of sight. Sometimes at one angle they look splendid, and at another quite poor, so you are torn with conflicting emotions in those few minutes of intense activity and excitement). This form of the chase, which I may appropriately call "river-hunting," offers both the easiest and the most difficult chances at deer. In the open marshes the caribou stag is generally at your mercy. You have time to circumvent him and to lay your plans. If you are anything of a shot and take care not to walk about too much, or give him the wind, he is yours. But by the river it is different. The stag appears; you must shoot at once or run like a hare to get into range, for he may disappear at any second, and generally, too, your shot is taken at the wrong end of the beast, though that is not of much moment, as in the old days of inferior rifles.

The following morning, 15th September, we continued to ascend the Gander. A strong head-wind was blowing, and the men experienced much difficulty in keeping on their feet and preventing our frail craft from breaking. I walked on for about five miles, and then sat down to spy as the country suddenly opened up, and I saw, for the first time since leaving the lake, a high, open, sparsely-wooded country. The men with the canoes arrived about midday, and, just as Bob came opposite to me, he slipped off a stone and fell in over his neck.

"This is my lucky day," he said philosophically; "only been in twice this morning."

We sat down to dinner on the bank, and, after much wrangling, I got him to change his clothes, which he did with many protests. Little Bob had half "shifted" when, it seems, he was overcome with curiosity as to the exceedingly "gamy-looking" nature of the mountain opposite, so, without saying a word, he captured my telescope, which he had now come to use with some success, and slipped off

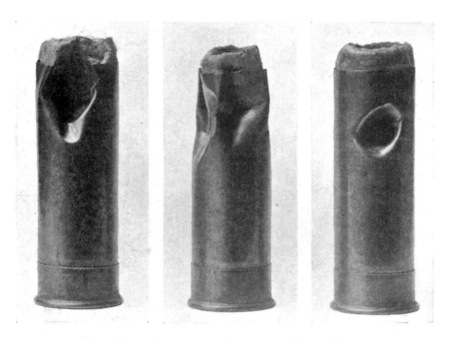

ELEY BRASS CARTRIDGES CHEWED BY BLACK BEARS

SANDY BUTT AT WORK

in the bushes. Like a good man he had gone to spy the hill from the only point it could be properly seen, namely, to the marsh on the north bank. In one minute he came running back, saying—

"Dere's a great lump of a stag above us, 'bout 300 feet."

There was only one way up on to this high ground, and that was up a well-worn caribou path, which seemed to lead directly down-wind to the point where Saunders said the stag was feeding. The wind was strong, and inclined to shoot our taint upwards, as I found on trying it with tobacco smoke. Nevertheless we decided to chance it.

The path itself was beaten down with fresh tracks crossing a hillside marsh. Then it became suddenly dry and stony, and we wound up on to a tiny plateau with small clumps of birch.

"'Twas 'bout here he was when I seen him," was Bob's remark, scarcely emitted than a loud rattle of stones proclaimed that the stag was started. Fortunately, he galloped up the hill and then alongside it, giving me a full broadside. I had time to see his head was large and sufficiently good, without many points; then, standing up to see him properly, I put the first bullet through his right horn. The chamber was immediately opened and closed, and I got in my second shot just as he was tearing into a droke of birch. The little missile went true, breaking both shoulders; the stag performed a complete somersault like a shot rabbit, and was nearly dead when we came up to him.

There was one thing remarkable about this deer, and that was his great size; and Saunders, who was well qualified to speak on the subject, said he was the largest caribou stag he had ever seen in his life. An immense brute, nearly as big as a wapiti, it took all our efforts to turn him over in the place where he lay, and had we the space to have carried the complete skin, I should certainly have brought it home for the museum.

Whilst Bob was attending to the head skin, I took the telescope to view the magnificent panorama that now spread itself before me.

At our feet, glittering in the sunlight, was the Blue Gander, and up this beautiful river, so like our Tay in Scotland, one could see for four or five miles to the entrance of Little Gull River away to the west. At the back rose the mountains known as Serpentine Hill, of some 800 or 900 feet elevation, and spread out below, though gradually rising away to the north, was a succession of woods and open marshes, on any of which there was a good chance of seeing the great white-necked stag or a black bear.

Bob had scarcely commenced his work, and I had not even begun to use the glass, for the prospect of the scene was in itself delightful, when looking down I saw another big caribou stag come out of the woods and walk quickly across a wide open marsh about half a mile below. One word to Bob was enough, and at a jog trot we set off downhill, passing through two small belts of timber and a mountain stream. Half the distance was overcome when it was deemed necessary to view the position of our quarry. Yes, there he was, right in the centre of the swamp, and either feeding or drinking, for his head was down. There was no particular hurry, so we advanced easily, and presently found ourselves overlooking the open marsh. Now there was nothing left but a good old-fashioned crawl with the cold water running in at your collar stud and out at your boots. This I did by myself till I reached a point within 200 yards from the stag, where seeing him so quiet I turned round and signalled to Bob so that we could discuss his respective merits. After examining the ground carefully I saw first that by making a flanking manoeuvre I could probably come in again on the deer and reach a small island of bush, with a stunted larch in the centre, and should then be within 100 yards of the stag. This required care, as we had to cross an open of about 20 yards within view of the deer, but old Roman-nose seemed absorbed in a brown study, so this insult to his sight and intelligence was unnoticed, and we reached the desired haven.

But what was the old fellow doing? His attitude indicated utter misery and woe. His head hung down, and ears flopped forwards like a sick donkey. He never moved from his position of dejection for ten minutes except once, when he lowered his nose into the marsh, and I could see him suck up the peat and muddy water. Now I had it: he was love-sick and taking in this stimulant to cool his passion. I daresay the reader, if he has killed deer in Scotland in October, will have noticed that certain stags when gralloched have nothing in their stomach but a peaty fluid. This is probably their only nutriment when in full rut, as the stag does not feed at this season, and seems to live for a week or two on his own previous condition. So, too, this old caribou stag must have been doing exactly the same, for when I cut him up I found nothing but this fluid in his stomach. It is probably a general habit of the whole genus *Cervidæ* during the season of love and war.

We looked his head over very carefully. Brows fair, bays very good and strong, tops very moderate. I hesitated, and had decided to spare his life, as I hoped to get better.

"You'll have to shoot him," said Bob; "he is very good, and a've seen many a season when a' should have been pleased if a' brought out a head like that from the Terra-Nova country."

Still I thought it best to spare him. "Whistle him up, Bob," I said; "we'll see what he looks like when he holds his head up." My companion whistled once, twice, and then gave a shout. Ye Gods! what a sudden change from the listless donkey to the alert king of the forest. His head was up in the air now, and he looked totally different; a fine heavy head, and certainly worth possessing. As I raised the rifle he bolted at full gallop straight away, and I made a very lucky shot as he fled in full career, the bullet entering at the back of his head and causing instant death. He fell so suddenly and with such force that he smashed the lower jaw to pieces and buried the antlers out of sight in the marsh, from which we had to unearth them. Like the other stag this was a very big old beast with a good massive head of thirty-two points. The work of cutting up the deer and preserving the head would occupy some time, so I accompanied Saunders back to camp, and then spent the evening spying from the hillside.

Just before sunset I saw a fine stag about a mile away across the river. I could see he had grand tops and very thick horns. He wandered into a thick forest, but the time being too late to go for him I returned to camp.

We were, however, destined to meet later.

A DREAM OF HOWLEY, BY ONE WHO HAS NEVER BEEN THERE

CHAPTER VI

HUNTING ON THE UPPER GANDER AND RETURN TO GLENWOOD

MY water babies both worked hard that night, Bob attending to the head skins and Sandy cleaning the skulls, so that next day we were able to make an extended expedition to the unexplored country to the south. About an hour's walk brought us to the summit, and the weather being delightfully warm and clear, we could see some ten miles in every direction. To the west a long silver streak embayed in forest disclosed a lake about four miles long running north and south, but whether Little Gull River flows through and out of this sheet of water I am unable to say, as I had no time to follow the river, which at its junction with the Gander is fully as large as the more important stream.[1] Beyond Little Gull River, and to the north, the country was once more blind and dense, which was something in the nature of a disappointment, as we had hoped to find it similar in character to our present surroundings. On reaching the summit of the southern hills, over which large numbers of female caribou had recently passed, we came within view of typical Newfoundland high ground scenery—an endless succession of small and large lakes, marshes, and scattered timber, all of which pointed east and west. The climb to the summit had entailed some exertion, though the going was good, so we sat and admired

---

[1] I afterwards found that the lake, which I named, was joined to the Little Gull by a brook.

H

the scenery till an exclamation from Sandy, and the direction of his gaze, caused us to turn our eyes towards a large open marsh about half a mile below. There was a white-neck stepping out proudly like Macgregor on his native heath. He seemed to carry fine horns, so Saunders and I made all haste to head him for a nearer inspection.

This was not quite so easy as it looked, for the stag was walking down-wind very fast and had already a considerable start. Moreover, a small forest rose about a quarter of a mile in front of the deer, and for this he was making to lie up for the day. We had to run, and run fast, over the worst kind of bog, into which we frequently sank to our middles; but, on the other hand, the chase lay downhill, and this was a distinct advantage to us. When we came within 400 yards of the stag I saw him looking about uneasily, so told Bob to sit and await my return, and, making an effort, ran right past and headed him. The sun was playing upon him, and I saw by his alert carriage and quick movement that he was not quite adult. His head, too, which looked fine from above, now underwent a considerable reduction on closer inspection. The brows and the bays were first class, but he carried only a snag on the left brow and the tops were short and undeveloped, so I let him pass by unmolested.

After this diversion we tramped for the whole day to examine the country to the south. The farther we travelled the worse the going became, till at last walking became a considerable effort. It was some time, in fact, before we could get back to the high and dry ground, from which we could alternately spy and cook our dinner; but nothing more was seen, so we returned to camp feeling that a hard day's work had been accomplished.

The next day, Friday, September 17, was rather an interesting one, because I killed a fine stag through a seemingly trivial piece of observation; and to show that in caribou hunting a man's ears are often as important as his eyes, I will give the circumstances.

It was an exquisite autumn morning, clear as crystal, and not a breath of wind stirring; a few golden birch leaves, early forerunners of coming decay, were floating down the river, and up on the hillside you could hear the jays whistling and talking to one another about the excellent food supply they had discovered. The great white-headed eagle passed overhead, coming from some of the fish lakes of the interior, and a belated osprey (who must have found fishing for his dinner in the shallows of the Gander a laborious necessity) circled round the camp. According to my usual custom, I started up stream soon after daybreak, leaving the men to follow when the canoes were packed.

Not one of the least important things in this form of still-hunting is to sit down frequently and, with senses alert, to interpret the manifold signs of nature—in fact, to sit and listen. After going for a mile, I found on the north bank the regular crossing-place of a big stag. Evidently, too, it had used the same spot to traverse the river morning and evening for the past two months, for the indentations showed a curious physical defect in one of the right fore hoofs, which was unusually elongated and bent inwards. That old fellow had been across the river about an hour before my advent. There was discoloured water in his spoor, and close alongside fresh droppings. So I sat down and listened.

The grey curtain of midges arose to float in a mazy dance in the sun. The black flies, though losing their viciousness, nevertheless attended to me personally; a few scattered ouananiche rose at the floating insects, and far away down the stream I could see my "wet bobs" lugging, drawing, and pushing their handy little craft against the swiftly-flowing stream.   It was delightful to sit and smoke, and enjoy the charming *dolce far niente* laziness of basking in the sun, and wondering whether the good people in Sussex were still shivering under umbrellas and mackintoshes, as they had been doing during May, June, July, and August in the year of grace 1903.   One or two of my friends had even cast eyes of pity upon me for coming to those "dreadful Arctic regions," as they fondly imagined Newfoundland to be.

And yet how different it was.   How nice to lie on the moss amidst the sun-warmed stones where thoughts were singing rivers and the dews of morning shone, and to listen for the bumping of the canoes round the bend.

But pleasurable thoughts and the contemplated enjoyment of ten minutes of that masterpiece, "The Experiences of an Irish R.M.," were abruptly terminated by the breaking of a small stick two hundred yards away on the far bank.   I only just heard it, it was almost a sound striking one's inner consciousness, yet when a man has hunted all kinds of birds and beasts, as I have done for years, the mind is soon alive to natural explanations and quick to read them.   It might have been caused by some small mammal, but except the varying hare, an ermine, or a small vole, there are no small beasts to speak of in the country.   A bird would not have done it, or the sound would be quickly repeated.   So I listened attentively.   Yes, there it was again.   This time unmistakable — the gradual crushing break of some large animal treading on dry wood.

The river was rather deep on the far side, so I had to

wait a quarter of an hour before Saunders came, and a ferry over became possible. Then telling the men to wait and not to make a sound, I climbed the bank, took off my boots, and crept into the dense timber.

At the very spot from whence the sounds had proceeded was the fresh track of old Curly Toe. He had trodden on a piece of rotten pine, the evidence of which was designated in scattered chips. I advanced as quickly as possible, fearful almost of placing my feet on the ground, for the stag was nearly certain to be within a hundred yards of me in that "droke" of spruce and alder. The track was easy to follow, and I made it out for three or four hundred yards going hillwards. Then I made a cast back, and stumbled on the home of the stag, scores of beds beaten hard and dry, with piles of old and fresh manure all around. There was one bed full of hairs that looked as if the stag had just sprung from it, and had been scared, for several pebbles of wet dung lay therein, often the sure sign of deer suddenly scared. I was looking at this, stooping down, when my ear caught the tinkle of stones being moved, followed by a subdued splash. My men I knew were too well trained to create this disturbance, so guessing its cause I rushed helter-skelter through the opposing stems towards the river. As I burst through the last alders I saw the stag looking about, very frightened, and standing up to his knees in the river about a hundred yards away. To fall into a sitting position was the work of an instant—good tops and thick horns at once decided that—and as the deer swung round to go I fired. The bullet took him about five inches too far back. Then off he went, full gallop, clattering up the shallows of the river, and sending the spray flying in all directions. I had a better shooting position than such a hurried seat usually offers, and so when I let go the next two shots, I had the satisfaction of seeing them both strike the flying deer. One went through his side, and the last raked him from end to end; so he stopped, floundered forward in the river, and was dead by the time I reached him. I looked upon the capture of this fine head as the result of simple reasoning, though Saunders regarded the affair in a somewhat more exaggerated fashion. Had I not heard that first gentle crack, led up to by the sight of those hoof-prints, old Curly Toe and his antlers would probably still be dodging backwards and forwards along the narrow leads of the Upper Gander.

This was without doubt the stag with the fine tops which I had spied late in the evening two days previously, and he must only just have returned to his lair when so rudely disturbed. The horns were not large, but very massive, and the head one of high quality, with thirty points.

At midday we decided to camp, as the country to the north seemed fairly open and worth a visit. As the canoes came to a halt, and we prepared to relieve them of their contents, a large stag came out on to the river bank, and stood surveying us within sixty yards. His horns were long and with few points, which accounted for the lack of evil intention on our part, so after a prolonged stare he swung round and disappeared in the forest again. In the afternoon a long tramp through a dense country resulted in nothing, and we returned to camp just in time to see two fine stags cross the river about a quarter of a mile below.

It was plain that real difficulties with the canoes had now commenced. Nothing but basswood, and that of the finest quality, would have withstood the bumping and hauling over sharp rocks that these little boats had undergone. Both were well "shaved," and the new one had swollen and burst

DIAMOND CUT DIAMOND

slightly at the bottom. With every care, they would not hold out long unless the river offered some "steady" water, and this it showed no signs of doing, but rather became shallower at every mile. There was now no part in the whole stream that would take a man above the knees, and the river was not narrowing; it was still about 120 yards wide, the same as twenty miles below.

The autumn of 1902 had been an exceptionally dry season, but that of 1903 was infinitely drier, and quite ruined my original project, which was to reach a point beyond the Partridgeberry Hills, portage our stuff across to Dog Lake River, thence on to the Big Lake river system of Round, Brazil, Long Lakes, down through Baie d'Est to Baie d'Espoir, where I could have got a boat from the Indians to take me to the weekly steamer which calls in Hermitage Bay, and so eventually to St. John's. Only one man has yet accomplished this journey, and if we had had water above Burnt Hill I think we should also have carried it out.

On the morning of 18th September, the men were in constant difficulties; one of the boats would catch on a sharp upright rock or narrow stony bar, and had either to be forcibly hauled over or some of the contents had to be taken out, portaged a few yards, and then replaced. It was slow, toilsome work for the men and disappointing, as I had now little chance of reaching the Partridgeberry Hills. By midday we had only accomplished three miles, having started soon after daybreak, and the Great Gander, which looks so important on the map at the inflow of the Little Gull River, was nothing more than a broad flat bank of stones, with a little water trickling through them. Little Gull River, where we stopped to have dinner, joins the Gander sixty miles from the lake and seventy-five from the sea. It is a much more important river than its marking on the map would indicate, for it brings down as much water as the main branch of the Gander does from the west.

The afternoon was glorious, so I walked ahead about two miles, and saw much fresh sign of big stags about the river bank. Leads came from the north, and after joining the river pointed due south in many places, and the whole country seemed to indicate that we were in the heart of the main trails. In one place they were particularly abundant, the dry timber on the bank slopes being beaten to dust by the tramp of many feet. I sat down here to enjoy the sun and "A Double Thread," keeping the while a desultory look-out, for it was as yet a bit too early for any of the old fellows to be up and stirring. Still you never know when a stag is going to appear, and they often do so at the most unexpected moments.

The canoes had just reached me, and I rose to resume the journey, when, looking up the river, I saw a stag walking swiftly out of the stream on the far side, and looking about for a path into the forest. It was hopeless to think of approaching a yard nearer, and he was a good 250 yards away. Instant decision was imperative, and as I could see that his tops were good, I sat down against a stone and put up my rifle just as he put his head into the forest. I fired, and distinctly saw the splash of the bullet on a patch of sand an inch above his back. He never winced, but his head and shoulders were now in the forest, and in another second he would disappear for ever. Taking the sight a trifle lower, I pulled again, and he came staggering down the bank, swayed for an instant or two, and plunged forwards into the river, into which he fell quite dead.

The head was not large, but carried a great number of

small points, many of which were so doubtful that it was difficult to say what their precise number was, although thirty-eight fulfilled the old watch-guard test.

After working on up stream for about three miles, the river suddenly became quite hopeless from the boatman's point of view. It was nothing but a bed of stones, and the men said they could proceed no farther without portaging. One of the canoes was full of water, and would stand but little more rough handling, so we decided to camp for the night and explore ahead on foot. A nice dry camping-ground was found on a steep hillside amongst a group of pines, and here Bob and Sandy set to work to cut supports for the lean-to, when, looking down the river, I saw a magnificent stag crossing it about a quarter of a mile below. He seemed to carry a fine set of horns, and marched up out of the water looking the picture of proud defiance, whilst his snowy neck and pendant ruffle shone like a star against the dark green undergrowth of the forest. In a moment he found his "lead" and disappeared, whilst I ran as hard as I could to try and catch him in a follow-on chase.

In a few minutes I turned in at his well-beaten road, took up his spoor through the pine belt and on out to some semi-open country, composed of hard, dry, quartzy hills. Here I lost it, and climbed a high larch, which led to no better results, and so in the dark, feeling very footsore—for I had no boots on, having taken them off as soon as we halted— I made my way back to camp. Perhaps the supposition was unwarranted, but only natural as the stag got away; yet for several evenings I cherished the idea that that stag was unusually fine.

An exploration of the river for eight miles ahead disclosed the fact that we were on the edge of "Burnt" country, which probably continued as far as the Partridgeberry Hills. About twelve miles up stream, on the left bank, rose the mountain marked in the map as Burnt Hill, seventy miles from the lake and eighty-five from the sea. This marks the farthest point reached by us, progress by means of the canoes being now impossible. In a moderately wet season there would be no difficulty in going much farther, but the drought had effectually stopped us, and we could do nothing more but pack ahead, which I had no wish to do. I only intended to kill one more stag, and that I hoped to get near my present camp. Evening came on, and I strolled up the river to meet Bob, who had gone on ahead. After waiting some time the shadows increased, and soon it would be too dark to see a deer, so I rose and tramped home. Turning the last corner I saw a stag crossing a shallow about 200 yards above my camp, and Sandy standing up black and prominent in front of the camp fire, lost in admiration. Having no wish to slay my excellent helper, I waited till the deer had moved half-way across the river, and I had time to thoroughly examine his head. It was a grand one, with splendid tops. The stag was a good 300 yards away, and I dared not approach nearer, as what wind there was blew straight down stream. A long rock with a ridge afforded a comfortable place to lie upon for the shot, and my coat a suitable rest, so raising the rifle I found I could scarcely see the foresight. Putting it under the deer which was now standing broadside, I raised it slowly and pulled; the bullet went over his back perhaps an inch or two; at the second shot the same thing happened, and the stag moved fast for the far bank. As he walked I fired again a little lower, this time with success. The ball reached him, passed through his neck, and he simply lay down in the river-bed without other movement.

SIDE VIEW OF FORTY-FOUR POINT HEAD SHOT ON THE UPPER GANDER,
SEPTEMBER 1903

THE FORTY-NINE POINTER AS HE FELL

The sight of this little episode was one of intense excitement to Sandy, who had watched the whole scene from the appearance of the stag opposite the camp. He had gazed upon it at about 60 yards distance, was prepared to swear to me on my return that he had seen the greatest stag that ever breathed, and was just becoming heart-broken as it walked away, when he saw me come round the bend of the river, "put three guns at 'um, and take 'um down."

On the death of the stag the excitable Sandy was to be seen rushing wildly out of the woods into the river, waving in one hand his somewhat dilapidated hat and brandishing in the other a huge knife, which followed every occupation, from cutting trees to opening tin cans. Sandy took the river with sportsmanlike enthusiasm, and was speedily at work taking off the stag's head, haunches, and rump fat.

This stag carried the first exceptional head which I had killed in Newfoundland. It was 42 inches long, and had very heavy "tops," with long points. The brows were each fully developed and of large size, and the whole head bore forty-four clearly defined points—a very unusual number. The only weak part was his bays or middle palms.

It was pitch dark when Sandy had finished his cold task, and we sat long admiring the beautiful horns, comparing it with others, and waiting for Little Bob. That individual turned up by-and-by, and, after a hearty supper and the head was skinned, we turned in just as the rain came down in torrents. During the night my faith in the excellence of the Newfoundland lean-to received a rude shock. The method of shelter with front open to the blazing logs is certainly brighter, warmer, and more cheerful than any tent, provided there is no heavy rain, and that the wind does not shift. If such unfortunate things occur there is nothing left but to get up in the middle of the **night**, rebuild camp in a fresh place, get wet through, and **try to** be as amiable as possible. On this occasion we were all **too** tired or sleepy to move, so we lay awake and let the **rain** come in upon us. My reindeer bag was soon soaked, **so I** put on my ulster and spent a miserable night in the uttermost corner of the cover sheet. The men also allowed themselves to be soaked, but that being the chronic condition of these human seals, they regarded the circumstances without comment.

The morning broke still and fine as usual, and at **very** early breakfast we had a pow-wow as to the best course to pursue. I had shot six fine heads, and had no desire to kill any more deer. The main object of my journey had been accomplished, so I decided to return. This was not quite so easy as it sounds, for in spite of last night's rain the river had fallen a foot since we had come to this camp. Nevertheless the men said they thought we could get out if the camp and canoes were portaged a mile down stream and over the worst of the stone banks.

It took all day to get as far as Little Gull River, **and** then when Little Bob appeared his face was long and aspect gloomy.

"One of the boats is completely bust up and t'other's cracked, and unless you shoot two more deer to lace **the** worst one in we'll never get down unless we build a raft **and** wait for the rain," he said.

"How far can you get the boats to-night?" I said.

"Perhaps another mile," he said; "but it's bale and shove all the time, and killing work."

I had no intention of waiting a fortnight or three weeks for rain and rafts, so decided to hunt about and kill **two** more stags as soon as possible. Nor was opportunity long deferred.

About half a mile below Little Gull River was an open stretch of the stream. To the eye it now looked just like a mass of pebbles, but the accession of the two rivers meeting had helped the Gander a bit, and there was a narrow thread of water about ten or twelve inches deep percolating through the stones. I sat down on the bank watching for a stag to appear down stream. There seemed little enough chance of killing one, as the wind was blowing hard towards the only likely part, and both evening and the rain were close at hand. It was already late, and I was about to walk up stream to see if any further accident had happened, when, taking one final glance towards the east, I saw a stag in the act of crossing the river about 800 yards away. He was gingerly picking his way through the stones of the river, and I could not understand how it was he did not get my wind. It seemed to be blowing directly towards him, and yet, as I afterwards found, must have been forced upwards after going for a hundred yards or so.

Strange things happen in stalking, and the vagaries of air are amongst the most curious. More than once I have succeeded in getting within shot of an animal by hard running and by simply relying on its being too confused to make out the object of attack. No other course was open, so I resolved to try it now. I ran as hard as I could, keeping my eye all the time fixed on the stag so as to know the exact moment he "had" me, and I should lie down and open fire—600, 500, 400, 300 yards—this was incomprehensible. At this distance I plainly saw the ripples of water going almost direct to the stag, which had now landed on a point and was feeding away stern-on. The river bank here bent inwards, and if I crossed in its "bay" the stag *must* get my wind, so I resolved to lie down and fire.

The stag was outlined against the water—always a good mark for the shooter, for he sees at once whether he has fired too low or too high. The bullet must have grazed his back, for he sharply raised his noble head and stopped feeding, whilst I saw the projectile flick up the stream in almost a direct line. A little lower, bang! The stag flinched, turned round towards me, and hobbled a few paces up stream. I now saw for the first time that he had a great head, which is a bad thing for a man to know when he greatly desires to slay a beast. I had broken his left hind leg, high up, so having now the exact range I prepared to give him another shot. At that moment he started, and, like nearly all wounded animals, made up-wind as hard as his three legs could carry him. Then it was that I thanked my stars I had not tried to go nearer to him at the first chance, for he came full tilt up the shore, almost towards me, and up the "bay" of the stream to my left. By a fortunate circumstance the river bank was here very steep, and though he kept watching for an opening as he ran, I saw he would come fairly close to me if I lay still, and so reserved my fire. About a hundred yards away a broad opening appeared in the bank, and here the grand fellow stopped, turned slightly, and was about to spring upwards into the bush, when I fired again, and he at once lay struggling on the stones with a bullet through the upper part of the neck. His fine horns were swaying from side to side as I ran up, and I stood contemplating what is in some respects the best head I have ever shot.

It is hardly necessary to say much about the head of an

animal whose portrait is given here, taken from various angles. It is enough to say that I had secured a perfect head of forty-nine points, the brows in particular being extraordinary. In his long experience Saunders said that he had never seen a more perfect caribou head, and that it was equal in quality to the head killed by Selous two years previously; although not quite so large in the beam as that head, the brows and bays are considerably finer. It is not often that a sportsman has secured two "great" heads in one season, and so I was grateful for the necessity that had compelled me to shoot this last stag. Had not the canoe broken down he would certainly have been left alone.

The men took about two hours doing the last mile from Little Gull River to where the fallen stag lay. It was becoming dark and threatening to rain, so, having no camera, I got out my sketch-book and made a rapid outline of the fallen monarch as he lay. Before I had finished heavy drops began to fall, so we made camp as quickly as possible, and had just got the shelter spread and a blazing birch fire started when the storm burst upon us.

The rain fell in torrents till midnight, when it suddenly ceased. Such a downfall, though severe, made little difference to the river, as the whole country was so parched that it would require two days of such rain to fill the burns and marshes, and so affect the main stream. All the next day (21st September) the men toiled down the river, and at dusk reached the Serpentine Hill, where, on the hills above, I had killed the two large stags. There was still about an hour of daylight left, so I went up the hill on the chance of finding a bear at the first carcase, immediately above our old camp. In the dusk I crept slowly forward through the bushes, and waited for some minutes to see if there was any movement. But nothing stirred, so I advanced to find that the remains of the first stag had been carried by bears about twenty yards up the hill.

From a ridge about fifty yards up the hill I could see the marsh and the remains of the other deer, about half a mile below to the east. The telescope showed that the carcase was untouched, and in the same position as that in which we had left it. I sat some time after the sun had sunk, and was just thinking of returning to camp when my eye detected a black spot to the right of the marsh, away in the valley below. The glass lay beside me, and as I raised it the dark object, a large bear, suddenly moved and galloped out into the open. At first I thought something must have scared him—he lolloped along so steadily and with such decision. Presently he took a turn, and I saw that he was circling round the carcase of the dead stag, to see if any one had been there recently. Twice he stopped, stood up on his hind legs, and tried the wind. Then he again dropped on the fore-paws and resumed his lumbering gait. The black bear gallops in a most peculiar manner. He looks like some ridiculous pantomime animal playing the buffoon. Nearly all large creatures hold the head and neck out or up in accelerated locomotion, but the black bear, which is the only member of the genus I have seen actually gallop, puts his head down and swings it clumsily from side to side as if he were enjoying some huge joke. Presently Mr. Bruin stopped and remained motionless for two or three minutes directly down-wind from the carcase. I think he was enjoying the delicious prospect of a hearty meal, and wondering whether it would be safe to approach. Then just as I thought it time to be making my approach, he set off on another circuit of inspection.

FORTY-NINE POINT HEAD SHOT NEAR LITTLE GULL RIVER, SEPTEMBER 1903

By the time I had passed the intervening woods, and had begun to creep cautiously down a depression in the marsh, the bear was still lumbering around about 400 yards away, and far on the other side of the dead deer. My position was clearly near enough to the carcase, for if the animal chose to make another circuit of the prospective dinner, he would doubtless come within easy shot. Accordingly I sat down behind a small larch and waited. At the same moment the bear approached his dinner, walking slowly and with evident apprehension. He was clearly of much cunning, or had at some time or another been greatly scared. I felt certain of an easy shot, however, and had settled myself in a good shooting position, when he suddenly stopped at about 200 yards distant, whipped round, and made off again as hard as his legs would carry him. There was a moment of doubt, and I did the wrong thing, which was to fire as he galloped away. A single moment of reflection would have told me that his fright was only simulated, and that he was only going for another final gallop, but I stupidly thought he was off for good, and so pressed the trigger and missed. He dashed round a small clump of trees, and then I saw him going over the marsh at his best pace for half a mile until he entered the northern woods and disappeared. It is easy to be wise after the event, but I shall know better next time.

September 22.—All day down through the worst kind of rocks. Till now the men have been pulling, hauling, and buffeting with the stoniest stream for a fortnight, with only one day's rest, and I had heard no complaints, but now, just before we reached Migwell's Brook, I found Bob, who had been long delayed, standing over his charge, sunk to the bottom of a small hole in the river, and smiling sadly as he waved the frying-pan in his hand.

"Guess this yer old thing (indicating his extempore baler) ain't much more use! 'less I bale out de whole stream, and that ain't surprisin' difficult now," he added, contemplating the shoal of rocks.

"Well," I suggested, "let us pack the stuff down to Migwell's Brook, and we will try and do a mend with the stag's skin and a biscuit tin." It was dusk as we reached our destination. Moving the water-logged goods and heads was no light task, but it was finished just as the sun set.

On our way up stream we had left the dried fat of two stags hanging on a tree at the Migwell's Brook camp. I had also placed out of reach a wooden box containing 100 Eley's brass shot cartridges. Knowing that bears were common round here, we thought that these things would be safe from their attentions, but such was not the case. The first thing that met our gaze was the broken cartridge box lying on the ground, and its contents scattered all over the camp. About twenty of the cartridges had actually been chewed and half-eaten by the bears, doubtless for the extraction of the grease-laden wads covering the powder, and the marks of their teeth were plainly indented on the outer coverings (see photograph). It was a curious diet in truth, for brass cartridges are not mentioned amongst the food of these omnivorous beasts. The results might have been even more interesting had our visitors bitten into the "cap" ends of the cartridges.

During the evening Saunders and I "tailed" a gun and a Mannlicher for the bears, but without result.

Next morning we spent in mending up the broken canoes. A Huntley and Palmer biscuit tin was flattened out and nailed over the break, into which, after removing the flooring, we poured about a pound of melted deer's fat. Saunders said that we could not utilise the skin until we had another, as the two must be laced together, and one was of no use. Accordingly I set out about midday, and made about four miles, when I reached the spot where I had missed the stag coming up the river. The view on either side was wide, and two well-used crossing places led across the stream within easy running distance. The afternoon passed away, and nothing appeared, not even the canoes, for on this day the rocks broke the strongest of the two boats and caused endless delays; so I took a book out of my pocket and was soon lost with Rider Haggard in the heart of Africa. In a country so peaceful, so still as the land of the northern forests, one is quick to recognise the slightest noise. That remarkable woman "She" was about to drink again the fires of eternal life, and her speech at this exciting moment simply grips the reader, for it is the best thing in a remarkable work. Yet it was in no spirit of disappointment that I dropped the book softly on the stones at my side—for had I not heard some pebbles roll down the bank on the far side of the river? I looked up, and there was a large brown doe coming down to drink. For a female she carried remarkable horns, about as large as the specimen I had killed in the previous year, and with thirteen good points. She entered the stream exactly opposite to the rock beside which I was seated, and, after drinking, marched slowly across the river towards me. It was a good opportunity for the camera. The sun was upon her, and I knew she would cross close to me, but the camera was far away at Glenwood. I lay under the shadow of the rock, and she came right on to within six yards, looking inquisitively at me as I crouched there with my arm in front of my face. Then she took a pace or two up stream, shook her head, ran a couple of yards, pretending to be frightened, and then seeing the fearsome object did not move, came back and smelt her way forwards. She was within three yards now, but working two yards to the right down stream, at once got the wind, and went off, sending the water flying in all directions. In two minutes she was out of sight, and I could hear her breaking through the forest up to the hills.

In another minute I resumed my book, and had hardly done so, when the sound of dropping water caused me to turn my head sharply and look up stream. There stood a very large stag, in the act of drinking, about 100 yards away. The sudden movement of turning to grasp my rifle did not escape his eye, and at once he was in a position of tense alertness. Slowly I put the bead on his heart and pressed the trigger. He scarcely winced, but, jumping out on to the stones, dashed away at full gallop. I was about to fire again, when it occurred to me that my shot was a fatal one, because he was going just a bit too fast for an unwounded beast. This conjecture was strengthened when I saw him shaking his head, a sure sign of a fatal blow. The next instant he wheeled round suddenly towards the river, and running along a ledge of rocks, bounded into the air, and fell dead in the stream.

So rapid was his descent into the river and blind the final plunge, that he broke his shovel, knocking off five points, as well as smashing his skull and lower jaw. A noble fellow with a massive head, but without many points. When the men came, we took his entire skin and head, and as much meat as we could carry, and made camp.

This ended our hunting for the year, and perhaps the most successful shooting trip I have engaged in. It took four days more before we reached the mouth of the Gander; but after passing the waterfalls the difficulties with the canoes ceased, for we reached water sufficiently deep to run the boats and their loads with care and safety. On the evening of the 27th a happy circumstance seemed to have brought the steamer to the mouth of the river, for she had not been there since she had brought us, so we got aboard, and next morning reached Glenwood and the railway line. Here I recovered my camera, and took a few photos of the heads, paid off Bob and Sandy, who had well earned their wages and a bit more. Better men to go anywhere, and turn their hands to anything, I have not found. Both had worked with untiring patience in cold water for twenty days, and would have been quite keen to " pack " on for another twenty had I wished them to do so.

The food provided by the Glenwood Hotel[1] was so bad that, after spending an unhappy hour there wrestling with some flaccid liquor named by courtesy tea, and a piece of chewed string, which at some remote period might have been a rabbit, I returned to my camp and had a simple yet clean dinner.

Travellers at some of these remote hostelries have only one idea in the world, and that is to get away from them as quickly as possible. An untruthful but humorous story tells of an unfortunate "drummer"—and "drummers" can stand most things — who, after partaking of two meals, decided to end his life. He lay down on the metals a minute or two before the express was due. After waiting for two days and catching a severe cold, he was reluctantly compelled to give up the idea of suicide, and is now instituting a claim for compensation against the railway company for the unpunctuality of their trains.

---

[1] I am speaking of the Glenwood Hotel of 1903. It has, I believe, twice changed hands since then.

Once upon a time there was a monarch whose kingdom was torn by dissensions, and, wishing for popularity, he offered as a reward to the guesser of a certain riddle half of his kingdom, and the hand of his lovely daughter. Of course there was no answer to the riddle, although the cunning monarch kept his people in a state of pleasurable excitement and peace from internal strife for the space of a few years, and so tided over a difficulty. In similar fashion the good folk of Newfoundland are apt to ask each other another conundrum which is also unanswerable, namely, "Why is the 'accommodation train' so-called, and whom does it accommodate?" At present the genius who can give a satisfactory answer has not been discovered. The people of the island regard the "accommodation train" with dread; strangers suffering a single journey resolve never to repeat the experiment. But the "accommodation train" must accommodate somebody—perhaps it is the Old Gentleman himself! Every second day that passes, Satan must bless the island's government for running such a show entirely for his benefit. Could the walls of those "First Class" carriages speak, what a tale of wicked thoughts and wickeder language they could tell, and how oft had the nature of the most gentle of men been turned to acid and gall through the bitter experience of a night's travel!

One evening, in 1902, little Mike, Saunders, Wells, a couple of station men, and myself were seated round a blazing fire near the line at Terra-Nova. We were waiting for the "accommodation train," which was only six hours late. The conversation turned on wild beasts, as it always does where two or three are gathered together in the backwoods.

"I seen a bear once here, close to the station," began little Mike. We listened with hushed expectancy to the

STAGINGS ON THE CLIFF

A TYPICAL VILLAGE OF THE OUTPORTS

eleven-year-old stationmaster's coming story, for he had an interesting way of putting things.

"He warn't walking away either, but come straight towards me."

"Weren't you frightened, Mike?" suggested some one.

"Sure," replied the little man; "but I stopped right still, and as I hadn't no gun I jes' said somethin' that I knew 'ud scare him proper."

"What did ye say, Mike?"

"Well, I ses quite quiet like, 'Go way, you black devil, or I'll send you to St. John's by the accommodation train,' and you should ha' seen him scoot." And Mike looked sadly upon me as a prospective sufferer.

We were due to leave Glenwood at 7 P.M., and punctually at five minutes past 1 A.M. the train, with its long string of baggage cars, steamed slowly into the station. Far away, and out in the darkness, overhanging a pool of water, was the passenger coach, on which was painted the curious legend "First Class." The train was designated as "mixed," not out of compliment to the passengers, but to individualise its component parts. It is really a baggage train, with a coach sandwiched between the trucks, so that the passengers may experience the full joys of shunting, which takes place at every heap of lumber piled beside the track between Bay of Islands and St. John's, a distance of five hundred miles. This journey is variously performed in two days, or, with the help of a snowstorm or a spring wash-out, in a week.

I opened the door of the "First Class" carriage, and was at once greeted with a terrible atmosphere. There were eight hard benches, capable of holding two passengers on each, and occupied by twelve men, four women, and three children. Of course there was no seat to be had, so I sat on a biscuit box and allowed the door to stand open a minute although it was freezing slightly. Soon a man from outside came and shut it. Then I opened it again, and then a passenger shivered, shook himself, got up and shut it. This went on for some time until there really was a little fresh air in the car, and I tried to get to sleep sitting on my biscuit tin. We remained four hours at Glenwood killing time and doing nothing in particular, then we were all thrown endways by the engine coupling on. All the men in the carriage woke up and swore. Then another fearful jolt, which put out the light and sent me into the arms of a perfectly innocent old lady, and off we went. These fearful shocks are caused by the engine's playful way of coupling on; this is effected apparently by adhesion, and it has to make a run at the train to make sure of sticking. This happened whenever the engine was required to detach for wood, coal, or water, or the driver went to gossip with the section man or the stationmaster.

After swinging, creaking, and swaying round the marvellous curves of the line I became sleepy, and so spread two weekly editions of the *Times* on the floor of the carriage, placed my ulster above these, and, lying flat out, had a very nice nap for several hours. When I woke up it was broad daylight, and somehow I imagined we had got on splendidly and were nearly at Port Blandford. I said as much to a pleasant-looking man sitting close to me, and the humour of the remark, quite unintentional, was received with roars of laughter by all the other men in the carriage.

"Why, we're nowhere near Gambo yet," replied my neighbour. (Gambo is about thirty-six miles from Glenwood.)

Quite as tiresome a feature as the train itself was the fact that it is well nigh impossible to get any provisions *en route.* Except at Whitburn (eight or nine hours out of St. John's), where it is possible to obtain a slice of corned beef and a cup of tea—that is, if the train will wait for you—there is no other halting-place where food can be obtained. My friends in the train had telegraphed on to Gambo to have breakfast ready at the hotel (*sic*). When we got there the "lady" in charge said she did not make breakfasts for travellers, but that they could have "a glass of whisky" apiece at an exorbitant price. At Gambo I managed to steal two pints of hot water out of a section man's house which I invaded, and so got enough to give the tired-looking women and children some tea. I also had a small supply of biscuits and cooked carabou meat, and this was all most of these unfortunate passengers had in thirty-six hours' travel. Near Terra-Nova we stopped an hour or two, and Dr. M'Pherson, myself, and the two St. John's boys turned out and helped to load lumber from the side of the track; we thought it would save time and assist us towards a decent breakfast at Port Blandford. When we reached that small village the passengers made a rush for the "hotel." "Breakfast," said the proprietor; "oh no, we received no telegram from Gambo, and we can do nothing for you in such a short time." The crowd then swooped down on a place that called itself a shop, and here met with better luck.

If the "accommodation train" and its attendant discomforts are a disagreeable experience, I must confess, in justice to the line, that the passenger need not take it unless he is obliged to do so. The regular passenger train, which runs every second day, is just as comfortable as any train in the Colonies. There are good sleeping-berths, and excellent meals are served on board.

CHAPTER VII

A VISIT TO THE OUTPORTS OF THE SOUTH COAST

WHEN I first visited Newfoundland, it was with the light heart of one who goes out to spend a short holiday in a new land, and to gain a few hunting trophies for his collection. Newfoundland, I thought, might prove worth a visit, and, like many another country, that one visit would be sufficient. But this was not the case. However, instead of a well-known and easily reached hunting-ground of only passing interest, I had found after my second trip a half-explored and altogether delightful country teeming with game; such a land, in fact, as men who love the woods speak of with respect, and which is, alas, generally mentioned with regret as belonging to the days that have gone by. I had found a way into the interior where other men had not attempted to go; and to me Central Newfoundland represented one great deer forest, over the greater part of which I could wander at will without the chance of seeing a human soul. To the general reader this may seem a selfish pleasure. To a certain extent I must admit it is, but on the other hand every big-game hunter of to-day is searching for such a land of promise, and can scarcely find it without travelling far.

It is one of the greatest truisms that when a fisherman has caught a twenty-pound salmon he can never rest until he has achieved the distinction of landing one of forty pounds; and when this notable achievement is reached, visions of fifty-pounders will ever afterwards float before his eyes. So, too, the caribou hunter cannot tamely sit down and gaze with

Fresh Cod

Drying Fish

satisfaction on the noble forty-pointer that adorns his walls when he knows that somewhere up in the sheltered "leads" of the Gander there are one or two fifty-pointers cleaning their horns. It is just the weird imaginings which poor human nature invents and sets us up some fetish that causes us to strive after the seemingly unattainable. Still it prompts us to pack up and go, and we obey.

On the other hand, my desire to revisit Newfoundland was not altogether connected with the acquisition of the fifty-pointer. A great part of the interior was, and is still, unmapped and unexplored, and I thought that I might add a little to our knowledge of this, the oldest of our Colonies, by surveying some new ground, as well as adding to that which had been so well mapped by Mr. Howley and Alexander Murray. There was work to be done, and this lent an additional charm to the pleasures of Nature and Sport. There was too, in the back of my mind, a feeling that on the last visit I had not accomplished all I had set out to do. I had intended to cross Newfoundland if possible, and had stuck in the middle, partly on account of the drought, and partly on account of the number of heads which had fallen to my rifle. The latter would have been impossible to transport to the Baie d'Est River, so I had given up the attempt for the year.

Before starting a fresh expedition into the interior, however, there was other work to do. For five years I had been grinding away at a large work on "The Mammals of Great Britain and Ireland." It was a book which seemed at the time almost beyond my strength, owing to the quantity of material in the way of first-hand knowledge and illustration which I had to supply, to say nothing of the outdoor work and the books I had to consult. It was necessary to see, study, hunt, and draw all the British species, including the whales, and this involved such constant work and **travel** that I feared a break-down under the strain. One mammal, the blue whale, it was absolutely necessary to examine in the flesh, and this, owing to its comparative scarcity in British waters, I hoped to find on the Newfoundland coasts. Accordingly I set out, at the end of July 1905, with the intention of spending a month in quest of this, the greatest of all living creatures.

On arrival at St. John's I learned that all whales were very scarce, and that only one blue whale had been killed in Newfoundland waters during the past month. This did not look well for success, as the blue whales, after leaving the south coast in June, generally work out to the Grand Banks in their pursuit of the red shrimps, and do not return until the late autumn. The difficulty in selecting a station, therefore, was considerable, whilst all the owners of the various factories admitted the impossibility of selecting a base where success was certain.

Eventually I chose the St. Lawrence Factory, near the point of Placentia and Fortune Bay, as this seemed to be well placed for distant sea trips. Moreover, I should have at this point the society and advice of Dr. Rismuller, the American-German savant, who has done more than any living man for the whaling industry. On applying to Mr. John Harvey for permission to stay at St. Lawrence, I was received with great kindness, and given every facility to study my subject. The owners of other factories, such as Mr. Edgar Bowring, Mr. Macdougall, and the Job brothers all extended such cordial invitations that I was sorry there was not sufficient time to visit their stations. St. John's people are nothing if not hospitable, and on this, as on other occasions, I was given every information by the Ministry of Fisheries and Marine, and personal friends such as Mr. E. C. Watson[1] and Judge Prowse.

Five hours' journey on the southern branch of the New-foundland Railway takes the traveller to the summit of the southern chain of mountains, and then you drop down to a great sea lagoon surrounded by broken hills which end in a sea beach, and the quaint old-world village of Placentia. The journey is comparatively safe, and if you know nothing about the railway or the state of the track, you can enjoy the beautiful scenery as you pass along the wooded cliffs—

> " Where the sea through all the mountains stretches up long arms between,
> Flashing, sweeping, with swift current, like a river rushing on,
> Till the tide turns, and the current, turning too, is seaward drawn,
> Skirting mountain brow and valley, changing still, yet still the same,
> Opening up unnumbered vistas, fairer far than lands of fame,
> Scenes to make an artist famous, to the world as yet unknown,
> Lovelier than that Lakeland region sung by poets of its own,
> Nestling in its sea-girt valley, 'midst its mountains forest clad,
> Lies Placentia rich in story, that might make an author glad."

Placentia is one of the most charming spots in New-foundland. The town itself is not attractive, as it lies scattered on a stony beach thrown up by the sea, and kept in place on one side by the Atlantic, and on the other by the swift currents of the north-east and south-east arms. The situation of the place and its surroundings are, however, delightful. To the north it is flanked by the summits of Castle Hill, where the cannon used to stand, and to the south there rise the wooded hills of the Strouter and Mount Pleasant. I have spent hours sitting on the beach watching the ospreys hawking and dashing down on the sea trout as they come in on the rising tide, and enjoying the play of light on hill and sea. At one

---

[1] Since these lines were written St. John's has to lament the death of Mr. Watson. A more charming gentleman or one more interested in his work as Secretary of the Fishery Board it will be impossible to find.

time Placentia was an opulent centre of the Grand Bank fishery, but it is now more or less neglected. Why, it is difficult to understand, because its great beach is more suitable for the drying of cod than any place in the island. The sea-trout fishing in the neighbourhood is excellent, and if protected it would be of great value to the residents. At Placentia live Mr. Albert and John Bradshaw. The former will show you the service of plate presented by King William IV., who visited this place during his travels, and a delightful collection of Indian and Esquimaux relics which he has gathered from the Labrador and Northern Newfoundland. He kindly presented me with a caribou charm of the Beothick Indians, which was supposed to carry good luck in hunting.

At Placentia I found the *Glencoe*, which performs weekly journeys along the south coast, and here too, lying like a veil, was the Newfoundland fog in all its density. In the evening we started westwards, and, leaving the land of sunshine, were at once lost in the gloom.

To find the various ports we had to enter was no easy task, but Captain Drake seemed to know his way blindfold. The steamer went full speed right ahead into Burin, and the captain took the most surprising liberties with his boat. Navigation was principally accomplished by the use of the steam-whistle, which kept blowing all the time, and by its use the old mariner could tell where he was by the echo on the surrounding hills. He bears the reputation of being the most accomplished fog captain in existence, and the skill with which he steered past anchored "bankers" and hidden rocks was amazing, even if appearing somewhat risky. The pace, about twelve knots, never slackened, and at 6 A.M. we entered the harbour of St. Lawrence, when the land greeted us once again. Here the fog was exceptionally dense. If there is no wind, or the wind is from the south, the coast is under its pall for months together in the summer, so the traveller must have a large stock of patience and a volatile temperament to withstand the constant rain and mist which obscure all things.

The entrance to St. Lawrence is dominated by a noble headland known locally as "Shaperu," one of those queer names which the traveller in Newfoundland constantly encounters, and for which he finds it difficult to obtain a derivation. The origin of nearly all these queer appellations are Norman-French, which has been vulgarised and perverted to suit local taste. To give a few instances. There is a beautiful little port in Placentia Bay which was called by the old Norman sailors *Tasse d'Argent* (The Silver Cup). This the natives transmogrified into *Tortello John*, and it is now called Tortello. *Cinq Isles* is made into Saint Kells; *Baie de l'Argent* into Bay de John; *Chapeau Rouge* into Shaperu; *Baie Facheux* into Foushy; *Baie d'Espoir* into Bay Despair; whilst many other instances could be given. This habit of doggerelising names has become a passion with the Newfoundlanders, and if a name is difficult, they make a short cut and apply the title of anything that sounds nearest to it. A poor woman brought her child to be christened by the Rev. Christopher Meek. On asking the name of the child, the mother replied that it was to be "Hyena." "Why, my good woman," said the parson, "I could not give the name of a wild animal to this lovely child. There must be some mistake." "Well," answered the mother, "my good man before he went up the Bay cuttin' wood, told me it were to be 'Hyena' and nothing else." Soon afterwards the clergyman met the father, who said, "Well, parson, that were a curious mistake between you and my missis about the baby. It were Joseph Hyena (Josephina) I told her to name the child."

Great St. Lawrence is a typical village of the outports. Imagine a little fiord surrounded by green hills covered with grass, tea-bush, pink calmia (*Kalmia Glauca*), blueberry, and stunted spruce and pine, amongst which the stone and granite outcrops. There are no trees of any size, because these have long since been cut for fuel, or blown down by the winter storms. Above high-water mark stands the village of wooden houses, many of them built on trestles after the Norwegian fashion. Some of these small crofts have a little hayfield surrounded by wooden palings, in a corner of which stands the cow-byre, whilst all possess on the sea front large staging and store-houses for the drying and curing of cod. The houses are roofed with wooden slates; they are of two stories and possess a loft. The best ones have little gardens, in which grow potatoes and cabbages, or, if the owner is sufficiently well to do, flowers. In August these gardens are quite gay, and I noticed quantities of meadow-sweet, foxgloves, sweet-williams, pæonies, pinks, violas, Aaron's rod and golden rod, monthly roses, and the common wild rose of the country. Neglected as a weed, and most beautiful of all, were great clumps of the blue monkshood, locally known as "Queen's fettle." In the wild marshes there was a great variety of berries and alpine plants, the most noticeable at this season being the pitcher plant, and a small and lovely snow-white orchis. Michaelmas daisies and golden rod give masses of yellow in the inland woods, whilst on all the roadsides grow pink and white spiræas.

On dull and foggy days no one in St. Lawrence seemed to have any work to do. Men could not go to sea, and women could not dry fish. All is silent and depressed, but when the sun comes out everything changes to life and movement. Dogs bark, children call at their play, and those at work on the "flakes" chat cheerfully together. In the still waters of the harbour the common terns (*Sterna hirundo*), like little sea-fairies, hover and descend upon their prey the sand-eels; American herring gulls (*Larus argentatus Smithsonianus*) sail aloft, whilst the common sandpipers and two species of *tringa* flit and call upon the beaches. The dogs, which seem to be well nigh amphibious, rush barking through the pools, and at low water search the shores for discarded cod-heads.

The best dogs are of the "Labrador" type. In winter they are used for hauling logs—one dog will haul 2 or 3 cwt. Seldom more than two are used together. The pure Newfoundland dogs are curly, and are a little higher on the leg than are the Labradors.

Everything eats cod in Newfoundland, even the cows. These cattle have the appearance of coming badly through the winter, and making up for it in summer with indifferent success. Their existence is one long struggle with the forces of nature, and in the battle of life they get the worst of it. Their lives are one long disappointment in the commissariat line. Just as the grass is getting sweet, it is denied them by means of wooden fences, so they do the best they can by nibbling various shrubs and by repairing to the beach at low water, where they eat seaweed, dulse, and the remains of cod. They are also very partial to whale flesh. The sheep are poor and thin, though why this should be so is difficult to understand, as there is abundant food for them in summer. I bought a good-sized lamb one day, and thought I had got a bargain at a dollar (4s. 6d.), but when two members of the whaling crew and I had finished the entire animal for breakfast one morning, its value seemed to be about three shillings, and dear at that.

Nothing has struck me so forcibly in Newfoundland as the miserable quality of their sheep, and the fact that a considerable part of the *fertile* coast-line would be made an excellent land for sheep-raising *if the right kinds were introduced*. It has been my lot to wander much in the barren northern lands of Iceland, Norway, the Hebrides, Shetland and Orkney, and in these wind-swept places I have seen flocks of different varieties of sheep in a flourishing condition —in spots, too, far more unsuitable in every way than the south and west coasts of Newfoundland. In most cases the farmers of these inhospitable wilds depend almost entirely on their sheep, and could not live without them. What is to be seen in Newfoundland? Only here and there, in widely separated places, one finds a few miserable sheep of some German extraction, carrying such a poor quality of wool and flesh as hardly to be worth the raising. Now, what is wanted is that the Government should take the matter in hand—for the Newfoundlanders themselves are much too apathetic and ignorant about such matters—and import a few flocks of the following sheep :—

The Highland ram of Scotland, which carries a magnificent coat of wool capable of withstanding the severest winter provided the snow is not too deep; Welsh sheep, Hebridean sheep, Shetland sheep, Icelandic sheep. All these varieties are extremely hardy, and would, I am sure, do well in the comparatively sheltered bays of the south and west coast.

One of the first things that would have to be done would be the shooting of *ownerless* dogs, and stringent laws would have to be enacted that the owners of dogs must keep their dogs in check and under proper supervision. A man who

NEWFOUNDLAND DOGS OF THE PRESENT DAY

THE FOWLS ARE FURNISHED WITH CURIOUS ATTACHMENTS TO PREVENT
THEM FROM ENTERING THE GARDENS

allows his dog to stray should be heavily fined. At present these half-wild "Labrador" dogs roam the country in spring and autumn, searching for anything they can kill. Once a dog has killed a sheep, it is very cunning, and will not murder in its own neighbourhood, but travels far afield to commit regular depredations.

Chickens are small and of a "speckelty" order. Some of them go about with curious attachments—a bar of wood tied across the top of the wings; this is done to prevent them getting into the gardens. Others are hobbled as an additional precaution.

On fine days a few butterflies are to be seen flitting about, but Newfoundland is not a good field for the entomologist. I noticed as common, the following species :— Cabbage white, red admiral, painted lady, and a large brown fritillary, which is very abundant on the rivers and woodland roads. Once I saw a small blue, and three times the lovely Camberwell Beauty.

The people are amiable and polite. It is a rare thing to pass a man or woman who does not wish you good day, and the children, too, are equally well-mannered. They are kind, sociable, and by no means reserved. The people of the outports make friends at once.

There was a sweet-looking old couple at Petty Fort, who, on my wishing to photograph them, said, "Yes, please, Mister, if it don't cost no more than a dollar." Then the old sweethearts took each other's hands in such a natural old-fashioned way to pose for the picture that I could not help thinking of the lines—

> "Now we maun toddle doon the hill,
> But hand in hand we'll go,
> And sleep thegither at the foot,
> John Anderson, my jo."

I met a fisherman one day at the same place, and he plunged into his wants at once, for of all things that young Newfoundland loves, it is a dance.

"Say, Mister," he said, "wouldn't you like a spree to-night?"

I remarked that I was not hunting for sprees just at that moment, but whales.

"But do just, there's a good man. Go up to the priest and ask the loan of the schoolhouse. You're a stranger, and he'll give it to you at once, though he wouldn't for me. I've got some whisky, and all the girls will come as soon as they know you've got the schoolhouse."

The offer was certainly enticing from his point of view, but as we might sail at any moment when the wind went down, I was forced to decline his hospitable suggestion. Most of the people stop and speak to you, and all ask if you are buying fish, and what is the price of cod in St. John's.

The women work on the drying stages as well as the men, laying out the fish whenever the sun shines, and piling into heaps under layers of bark whenever it threatens to rain. They all talk a good deal about their poverty, but personally I could hear of little genuine distress in this part of the island. One day two little boys, plump and well fed, but dressed in rags, stopped me and demanded cents. On asking them why they begged, and if it was for money to buy sweets, one of them said that they had had nothing to eat that day.

"What is your father?" I asked.

"We ain't got no father," the eldest replied, looking down. "He's got drowned."

"And your mother?"

"She can't do nothing; she's sick wi' the chills."

"Why don't you fish in the harbour?" I suggested; "it's full of flat fish."

This idea seemed new to them, and to present certain possibilities as yet undreamed of, and, after further conversation in which I found that their poverty was genuine, I was glad to give them some help.

It may seem extraordinary, but here was a bay simply crawling with beautiful flounders, but not a soul dreamt of catching and cooking them for their own use. Those who know best the outport Newfoundlander are aware of his conservatism and pig-headed objection to all innovations. Their fathers never ate flat fish, so why should they? They would rather starve than do such a thing. I asked a fisherman one day what his objection to them was, and he said, "People say they're poisonous."

I assured him to the contrary, and asked him if he had ever tried one, and he answered, "Yes, once, out of curiosity."

There are many other excellent fish, which they neither eat fresh nor cured, such as herring, wrasse (conors), skate, ling, hake, and halibut.

Like all seafaring people, the Newfoundlanders are exceedingly childlike and superstitious. Their fathers fished cod before them, and they do the same for four months in the year, often doing absolutely nothing for the other eight months, except to set a few traps for lobsters. If the Government offers them wages for making a road through the country they work splendidly—for one day—and then sit down contentedly and expect to declare a permanent dividend.

On the whole the men look strong, but the women are generally pinched and narrow-chested. Consumption is rife, and in no way lessened by the dirty practice of expectoration, so that if one member of a family acquires the dread disease it rapidly spreads, as the germs are fostered by hot rooms and damp weather. The purity of the air of Newfoundland is without doubt due to the fact that the people of the outports never open their windows.

Taking all things into consideration, the lot of the Newfoundlander who cares to work a little is an exceedingly happy one. He makes little or no money, but Nature offers him her gifts with no ungenerous hand. It is quite easy to go into the country in November and December and kill three deer. This can be done in a few days, the carcases being hauled out by dog or ox sledge. A supply of fresh meat is thus assured for the winter months.

When spring comes on and the ice breaks up,[1] large numbers of the more able-bodied take to the woods for the purpose of cutting logs. In many cases they work on their own account in the virgin forest, cutting in such sections as have not already been claimed by lumber companies, and hauling or floating their logs to the saw-mills, where they sell them, wages averaging from one to two dollars a day. The majority, however, take employment with some of the larger or smaller timber owners, and they prefer this method, as they are housed and fed at the expense of the owners. A good "riverside" boss—that is, the man who keeps the others at work and superintends the movement of the logs on the rivers—will earn as much as three dollars a day. During the summer the men fish, mostly in "bankers," off the coast or away north along the Labrador, whilst the

---

[1] Few of these south coast men go to the seal-fishing in spring. They are too independent, and are not forced to board the seal vessels as the men of the east coast are.

women attend to the home croft, and the planting and care of the land. In August most of the fishermen return and reap the hay or rough corn, which is only used as cattle food. On the east and west coast, in September, if the men are acquainted with the interior of the neighbourhood of their homes, they are often employed as "guides" for caribou hunting; at this they can earn from one to two dollars a day, sometimes even getting parties in October for the second season. No shooting parties—that is, sportsmen— enter Newfoundland from the south coast or northern peninsula, so this does not apply to them.

Thus we see that on the whole the Newfoundlanders, except the poor of St. John's and the islanders of the east coast, are exceedingly well off in the literal sense of the word, and would be in clover were it not for the overpowering taxes, for which they get absolutely nothing in return.

Cod-fishing being the principal industry of Newfoundland, it may be as well to briefly survey the various methods of taking this fish.[1] The men of the outports begin to fish about the 1st of May, for it is at this season that the cod move in from the ocean. The usual method is to fish from "bankers," small ocean-going schooners, carrying little boats with trawls. A "trawl" is not such as we understand it in England, but five dozen cod-lines, each 30 fathoms long, and baited in spring with herring. This method goes on till about the 15th of June. Then a large number of men desert the "bankers" and employ "cod-traps," seine-

---

[1] Cod rarely exceed 60 lbs. in weight, but there are authentic records of fish of 90 lbs. One was taken at Smoky Tickle, Labrador, in August 1906, which, according to the Newfoundland newspapers, was said to be 9 feet long when spit, and 5 feet broad. It is said to have weighed, when dry, 230 lbs. Doubtless these figures were exaggerated.

nets, or nets, hand-lines, and trawls all together. At this season the fish are at their best quality, as the caplin are in, and on these the cod largely feed. Caplin strike on to the south coast about the 10th of June, and last till 1st August, dying in myriads on the shore after spawning amongst the seaweed.

In shape a cod-trap is very like a house, with a large door at which the fish can enter. In the water it is 15 fathoms square on the ground plan, and 10 to 12 fathoms deep, the mesh of the net being 7 inches. The trap is set in 10 to 12 fathoms of water, and a long net stretching landwards, and called a "leader," guides the fish in at the front door. Once they go in they seldom return. This effective trap is hauled up twice a day, and generally it will contain anything from 1 to 150 quintals of fish.

Cod-nets are of somewhat different construction, the mesh being small, only 6 inches. They are about 100 fathoms long, and are about 20 feet deep. Weights are attached to the bottom, and they are sunk in from 18 to 20 fathoms of water. The cod run their heads into the net, and get their gills entangled. These nets are hauled once a day, and contain from a few fish to 10 quintals.

A cod-seine is a long net 102 to 130 fathoms of still smaller mesh, 4 inches in the centre and 5 at both ends. It is coiled in the stern of a small boat, and two men cast it out as the boat is rowed in a circle. The men, by means of a water-glass, see the school of fish before casting their net, and are sometimes very successful at this method of fishing. The cod-seine net can be cast several times during the day.

Hand-line fishing from small boats is somewhat precarious. The men usually average about fifty fish a day, but as many as 20 quintals have been taken in one day by two men, who happened to strike a shoal of hungry cod.

The cod-traps, cod-seines, and cod-nets all stop about 1st August, but the hand-line men and "bankers," with trawl lines, go on till about 1st October, when the weather usually becomes too bad for fishing.

Having brought the fish ashore, it may interest the reader to follow the history of the fish until it is eventually distributed.

As soon as the cod are brought ashore they are treated as follows. One man cuts the throat, another cuts the head off, a third splits and cleans the fish, and a fourth salts it. These "green" fish are then arranged in piles for a week or a fortnight. They are then taken out and washed in salt by boys and girls, and again packed in bulk for twenty-four hours. After this they are spread out to dry in the sun on the fir-branched trestles or flakes. It takes about five fine days to dry a cod. The dried fish is then packed in bulk and stored in the house, ready for removal. A usual price for outport curers is five dollars a quintal. (A quintal is 112 lbs., and it takes about fifty trawl fish, or a hundred trap fish, to realise this weight.)

The cod-fishing has for centuries been the mainstay of the island, and when all other things fail, this (and the caribou) will last, if taken care of. Of course seasons fluctuate owing to the irregular movements of the fish, but it may be taken as a general rule that if the season is bad off Newfoundland it is good on "The Labrador," or "Down North" as it is always called, where a large percentage of the Newfoundlanders go to fish.

The report of the Fisheries Board will give some idea of the great number of cod which are usually exported.

The total export of cod-fish by customs returns for the past five years was as follows, showing an average annual export of 1,322,466 quintals :—

Season 1899–1900	. . . . . .	1,300,622
„ 1900–1901	. . . . . .	1,233,107
„ 1901–1902	. . . . . .	1,288,955
„ 1902–1903	. . . . . .	1,429,274
„ 1903–1904	. . . . . .	1,360,373

The Grand Banks extend from Labrador southwards past Newfoundland to the Massachusetts coast, a distance of over 1000 miles, and every year some 1200 vessels, carrying crews of 20,000 fishermen, go out to battle with the surges as they have done for the past four hundred years. The fishermen of all lands have to encounter the perils of the deep, but none have to face the risks that the "bankers" do. Their special dangers are swift liners, that steam full speed through the fog, ice-bergs, ice-floes, chilling frosts, and furious storms. The fishing zone lies right in the track of great liners plying between Europe and America, and many a poor fisherman has lived to curse

> " Some damned liner's lights go by
> Like a great hotel " ;

whilst nearly all have some heartrending tale to tell of the destruction of fishing craft of which he has been an eye-witness. There is an ever-increasing record of sunken ships, of frosts which overpower, and of dory crews driven from their schooners by sudden tempests, and, during the fishing season, hardly a week goes by without some tale of misfortune. Of the method of fishing and the disasters which overtake the ship I must quote a passage from one of Mr. P. T. M'Grath's articles,[1] which are full of interest and accurate information.

[1] *St. John's Herald*, 28th August 1906.

"When fishing is actually in progress, the smacks always anchor, for the shoals carry only thirty to sixty fathoms of water, and hempen cables are used instead of iron chains to moor them, as the latter would saw their bows out from the lively pitching they do in these choppy seas. The fishing itself is done from dories, light but strong flat-bottomed boats, each carrying two men, who set their lines or trawls overnight, and examine them next day, removing the fish impaled on the hooks with which the trawl is furnished, and then rebaiting them for another night's service. The ship is therefore like a hen with a flock of chickens, the dories standing in this relation to her, while the trawls radiate from her as spokes from a wheel-hub, being laid outward from her at a distance of one or two miles, the ship serving as a depôt for feeding and housing the men and for cleaning and storing their catch. In setting and cleaning his trawls and cleaning his catch the doryman finds abundant occupation, and rarely gets more than a few hours' sleep in a night, sometimes none at all.

"Thus it is that when fogs obscure the water, vigilance is relaxed by the toil-worn look-out, to whom is entrusted the lives of a score of comrades, tiredly sleeping below. Though the fog-horn each vessel carries is sounded regularly, still many a horror is enacted amid this curtain of gloom, when a mighty steamship splits a hapless fisher-boat and, like a marine juggernaut, rushes on over the wreckage and bodies she sends to the bottom by the stroke of her steel-clad prow. Often at night a sudden crash rends the stillness, and a shriek of despair rises from the stricken schooner's crew, a swirl of splintered wood in her wake to mark the eddies for a while, and then vanish, a tomb for fifteen or twenty men.

"Last summer one of the German liners cut down a trawler on the banks, but it was in the daytime, and the crew fortunately escaped. The previous year two similar occurrences took place with equally harmless results. The freighter *Endymion*, however, bound to Montreal, crashed into the smack *Albatross* off Cape Race last July, and of the nineteen on the latter only one was saved. In September 1902 the collier *Warspite* sank the smack *Bonavista* on one of the banks, three only surviving out of twenty-two on board. In 1898 the *City of Rome* ripped the stem off the smack *Victor* of St. Pierre Miquelon, but she kept afloat, and a relief party from the liner got her safely to land after three days of trying endeavour, as she was leaking badly from the shock. This humane action on the liner's part is agreeably remembered yet among the fishing fleets, for, if the bankmen are to be believed, steamers usually keep on as if nothing had happened, and tell the passengers who may have felt the shock that it was caused by striking loose ice or suddenly changing the course. It is, indeed, alleged among the bankmen, that crews of foreign steamers will beat off with belaying pins the wretches from the foundering vessels who try to swarm on board, that the name of the destroyer may not be known, and local complications be thus avoided.

"How many of the missing bankmen meet their end in this way can only be conjectured, but certain it is that far more are sunk than are reported to the world. Frequently the steamer's people scarcely know what has happened when such a catastrophe occurs to the accompaniment of a midnight storm, so slight is the shock of impact on her huge hull, and with spectators few at these times, and look-outs and watch-officers having every reason to escape inquiry and possible punishment, the temptation to hurry on and make no alarm is usually yielded to. Many lives are certainly sacrificed every year because of this which could otherwise be saved, for the fishing schooners are all wooden-built and, unless mortally smitten, will float for some time. Even at the worst the men can cling to planks or spars long enough to be rescued if the steamer would stop to launch a boat, which, of course, is always done when the collision occurs while passengers are on deck or in daylight.

"The fishermen take every ship that strikes them to be a liner, but, during the last few years, the greyhound track has been moved south of the Grand Bank to avoid them, so fearful from these mishaps previously, and now most of the tragedies are due to freighters, which swarm across this area during the summer. Not a few of the unrecorded disappearances there of splendid trawlers must be assigned to these racing steamboats, such as the loss of the *Cora M'Kay*, in October 1902, one of the finest vessels that ever sailed out of Gloucester, which disappeared with her twenty-two men under conditions which would warrant the belief that she was run over and sent to the bottom. Eight French smacks from St. Pierre were damaged by steamships in 1900, and there is every reason to think that three others were sunk with all hands by them the same year.

"So frequent are these collisions, that the recent comic papers had a rather ghastly joke about a tourist returning to America and bemoaning the uneventful passage, as the ship 'ran down only one fishing smack, don't you know.' All steamers are supposed to slow down to half-speed during a fog, but this rule is rarely observed, and it is to its ignoring that most of the fatalities are due.

"Equally terrible destruction is often wrought by the gales which sweep the banks in the fishing time. Chief among these, in its appalling fatality list, was the 'Seventh of June Breeze' of 1896. The day was fine and fair for fishing, when the tempest broke and caught hundreds of dories far from their ships, imperilling not alone the skiffs and occupants, but also the vessels themselves, because only the captain and cook remain aboard while trawling is on. Scores of boats and several vessels sank, and over 300 lives were lost. Three Newfoundland, two Canadian, and three Americans were sunk at their moorings, and all hands were lost."

It is sad to see a grand old man like Lord Roberts trying to arouse the nation to a sense of its military weakness, but, thank heaven, those in power in the Navy are not so blind or foolish as to overlook the splendid reserve of naval seamen that can be made from the Terra-Novan fishermen. We have great and powerful colonies full of virile men capable of making excellent soldiers, but where can we find sailors that are experienced and used to the sea beyond our own coasts, except in Newfoundland? Here we have a people, bound to us not only by the ties of kinship, but of love. It is a land where the portraits of our beloved King and Queen hang in every humble cottage, not as nominal rulers of some visionary power, but as the heads of the great motherland for which the islanders have both pride and respect. Newfoundland will gladly give of her best when the great day of war comes, as come it surely will, and her bluejackets, I feel sure, will acquit themselves with honour. I cannot do better than conclude this chapter with some stirring lines by James B. Connolly :—

OLD SWEETHEARTS

THE CAPTAIN ABOUT TO FIRE AT A FINBACK

" Oh, Newf'undland and Cape Shore men, and men of Gloucester town,
With ye I've trawled o'er many banks, and sailed the compass round ;
I've ate wi' ye, and watched wi' ye, and bunked wi' ye, all three,
And better shipmates than ye were I never hope to see.
I've seen ye in a wild typhoon beneath a Southern sky,
I've seen ye when the Northern gales drove seas to masthead high ;
But summer breeze or winter blow, from Hatt'ras to Cape Race,
I've yet to see ye with the sign of fear upon your face."

The total strength of the Newfoundland naval reserve is at present 573, and it ought to be treble this number. The men enrol for a period of five years, at the expiration of which they can enrol for a further period or obtain their discharge. The reservists between the age of eighteen and thirty are of two classes, " Seamen " and " Qualified Seamen "; on entry he belongs to the former class.

CHAPTER VIII

MODERN FIN-WHALING AND THE GREAT WHALES

BEFORE introducing my readers to the business and excitement of modern whale-hunting, it is necessary to give a slight review or history of Newfoundland's advance in this respect, and to see how the industry gradually developed since the first discovery of the island by Cabot in 1497.[1]

Soon after this important discovery great tales of the Newfoundland seas and their riches excited the Devon and Somerset men to cross the Atlantic in their crazy fishing boats to filch the treasures of the deep in the shape of walrus, seal, and cod from the waters of the west. Owing to the rapacity of those in power these early mariners kept their catch secret for a long time, carrying their salt cod to Spain and Portugal, just as they do to-day, and reaping a rich reward. Judge Prowse, than whom there is no better authority on the island's history, tells us that "the proofs that the trade was both extensive and lucrative are abundant. In 1527, the little Devonshire fishing ships were unable to carry home their large catch, so 'sack ships' (large merchant vessels) were employed to carry the salt cod to Spain and Portugal. In 1541 an Act of Henry VIII. classes the Newfoundland trade among such well-known enterprises as the Irish, Shetland, and Iceland fisheries. Soon after 1497, the great trade between Bristol and Iceland declined, and the price of fish fell. We have further transactions in 'barrelled fish' from Newfoundland.

[1] Our information on this point is derived from Italian and Spanish letters written soon after his arrival in 1497.

THE CAPTAIN OF THE WHALER

DUSKY MALLARD OR BLACK DUCK

In 1583 Sir Humphrey Gilbert came to St. John's especially to obtain supplies for his impoverished fleet, and it is then mentioned as a 'place very populace and much frequented.' 'The English command all there.'"

Sir Walter Raleigh declared that this trade was the mainstay and support of the western counties, and "that if any misfortune happened to the Newfoundland fleet, it would be the greatest calamity that could befall England." The value will be seen from the fact that the Newfoundland business employed over 10,000 men, who earned annually over £500,000—a very large sum in those days, and amounting to a half of the national assets.

One is apt to forget that the great Chancellor Bacon was not only famous for his literary gifts. He was also, as Ben Jonson tells us, a great public speaker, and, far in advance of his age, believed in the value and success of our colonies. He was the chief organiser of "The London and Bristol Company for Colonising Newfoundland," and drew up both its prospectus and the rules of the new enterprise. In one passage he refers to "The Goldmine of the Newfoundland fishery, richer than all the treasures of Golconda and Peru," and thus predicted a success for the industry which has since come true. For as Prowse remarks : "This wonderful harvest of the sea has been producing millions upon millions every season for four hundred years, as productive to-day as when John Cabot and his West-country fishermen first sighted 'the New-founde-launde,' and told their countrymen marvellous stories about the fish that were dipped up in baskets, of the great deer, and of the strange birds and beasts in this wonderful new island of the West. These tales of wealth in fur, fin, and feather in our most ancient colony are as true to-day as in the Tudor age."

L

These hardy old sea-rovers, together with a small per-
centage of French and Portuguese, fished on the Grand
Banks, or killed the seal and walrus in early spring to the
north and west. It was not, however, until about 1550, that
the Spanish Basques, who had long chased the Great Southern
Right Whale (*Balæna australis*) in the stormy waters of the
Bay of Biscay, inaugurated the whaling industry in the
Newfoundland seas.

It is a common fallacy amongst the British, that we were
the first nation to commence whaling. It was the Basques
who first chased the seal and the walrus,[1] and afterwards
taught our people the dangerous business of whale-killing.
The very word "harpoon" is derived from an old Basque
word "harpon." Yet though the English ruled all then in
Newfoundland, as they had maintained their supremacy
hundreds of years before in the Iceland cod-fishery, whaling
was a trade they had to learn and did learn. For courtesy
the chief post, that of whale-killer, was held by a Basque
"harponier," just as the Norwegians are the first of whale-
men to-day.

Up to 1800 the whales were pursued in open boats, and
struck with the hand harpoon; about 1830 the small bomb
came into use; soon after which date whales were found too
difficult and dangerous to hunt, the Right Whale (probably
Balæna australis, not *Balæna mysticetus*) having almost completely disappeared. The last Right Whale killed in Newfoundland was taken near Gaultois, on the south coast,
in 1850.

In the year 1880, a Norwegian sailor named Svend Foyn,
after several ineffectual attempts to kill the great *Balænoptera*

---

[1] This of course only refers to our colonial hunting. The Norwegians had for
long exploited the waters of Spitzbergen for the chase of these animals.

with ordinary lines and bomb-guns, invented the cannon and harpoon with exploding head. This was at once found to be effective on the greatest of all whales, such as Sibbald's Rorqual, the Common Rorqual, and the Humpback. These enormous creatures had never previously suffered from the attacks of man to any serious extent, because the attempt to strike and hold them with the ordinary methods employed on the Greenland, the Southern Right, or the Sperm Whales, would have led to disaster.

Svend Foyn commenced operations at once on the Finmark coast of Norway in 1880, and his immediate success was quickly followed by a crowd of small vessels which, killing sometimes as many as five or six *Balænoptera* in a single day, rapidly depleted the northern grounds. Many thousands were slain until the Norwegian Government stepped in and put a stop to further operations by appointing a close time until the year 1907. This industry, however, was profitable, so the gallant Norwegians, having found a trade after their own hearts, at once set out to look for "fresh fields and pastures new." *Balænoptera* were reported as being numerous in the Gulf of St. Lawrence and Newfoundland waters, and in 1897–1899 the Cabot Whaling Company commenced hunting, and began operations at Snooks Arm, and at Balæna, in Hermitage Bay. The first whale was killed on 25th June 1898 by the steamer *Cabot* (Captain Bull), and she killed 47 in that year. In 1899 she took 95 ; in 1900 the total was 111 ; in 1901 the *Cabot* and another boat killed 258 ; in 1902 three steamers slew 472 ; and in 1903 four steamers slaughtered the enormous total of 858 large whales. In 1904 more ships took the sea, the total catch of fourteen factories being 1275 whales, made up as follows : 264 Sibbald's Rorqual, 281 Humpbacks, 690 Common Rorqual, 39 Rudolphi's Rorqual, 1 Sperm Whale.

In spite of this great slaughter, whales were reported to be quite as plentiful as usual in the spring of 1905. In fact, in April and May Sibbald's Rorqual and Common Rorqual were abundant along the edge of the ice at the mouth of the St. Lawrence, and on the south coast of Newfoundland, as far east as Placentia Bay. In June, however, whales suddenly became extremely scarce, owing, said some of the owners and St. John's people, to the excessive slaughter, but in reality to the trend seawards of the stream of "kril" or red shrimp, on which the great *Balænoptera* subsist.

The whales which are hunted are: Sibbald's Rorqual (*Balænoptera Sibbaldi*), called by the Norwegians "the Blue Whale," and by the Americans and Newfoundlanders by the stupid name of "Sulphur-Bottom"; the Common Rorqual (*Balænoptera musculus*), generally known as "the Finback"; the Humpback Whale (*Megaptera* boops); and Rudolphi's Rorqual (*Balænoptera borealis*), known to the Norwegians as "Seijval," or Seiwhale. The Lesser Rorqual (*Balænoptera rostrata*), or Minkie's Whale, and the Sperm Whale, are also killed on rare occasions.

Sibbald's Rorqual, or, as I shall call it in future, the Blue Whale, is the largest of living creatures, and larger than any mammal or reptile that the world has ever seen. Zoologists who revel in piecing together the extinct creatures of the past, and giving them an undue prominence, are somewhat apt to overlook the more interesting forms which still live and frequent our seas close at hand. Consequently the distribution and habits of the most wonderful things that have ever breathed have not received the attention they deserved. On commencing the study of whales some years ago, I found the literature of the *Balænoptera* so meagre that much study and personal experience would be necessary to ascertain new facts

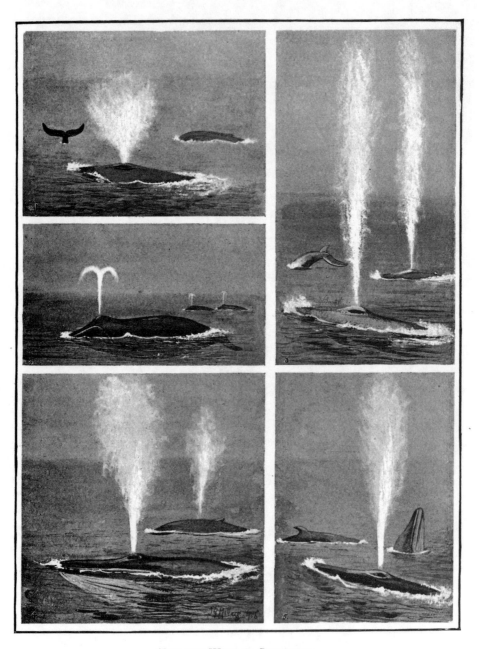

VARIOUS WHALES SPOUTING

1. The Humpbacked Whale.   Spout like the smoke of a cigar, round and evanescent.
2. Atlantic Right Whale, redrawn by the Author from a sketch by a Nordkaper hunter.
3. Blue Whale.   Spout from 15 to 30 feet in height.
4. Common Rorqual.   Spout from 10 to 15 feet.
5. Rudolphi's Rorqual.   Spout from 8 to 10 feet.   Rudolphi's and the Common Rorqual do not show the tail when "sounding."

about them and their ways. Since the introduction of the whaling steamer, and the publication of Dr. True's admirable monograph on the "Whalebone Whales of the North-West Atlantic," our knowledge has advanced by leaps and bounds, and now we know a good deal about these animals, although many points still remain to be cleared up, especially with regard to the distribution and movements of the several species, which I have carefully studied at home and abroad.

In a work of this kind I shall not inflict on my readers the dry bones of scientific lore, but shall only place before them just as many details as are necessary to allow them to understand superficially the animals we are about to hunt.

The Blue Whale is distinguished from the other Rorquals by its superior size and rich colour. All the upper part is a rich zinc-blue slate, the lower a dark blue-grey, whilst the interior parts of the throat and belly grooves are brownish-grey. The pectoral fins are blue-grey with snow-white outer edges. The baleen plates, about 4 feet in length, are black, and number up to 400. The Blue Whale feeds almost exclusively on a small red shrimp (*Euphausia*), known to the Norwegians as "kril," and "swamps" (*Temora longicornis*). Adults measure from 70 to 102 feet, and weigh approximately from 150 to 200 tons, and yield over 100 barrels of oil. This whale occurs both in the Atlantic and the Pacific. It has been observed off the fringe of the Antarctic ice, and all along both coasts of America, whilst many winter to the east of the West Indies. In March and April large numbers approach the Gulf of St. Lawrence, just keeping outside the ice. Here the main body of these western whales separate, one gathering going right up the estuary as the ice breaks, the other turning east along the south coast of Newfoundland, slowly, but closely, fishing the banks of "kril" as far as Cape St. Mary, in

Placentia Bay. As a rule, in the month of June, the "kril" move out from Cape St. Mary to the Grand Banks, where the whales scatter and feed about over a large area, and do not return to the Newfoundland coast until September and October. They do not go north along the Newfoundland east coast, or along the Labrador. It is still uncertain whether these whales, which return in September, are the same as those which left the south coast in June, or fresh comers from the south. It is also uncertain where this herd of whales winter, but the Norwegian captains, who are the best judges on these matters, are all inclined to think that they do not go very far, but winter about the Grand Banks,[1] some two hundred miles off south-east Newfoundland, and scattered over a large area. Certainly, many solitary Blue Whales have been seen by ships in this range during the winter months.

The range of the Blue Whale in the eastern Atlantic may be briefly summed up as follows. They appear in large numbers in early May off the west coast of the Hebrides, where one factory in Harris killed no less than forty-two in 1905. They then strike due north, passing the Faroes, where a few are killed; and make their summer home in the seas off Finmark, Spitzbergen, the White Sea, and the north-east coast of Iceland. Captain Larsen, who has made five trips to East Greenland in summer, has also seen many there. In October all these Blue Whales strike due south, going at full-speed, holding out for the main Atlantic, into which they disappear for the winter.

In the water the Blue Whale, doubtless owing to its vast bulk, is somewhat slow and stately in its movements. It

---

[1] I saw two individuals about two hundred miles east of St. John's in November 1906.

travels in search of food at the rate of about six miles an hour, but when frightened, travelling, or struck by a harpoon, it can go at twenty knots, a speed which it can maintain for a long period. In feeding on a bank of "kril," it swims on its side, erects a fin, and gives a sudden movement of "full-speed ahead"; at the same moment the vast mouth is opened and slowly closed, encompassing about twenty barrels of shrimps. As the mouth closes the water is forced outwards, and may be seen rushing in a white stream from the sides of the baleen, whilst the food remains resting on the inside of the "plates," to be swallowed at leisure. All the *Balænop-tera* feed in this manner, and I have seen a large Finback rolling round and round the steamer, taking in its huge mouthfuls with evident satisfaction, and caring as little for our presence as if we were not there at all—in fact it seemed a miracle that he could avoid striking the vessel with his great jaws.

The Blue Whale generally remains under water during his great dive, according to my watch, for ten to twenty minutes. On reaching the surface he "blows," sending up a spout of air and steam to a height of from 20 to 30 feet. He rolls over, slowly exposing the blow-hole, and afterwards the small back fin. Then he makes a series of from eight to twelve short dives on the surface, occupying four minutes. When making his great dive he often raises his tail right out of the water, but not at such a perpendicular angle as the Humpback. It is during the time the whale is making these short dives on the surface that the steam whaler races in and endeavours to get the shot. When struck by the harpoon and its bursting charge, the great Blue Whale often dives at once and sinks to the bottom of the sea. Frequently it rushes off at high speed, and then, coming to the surface, dies after a short "flurry." Sometimes, however, when the whale is hit too far back or near and under the backbone (in which case the bomb does not explode), a long and difficult chase, protracted for hours, ensues. On the whole this is a fairly tame whale, and not considered dangerous, if ordinary precautions are observed. The value is from £100 to £150.

Although not so difficult to kill as the Finback, this species is possessed of greater strength and staying power than any whale, and some exciting experiences have fallen to the lot of the Fin-whalers engaged in its chase. The most remarkable and protracted hunt on record after a whale was experienced by the steamer *Puma* in 1903. The most exaggerated accounts of this appeared in the American and English papers, where the journalists went so far as to say that the whale had towed the ship from Newfoundland to Labrador, and other wild statements. The following particulars were given to me by Hans Johanssen, mate of the *Puma*, and Captain Christopherson himself, so they are, at any rate, first-hand.

The *Puma* spied and "struck" a large Blue Whale, six miles from Placentia, at nine o'clock in the morning. The animal immediately became "wild," and it was found impossible to get near enough to fire another harpoon into it, as it came on to blow hard. For the entire day it towed the steamer, with engines at half-speed astern, at a rate of six knots. Towards evening a second rope was made fast to the stern of the vessel and attached to the first line, now "out" one mile. The steamer then put on full-speed ahead. This seemed to incense the whale, which put forth all its strength, and dragged the whole of the after part of the vessel under water, flooding the after cabin and part of the engine-room. The stern rope was immediately cut with an axe and the danger averted. All through the night the gallant whale dragged the steamer, with the dead weight of two miles of rope, and the engines going half-speed astern, and at 9 A.M. the following morning the monster seemed to be as lively and powerful as ever. At 10 A.M., however, its strength seemed to decrease, and at 11 it was wallowing on the surface, where, at 12.30, it was finally lanced by the captain. This great fight occupied twenty-eight hours, the whale having dragged the steamer a distance of thirty miles to Cape St. Mary.

The Common Rorqual, or "Finback," is the second largest whale. Adults are from 60 to 70 feet in length. The upper surface is a dark amber-brown, the lower white. In a few examples, a grey-brown colour covers the whole of the lower parts, and these are known to the Norwegian whale-men as "bastards," and considered by them as separate species. This is, however, an error, as the dark colour is merely an individual variation. The baleen plates are 3 feet in length and 375 in number on each side, being of two colours, blue-grey and yellowish-white. They are more valuable than those of the Blue Whale or the Humpback, but fetch less than the "plates" of Rudolphi Rorqual, which are considered the best quality amongst the *Balænoptera*.

The distribution of this whale is very wide. It travels all over the temperate seas of the northern and southern hemispheres. It is abundant off the Antarctic ice, and num-bers pass up and down the Pacific, and go as far north as the Aleutian Islands and Behring Straits. On the western Atlantic side many winter to the east of the West Indian Islands, and appear off the Massachusetts coast about March, working up into the St. Lawrence and off the south and east coast of Newfoundland, where they stay until August. The main body seem to scatter out on the Grand Banks,

or move north along the Labrador, where they are very
numerous in August and September, in fact until the northern
ice comes down and drives them south again. On the British
coasts they appear in large numbers off Harris and West
Shetland in May, and move north-east very slowly throughout the summer, following the banks of "kril." By September
the main herds are still only about 100 miles due north of
Muckle Flugga (Unst), where I saw 200 all in view at once
in 1904. After this the whalemen think they slowly continue their journey north-north-east, and that they turn south-
west again in October, bringing with them the main body,
which has summered up on the Finmark coast, Spitzbergen,
Iceland, and the White Sea. In general habits this whale
is very similar to the Blue Whale, but it is a more active
creature. It swims faster, and remains under water for a
shorter period (about eight to twelve minutes).

Its superficial dives are also made more quickly, only from
six to ten appearances taking place.

In the midst of "kril" or caplin it moves very slowly,
and drives the "bait" together by circling round it. When
thus engaged Finbacks seem to be quite oblivious of the
presence of ships, and roll under the bows and body of the
ship with a disregard of their own safety which is truly
astonishing; and yet so delicate is their judgment of distance
and sense of proportion that they seldom, if ever, come into
collision with a vessel.[1] Strange as it may seem, these feeding
whales are sometimes most difficult to fire at from the ship. I
have been in a whaler within a stone's-throw of a big Finback
for a quarter of an hour, and the captain, with all his skilful

---

[1] A Finner moving in a mass of "kril" struck a whaler on the coast of Finmark
in 1890. The whale was stunned, and the vessel sustained little injury beyond
some bent plates.

manœuvring, has been unable to obtain a shot, the whale never once rising within proper distance of the firing circle. When feeding, the Finback turns on its side, gives a " start " forward, and erects the pectoral. As it rolls slowly over, it also shows the whole of one side of the tail. About six to ten feet below the surface it opens its enormous mouth, and closes it slowly, to take in vast numbers of "kril." As the mouth shuts one sees a white stream of water rushing from the outer sides of the baleen plates. The whale opens and shuts its mouth several times before coming to the surface. In the vicinity of the feeding operations the sea is suffused with a mass of oily matter, in which numerous small marine creatures, too small for the eye of man to see, are present. On these descend swarms of kittiwakes, Leach's petrels, and Manx greater and dusky shearwaters, which are for ever scouring the seas on the look-out for such provender. Finbacks sometimes associate in scattered parties, or even in one great herd, the individual members of which keep at a considerable distance from one another. Often they are met with singly, or in family parties consisting of the bull, cow, and calf of the previous year. Off the coast of Shetland they are usually found from thirty to ninety miles distance in 120 fathoms of water (Foden), but are sometimes seen within a mile of the land. Like the Blue Whale and some of the dolphins, they seem fond of the company of large vessels, and will play round these without alarm.

The food consists of a few herrings, caplin, *Mallotus arcticus*, white fish, small squid, and various crustaceans. It is the general opinion of the whalers that this species only eats herrings when crustaceans are unobtainable. Very few Finbacks have been obtained in Shetland whose mouths or stomachs contained herrings, but one was taken at the

Norrona Station, on 8th June 1905, which had devoured a small quantity of herrings.

On being struck the Finback is either killed dead on the spot, or rushes away at a speed of about 15 knots for a distance of two or more miles. Most of the steamers carry about 3½ miles of line. When it is exhausted the rope is "clamped," *i.e.* held fast by the winch, and the steamer is towed at a rate of 6 to 10 knots. As the efforts of the whale slacken, quarter-, half-, or full-speed astern is employed by the steamer to act as a drag, and so the battle goes on until the monster is exhausted, or the harpoon "drawn." Space will not allow me to give any of the numerous stories of the exciting hunts to which one listens in the galley and the cabin of the Atlantic Fin-whalers, but they prove that the chase of this great whale calls for the sternest courage and readiest resource. To stand up in a tiny "pram" amidst a whirl of waters and lance a fighting Finback is no child's play, and requires that three-o'clock-in-the-morning pluck that the Norsemen possess in a high degree. Many accidents have occurred to the boat crews when engaged in "lancing," and one or two to the steamers themselves. The whaler *Gracia*, belonging to Vadso, was sunk by a Finner in 1894 in the Veranger Fjord. In 1896 the *Jarjford* was sunk in ten minutes by one of these whales charging it when about sixty miles north of the North Cape. A heavy sea was running at the time, and the crew crowded into two small prams which would probably have been overwhelmed had not Captain Castberg, hunting in another steamer, come to their rescue.

The following notes from my diary were made when, as guest of Mr. Haldane, I shared in the chase of the Finback in August 1904 :—

A Shot at a Finback

After a day of fruitless battling with the wind and sea we lay up in Balta Sound, Unst, for the night. At midday the wind went down, and the captain and mate, who had gone to the summit of a mountain to spy, were seen running at full-speed for the boat. Steam was up and the anchor weighed as soon as their feet touched the deck, and we ran out for one mile eastward, where we found a large bull and cow Finner. Several times a shot seemed imminent, but the whales went down. After two hours' pursuit the captain decided that these whales were too "wild," so we stood out to the north, encountering several herds of Pilot Whales and three Lesser Rorqual, the first I had seen. About six o'clock in the evening we encountered the fringe of the main herd of Finbacks, which were spouting in all directions. We pursued whale after whale, but all seemed wild except one monster which refused to leave the side of the vessel, and in consequence could not be shot at. At last the mate got a shot at 7 P.M., and missed. He was much crestfallen, and retired to the galley to enjoy the healing balm of coffee and potatoes. At 7.30 it was bitterly cold when Captain Stokken again stood beside the gun, and we were in full pursuit of a large female Finback that seemed tamer than the rest. Eventually in its final "roll" the whale raised itself about ten yards from the gun, and the whaler tipping the muzzle downwards fired and struck the quarry under the backbone.

At first the Finback was rather quiet, and then it began to run, the strong line rushing out at a speed of about 15 knots. When some two miles of rope had gone over the bow I turned to Captain Stokken, and said:

"How much line have you got?"

"About three mile," was the curt reply.

"But when that three miles goes, what then?"

"Oh, well," was the imperturbable answer, "then I check line, and we see which is strongest, whale or rope. Perhaps harpoon draws out."

In the course of a minute the captain gave the order to check the line. The strain now became terrific, the two-inch rope straining and groaning as if it would burst. At the same moment the little steamer leaped forward and raced over the seas at about twelve miles an hour. There was a feeling of intense exhilaration as we rushed northwards, the spray flying from our bows as the ship leapt from crest to crest in the heavy swell. I have enjoyed the rushes of gallant thirty and even forty-pound salmon in heavy water on the Tay, the supreme moments in an angler's life, but that was mere child's play to the intense excitement which we now experienced during the next three hours. To be in tow of a wild whale is something to experience and remember to one's dying day. You feel that you are alive, and that you are there with the sport of kings. No wonder the Norwegians are full of life, and the men, from the captain to the cook, run to their several tasks with eyes and hearts aflame. This is a trade which will stir the blood of the dullest clod, and to men who are one and all the finest seamen in the world, it is the very life and essence of the Viking nature.

Three hours of this fierce race went on, and the whale seemed as if it would take us to Iceland. The gallant Fin-back was as fresh as ever when the captain gave the order, "Quarter-speed astern." Another tremendous strain on the rope, the churning of the backward-driving screw, and our speed was at once reduced to 10 knots. It was marvellous the strength of the animal. The minutes and even the hours fled by, still the great cetacean held on its northward course without a check. Three hours went by; then came the order,

"Half-speed astern," and we were down to 6 knots, the vessel and the whale still fighting the battle for the mastery. In another hour the whale showed visible signs of weakening, when "Full-speed astern" brought matters to a standstill. The machinery of man and the natural strength of the beast still worried on for another hour, and then we saw the steamer moving backwards; the whale was done, and could pull no more.

The rope was then slackened, hoisted on to a "giving" pulley, and then wound on to the powerful steam winch, which, acting like the fisherman's reel, at once began to "take in." Nothing was heard for another hour but the monotonous throb of the engine, until at last on the crest of a wave, about 300 yards to windward, was seen the great Finback, rolling over and over, spouting continuously, but so tired that it was unable to drag or dive.

The captain now gave the order, "Lower away to lance." There was a fairly heavy sea running, as there always is off Shetland, and yet I never saw anything more smartly done than the way in which those Norwegians flung their light "pram" into the water and jumped in from the bulwarks. Other men were ready with the oars, which they handed to the two rowers, whilst the mate seized the long 15-foot "killing" lance, and the small party rowed rapidly away towards the whale. This is the dangerous part of whaling; the killing of the Finback, and more especially the Humpback, is neither a safe nor an easy matter. If the whale is not quite exhausted, it rapidly rights itself, and goes for the boat and its occupants, whom it endeavours to strike with its flippers; sometimes it turns away from the boat and brings the tail sharply downwards on boat and men. Many fatal accidents have occurred on such occasions.

Hans Andersen, the mate, stood up in the stern, holding his long lance, as the men rowed slowly up to the leviathan. Then the rowers turned the boat round, and backed it in towards their prey. At times they were lost in the great swell, and then they would appear apparently beside the sea-monster, whose pathetic rolling was at once changed into spasmodic life. The whale, churning the water, now righted itself, and at once turned on its attackers, who retreated at full-speed. Now on one side and now on another, the plucky mate tried to approach and bring off his death-thrust, but all to no avail. Every time the exhausted cetacean had just enough strength left to carry the war into the enemy's country, and to turn the tables on its opponents. Mist and darkness were rolling up, the sea was rising, and still the duel of attack and defence went on. Full twenty times Andersen got within 25 feet of his objective, and yet dare not give the thrust, which, if attempted too soon, would mean his own death. At last darkness hid the combatants from view, when Stokken turned to me and said :

"This very wild whale. Must give him another shot, or Andersen will get hurt." He reached up and blew the steam whistle three times as a signal for the boat to return. In a few minutes Andersen's cheerful face was looking up at us, the lance held high and streaming with blood.

"Ha, so you stab him," said Stokken.

"Ja, just as you blow the whistle," replied the mate, with a smile. The pram and its occupants were soon aboard, and the whale rolled in and lashed alongside by the tail. The chase had lasted seven hours.

Few Finbacks fight so well as this, but it was a sight to see, and one I shall never forget.

Rudolphi's Rorqual, commonly called the "Seijval," or

A FIGHTING HUMPBACK

(*From Millais's " The Mammals of Great Britain and Ireland"*)

"Seiwhale," is another common species in northern waters, but is not so much sought after owing to its inferior size. The baleen, however, is most valuable of all, next to that of the two Right Whales. Its general habits are similar to the last named, but it is much swifter in its movements than either of them. When first struck it races off at great speed — Norwegians say 25 knots an hour; but this is seldom maintained for more than a quarter of an hour, and it is then easily killed. This whale often comes close in shore, like the Humpback, and may often be seen in the tideways of Scotland close to the northern islands.

The last of the whales which form the prey of the *Balænoptera* hunters is the Humpback (*Megaptera* boops). It is a very strong, thick-set animal, 50 feet long and often 40 feet in circumference. It varies in colour from jet black all over with white outer edges to its 15-foot pectoral fins to black above and white underneath. The throat and breast grooves are deeper and not so numerous as in the other varieties of this group. No whale has so wide a distribution as the Humpback, and it is safe to say that it is found in all the large waters, whether warm or cold. It is very numerous along the Antarctic ice, the Indian Ocean, the sea off the Cape, and south to New Zealand. In the Pacific Islands it is numerous, and there it is hunted with small boats; in the Vancouver and Behring Straits it is found in summer. In the North Atlantic it is abundant on both sides and, I believe, constantly passes from America to Shetland and Norway. It also frequents the White Sea, Iceland, Greenland, and the coast of Labrador at various seasons.

At Tobago and Santa Lucia the Humpback fishery is worked by Americans. Captain Scammon gives an interesting account in his book of the Humpback in the Pacific, and

M

the methods of taking it employed in the sixties and seventies, and for a reliable narrative of the chase of this whale in Friendly Islands the reader will find "My First Whale," by Stanley Mylius, most entertaining.

In Europe the Humpback was not hunted until the introduction of the little steamers and the bomb-gun invented by Svend Foyn (1865), but now some hundreds are annually killed in the northern waters of the Atlantic. In Shetland about four or five per station is the usual take. Between the years 1865 and 1885 large numbers of Humpbacks were killed off the Finmark coast by the Norwegians; in fact, so successful were these steamers that they have decimated the *Balænoptera* in the neighbourhood of the north-eastern waters. A close time is now, however, in force.

Humpbacks appear in spring in the northern waters, and often come close in shore, where they have been seen rubbing their noses, lips, and fins on the rocks to free themselves from the objectionable barnacles which grow on these parts. They feed principally on "kril," but also eat a variety of fish, such as caplin, &c.

The Humpback may be described as the clown of the sea. It is of a joyous, lively disposition, rollicking and sporting in the ocean with all the happy irresponsibility of a monstrous child. We can hardly imagine a huge creature like a whale being frolicsome, but such is the case, and within the limits of its vast bulk it contrives to get a lot of fun out of life. In fact it is a sort of Marine White-tailed Gnu. The animal loves to fling itself clear out of the water, coming down with a huge splash, and to see two or three playing and romping in a summer sea is quite an education in elephantine joy.

As a rule these whales are of a fearless disposition, and will permit the close approach of a boat or small steamer.

They seem to have no regular mating season, but the young are born during the summer months. " In the mating season," says Captain Scammon, "they are noted for their amorous antics. At such times their caresses are of the most amusing and novel character, and these performances have doubtless given rise to the fabulous tales of the sword-fish and thrasher attacking whales. When lying by the side of each other, the Megapteras frequently administer alternate blows with their long fins, which love-pats may, on a still day, be heard at a distance of miles. They also rub each other with the same huge and flexible arms, rolling occasionally from side to side, and indulging in other gambols which can easier be imagined than described. The time of gestation is not known, but in all probability it is the same as that of other large cetaceans, not exceeding ten or twelve months. The calf, when brought forth, is about one-fourth the length of the dam ; and it suckles by holding the teat between the extremity of the jaws or lips, while the mother reclines a little on one side, raising the posterior portion of her form nearly out of the water, and lying in a relaxed condition. This peculiar manner of suckling the young appears to be common to all the whalebone whales.

When the whales first arrive on the Finmark coast the Humpbacks are the only species of the large whales which will voluntarily come into shallow water. They do so, so say the Fin-whalers, to rub their heads and pectorals against the rocks so as to free them from the barnacles which at this season seem to cause them great annoyance. Captains Castberg and Nilsen state that they have seen the Humpback rubbing their heads against rocks so close in shore that a stone could have been thrown upon their backs. At this season, too, they have often been observed dozing on the surface of the sea in exactly the same curious position as the Californian Grey Whale, *Rhachianectes Glaucus* as figured by Scammon.[1] This attitude of the Humpback at rest was first described to me by Captain Nilsen, and its accuracy is confirmed by Captains Larsen and Bull. Humpback will drift about motionless for half-an-hour, with the head held in this perpendicular fashion, respiring the while after the manner of other mammals.[2]

These whales exhibit unusual attachment to their young, and will stand by and endeavour to defend them even if seriously wounded. This affection is reciprocated by the calf, as the following incident will show.

Captain Nilsen, of the whaler *St. Lawrence*, was hunting in Hermitage Bay, Newfoundland, in June 1903, when he came up to a huge cow Humpback and her calf. After getting "fast" to the mother and seeing that she was exhausted, Captain Nilsen gave the order to lower away the "pram" for the purpose of lancing. However, when the boat approached the wounded whale, the young one kept moving round the body of its mother and getting between the boat and its prey. Every time the mate endeavoured to lance, the calf intervened, and by holding its tail towards the boat and smashing it down whenever they approached, kept the stabber at bay for half-an-hour. Finally the boat had to be recalled for fear of an accident, and a fresh harpoon was fired into the mother, causing instant death. The faithful calf now came and lay alongside the body of its dead mother, where it was badly lanced, but not killed. Owing to its position it was found impossible to kill it, so

[1] "Marine Mammalia and American Whale Fishery," by Captain Scammon, p. 32.
[2] Fabricius noted something of this kind, for he says that when the sea is calm the Humpback rests as if it was asleep ; at other times on its side and beat itself with the pectorals.

another bomb-harpoon was fired into it. Even this did not complete the tragedy, and it required another lance-stroke to finish the gallant little whale.

Unlike the *Balænoptera* which seldom eat fish, the Humpback consumes quantities of the little white fish on its first appearance in northern waters. It is also very partial to the common squid and various small crustaceans. Its principal food, however, is the small crustacean *Euphausia inermis*,[1] on which it feeds almost exclusively from June to September. If caplin are encountered and "kril" are absent, it will eat no other food. Herrings do not seem to be a part of the diet.[2]

Like the Finback, this whale usually takes its food sideways, but Nilsen has seen two in the act of feeding and with mouth open in the usual attitude.

Humpbacks may be easily recognised at a distance by the form of the "spout." This rises in two separate streams, which are, however, united into one as they ascend and expand. At the top it disperses freely into vapour, and looks larger than that emitted by any of the other species of large whale. It "drifts" out at once into a puffy ball of spray. An apt description by the whale captains is that the "blow" is "like the smoke of a cigar." When moving to windward the respiration dissolves into smoke at once, and almost obscures the animal. In still water it rises to a height of 12 to 15 feet. Scammon says 20 feet and more; but this is, I think, slightly exaggerated. On rising to the surface the number of respirations is exceedingly variable, more so in fact than in any of the larger

[1] Sometimes called *Thysanopoda inermis*.

[2] Mr. Southwell mentions a case of a Humpback Whale which was found dead after indulging too freely on cormorants. *Ann. Scot. Nat. Hist.*, April 1904, p. 86.

species of whales. "Sometimes the animal," says Scammon (p. 42), "blows only once, at another time six, eight or ten, and from that up to fifteen or twenty times." This is, I think, correct. A Humpback which I observed on the Greenbank, Newfoundland, spouted eight, ten, and twelve times. The periods of absence under water during the big dives average about five minutes. Baer, Lilljeborg, Jouan, and Racovitza all bear testimony to the warm and fœtid breath of this whale. In fact all the large whales are foul in this respect, the Humpback particularly so." [1]

The Norwegians considered this a somewhat difficult animal to kill and by far the most dangerous whale to lance, not even excepting the Sperm. Unless mortally struck it rushes off at great speed and dashes about in an irresponsible manner, at one time forming great circles, at another heading straight for the ship.

Humpbacks sometimes give trouble when struck too high in the body or only slightly wounded, and several serious accidents have occurred both to steamers and to the men in the small "prams" when trying to lance the wounded whale. Owing to its sudden rushes and free use of tail and pectorals the Humpback is more feared by the Norwegian whalemen than any other species. The following authentic instances have been given to me by Norwegian captains:—

In May 1903 the whaling steamer *Minerva*, under Captain Johan Petersen, hunting from the station in Isafjord, made up to and struck a bull Humpback. The beast was wild, so they fired two harpoons into it, both of which were well placed. In the dim light the captain and two men went off in the "pram" to lance the wounded whale, when the latter suddenly smashed its tail downwards, breaking the

[1] "The Mammals of Great Britain and Ireland," vol. iii.

boat to pieces, killing the captain and one man, and breaking the leg of the other. The last named was, however, rescued clinging to some spars.

A most curious accident happened on the coast of Finmark about ten years ago. A steamer had just got fast to a Humpback, which, in one of its mad rushes, broke through the side of the vessel at the coal bunkers, thus allowing a great inrush of water which put out the fires and sunk the ship in three minutes. The crew had just time to float the boats and were rescued by another whaler some hours later.

Other whales which are occasional visitors to Newfoundland are the Lesser Rorqual (*Balænoptera rostrata*), the Pilot Whale (*Globicephalus melas*), and the Sperm Whale (*Physeter macrocephalus*), of which a few males are killed annually. Until 1830 the Southern Right Whale (*Balæna australis*) was an irregular visitor, but of late years it has not been observed although still known about Long Island, New York State.

CHAPTER IX

THE CHASE OF THE BLUE WHALE

ON reaching the whale factory of St. Lawrence, on 15th August, I found the most perfect plant for the manufacture of whale products. Even the land about the buildings had been dressed with whale-guano, and was growing a crop of hay that any English farmer might have envied. St. Lawrence is an up-to-date whale factory under the immediate super-vision of Dr. Rismuller, the German-American scientist, who has done more for whaling and the use of whale products than any other living man. To him is owed the utilisation of every part of the whale, including the flesh, the blood and liver, and parts of the skin which were only regarded as wastage a few years ago.

The cost of building and running a whale factory is very great. The outlay on the buildings, engines, steamer and appurtenances, and boiling houses cost from £8000 to £10,000; labour and coal for one season, £800—so that a good supply of whales is necessary to make the business pay. In addition to this the Government charges an annual licence of £300 per factory.

The manager told me that they had not killed a Blue Whale (Sulphur-Bottom) since May, and that my chance of seeing one was most remote, even if the fog lifted. The hunting steamer was to leave in the evening for a cruise, and might be away for any time from one to six days, so I made a few preparations, and went aboard as the sun was setting.

The little steamers used in the pursuit of the *Balæn-optera* are vessels of about 100 tons burthen and 95 feet in length. They can steam fast—from twelve to fifteen knots —and can turn in their own length. Up in the bows is the heavy swivel gun which has back and front sights. The charge is half a pound of powder. The harpoon is four and a half feet long, furnished with a diamond-shaped head, which flies open when the time-fuse explodes. The main shaft has four iron flukes which are tied with string, and these open and anchor the main shaft in the whale on the explosion. The after part of this iron shaft is divided, and in this opening runs the iron ring to which is attached a strong manilla rope, two or three inches in diameter. It is unusual to fire at a whale at greater distance than forty yards, the shots being generally taken at about ten to twenty yards range. To the uninitiated, it may seem difficult to miss a huge creature like a whale at a distance of twenty yards, but such is often the case, as the roll and pitch of the ship, which in these vessels is very quick, renders accurate shooting by no means easy.

The crew of the *St. Lawrence* consisted of—Captain Nilsen, who was also first gunner; a mate, Christian Johanessen; an engineer, and four seamen, each of whom could take any part, from shooting the whales to cooking the dinner. They were all Norwegians, and very cheery, modest fellows. I felt I would like to sail about the world amongst unvisited places, and hunt all kinds of wild beasts, with none but Norwegians as my companions. They are the best of all comrades, always good-natured, loving sport, especially if it is dangerous, and absolutely self-reliant.

We steamed out of the harbour of Little St. Lawrence at 9 P.M., and at once entered dense fog and a heavy swell.

The vessel pitched so abominably that sleep was out of the question. Next morning we were about thirty miles off, steaming about, and peering through the mist without seeing a single spout; and the next day was but a repetition of the previous one. On the third night it began to blow great guns, and I was flung out of the bunk right across the cabin, narrowly escaping some broken ribs; at any rate I was sore for a week afterwards.

Those who have been across the Atlantic in a breeze in one of the great floating palaces have no conception of what it meant to weather out half a gale in a little 95-foot whaler. On the one you can sleep, walk, and eat in comfort; in the other you are tossed about like a floating cork. Once, whilst crossing the cabin, I was flung clean up to the ceiling, and just saved my head from striking the wood by putting up my arm. The only way to obtain any rest was to be nailed in one's bunk, which, with straps and ties, I did with comparative success.

During the third night Captain Nilsen decided to run to the coast for shelter, and we only reached a pretty little bay, called Petty Fort, in time, for it was now blowing a full gale. Here we lay for twelve hours, and I went ashore to try and buy some fresh meat, as a diet of salt junk, ship-biscuit, and doubtful coffee had somewhat chilled my enthusiasm.

Sheep were scarce, and the houses of the owners had to be hunted for amongst the rocks, there being no roads; but at last I discovered a man whose wife, he said, would be only too willing to sell me a lamb. The good lady, however, at first refused point-blank to sell, as she required the four she possessed for her winter knitting. A loud argument now ensued between the wife and her lord and master, each taking opposite views, till at last the man seized her and retired to the next room, where the discussion became so heated that I feared it would end in blows, so I rose to interfere. It appeared that the woman did not wish to sell the lamb, but if she did she could not possibly ask more than one dollar (about 4s. 6d.) for it; a price she considered it doubtful I would pay. "Besides," she added, "it's as wild as a deer, and no one can catch it." Finally I was allowed to have the lamb if I could catch it, and would return the skin to her; a decision which pleased all parties. The woman had said the lamb was wild; it was wild—as wild as a hawk. The captain and I pursued that wretched animal amongst the hills, the woods, and the rocks for the best part of two hours. I longed for my rifle, but it was far away, and we had to resort to the armament of primeval man, with which we were at last successful. Next morning at breakfast the captain, the mate, and I devoured the whole lamb in a few minutes, and we *then* understood why the price was one dollar.

At midday the glass went up rapidly, and the captain said that though there was much sea outside, fine weather might be expected in a few hours. It was, therefore, his intention to steam right out about seventy miles south-west to the Saint Pierre bank, off the coast of St. Pierre, where he expected to find Finbacks and, perhaps, a Blue Whale. Next morning we were on our hunting ground. The sea had moderated considerably, and the air was clear. We could now see for several miles, and soon observed two Finbacks of moderate size. These we pursued for three hours, but they were both exceedingly wild and quite unapproachable. When "kril" is scarce whales always travel fast and make long dives, and it is difficult to make up before they dive again; also if the steamer is put after the quarry at full speed it makes some noise which the whales hear and, in consequence, accelerate their speed. In the afternoon we found a very large Finback, whose course was followed by a cloud of Leach's Petrel. At one time, as the whale dived slowly in a mass of "kril," these birds were to be seen gathering in a perfect swarm in its wake, and picking the floating crustacea off the sea. It was a most interesting sight, and I made a sketch of it, which is given here. However, the whale defeated us just as we seemed about to get a shot, and as evening drew on we lost it.

Friday, 18th August, is one of the red-letter days of my life, so I give it just as it is entered in my diary.

During the night the captain decided to steam right out for the Greenbank (about one hundred and twenty miles due south of St. Lawrence). The wind had fallen, and I was eating my breakfast and reading Dickens, when at 9 A.M. I heard the engines slow down, and knew that meant whales, so I ran on deck.

It was a glorious morning, with bright sun and the sea like oil. Far ahead were two spouts of silvery spray, and as we approached I could see they were higher than those of Finbacks.

"Yes, those are Blaa-hval" (Blue Whales), said Johanessen, "and we shall kill to-day."

We were within three hundred yards of the larger of the two whales when it rolled over, showing its enormous tail, and disappeared for the "big" dive.

"That's a ninety-foot bull," said the captain, as I stood beside the gun. His eyes glistened as he swayed the swivel to and fro to make sure that the engine of destruction worked well. Both whales were under the sea for a quarter of an

hour by my watch, and then burst up about a quarter of a
mile ahead, throwing a cloud of spray thirty feet into the air.

"Full speed ahead and then 'safte'" (slowly), and we ran
up to within fifty yards of the rolling slate monsters, which
were now travelling fast, although not wild. When a shot
seemed imminent they both disappeared from view, after about
twelve surface dives, and we lost them again for another ten
minutes. When next viewed the larger whale was half a
mile astern, so we turned and went for him again, only
reaching the animal in time to see him disappear for the
third time. The actual big dives of this whale lasted 10, 15,
14, 12½, and 20 minutes, and we then left him, as the captain
considered the other one might be tamer. This, however,
did not prove to be the case. Whilst racing to cut off the
whale during its surface appearance we spied a third Blue
Whale spouting about half a mile to the east, so the order
to turn was given, and we approached and hunted it (another
bull) for some time. Luck seemed quite against us, when the
Blue Whale was suddenly joined by two very large Finbacks
which we had not previously seen. The advent of these new-
comers seemed to quiet the larger animal. They made several
dives, and then disappeared almost under our bows, and yet
passing onward, so that a shot seemed certain if they rose
again.

It was a moment of intense excitement when the two Finbacks rose right in front of the bows and within easy shot,
but the captain and I were gazing fixedly into the green and
clear depths, looking for the Blue Whale, when far away down
beneath the water I saw a great copper-grey form rising
rapidly right underneath the ship. The captain signalled with
his hand to the man at the wheel on the bridge, turning the
vessel off a point just as the ghostly form of the whale,

growing larger and larger every moment until it seemed as big as the ship, burst on the surface beside us, and broke the water within ten yards.   In a moment we were drenched in blinding spray as the whale spouted in our faces.   I turned my arm to protect my camera and to click the shutter as the captain fired his gun.   The latter planted the harpoon fairly in the great creature's lungs.

"Fast!" yelled the cook, who had rushed on deck brandishing a kettle of potatoes in one hand.   Crimson flecks of blood floating on the emerald sea alone told of the success of the shot.   When the crew had seen all they wished then there was a lull of silence.   The captain heaved a sigh, the sigh of one who obtains relief after some tense and long-drawn strain.   Nothing was heard except the flop, flop of the line as it rolled slowly out, and the movement of the men as they ran quietly to their posts beside the steam-winch and the line-coil down below.

"Was that a death-shot?" I asked the captain.

"Don't know, sir," he answered; "I think it run a bit. The bomb did not burst."

It was so.   The line at first slowly dribbled out, and then it began to go faster and faster, until it rushed from the bow at such speed that I thought it would catch fire.

"He's going to travel now," said Nilsen, pulling me away from the smoking rope.   "You must not stand there. If the rope breaks you might get killed."

We repaired to the bridge to get a better view.

"Two lines gone now" (about 500 yards), said my companion.   "I fear I hit him too far back."

At this moment all eyes were riveted on a great commotion in the sea about 500 yards away.   The next instant the whale appeared, rolling and fighting on the surface.

It lashed the sea into white spume with its flippers and raised its head frequently right out of the water, opening its immense jaws. The leviathan of the deep was fighting hard with death, but the harpoon had penetrated its vitals, and its struggles only lasted about two minutes. Soon it grew weaker and weaker, until, casting forth a thin spout of red blood, it threw up its tail and sank in one mighty swirl.

The first operation in raising the dead whale from the bottom is to take in the slack line. This is done by one man mounting the rigging and placing the rope over a strong running pulley, which receives play by means of a powerful spring or heavy lead concealed in the hold of the ship. At first all is easy, and then the line receives a tremendous strain as it lifts the carcase from the depths.

The winch is set in motion, and with each rise of the ship we notice the "give" of the line and the utility of the spring which prevents the strain being either sudden or excessive.

For half-an-hour the powerful steam reel goes pounding on until the finer line of the gun rope comes up over the side. Then looking down you see the yellow grey ghost appear far below in the limpid depths. In another moment the mystery has developed into form, and the great Blue Whale comes floating to the surface, with the hilt of the harpoon buried in its side.

Johanessen now passes a rope over the tail whilst I make some colour sketches and notes immediately after death—an important point for the artist, as whales lose their rich colour very rapidly, and are generally inaccurately represented in books.

The rope on the tail is attached to a strong chain which

loops round the huge member and fastens it securely to the bows of the ship. The flukes of the tail are now cut off. We decide to look for another whale, so the carcase must be set afloat. To achieve this it is necessary to blow it up with steam. This is effected by driving a sharp hollow spear into the stomach; to this is attached a long rubber hose pipe which connects with the engines of the ship. The whale is then blown up with steam. As soon as a sufficient quantity has entered the iron pipe is withdrawn and the hole plugged with tow.

A long harpoon, on the top of which floats the Norwegian flag, is now fixed to the carcase, and the floating whale is cut adrift. The ensign can be seen twenty miles away on a fine day.

It took us about half-an-hour to find the big bull which we had hunted in the morning, and for three hours we pursued him relentlessly but without success. No other whales appearing in sight, the captain considered it best to return and take our "kill" to port, as decomposition takes place rapidly in these large cetaceans.

As we approached the carcase, Johanessen, who was standing beside me, suddenly exclaimed, " Look at the big shark !"

There, sure enough, was the ugly head of a large shark, tearing off great strips of blubber from the breast of the whale. My companion at once rushed for one of the long stabbing lances, but ere he could use it the shark had slipped off and disappeared.

On the Labrador coast sharks and killers (*Orca gladiator*) are so numerous and fierce that they will tear to pieces the carcase of a floating whale in a very short time, so that when a whale is shot it must be taken to the factory at once. These wolves of the sea are so bold that they will tear at

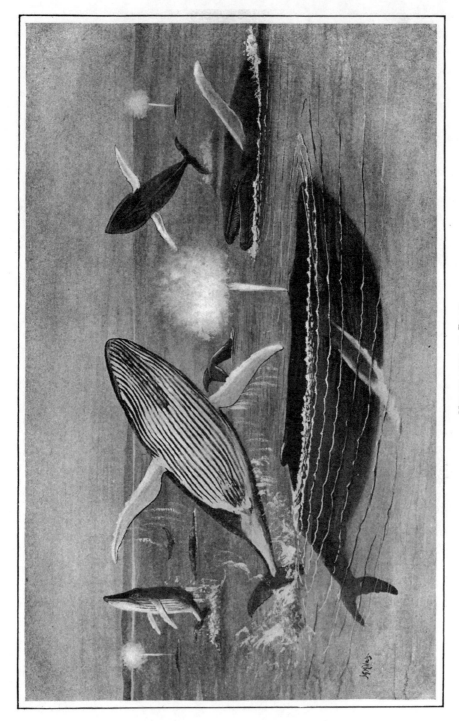

HUMPBACKS AT PLAY

(From Millais's "The Mammals of Great Britain and Ireland")

a whale even when it is fastened to the ship, and Andersen, one of the sailors of the *St. Lawrence*, told me he had killed with the lance as many as ten killer whales in a few minutes, by standing in the ship's bows.

Our arrival at Little St. Lawrence was hailed with delight, for a "Sulphur" had not been slain since May. The present example measured 78 feet, being considered a fair-sized adult bull. On the following morning, after making some drawings, I witnessed the whole process of disintegration. Every part of the whale was utilised, even the blood, which ran in rivers into a huge vat.

The various processes through which whales pass before being converted into oil, fat, soap, and guano are not of much interest to the general reader, so I will omit them.

With the man who devised the utilisation of these products, Dr. Rismuller, I spent eight days. He insisted on my remaining as his guest, and gave me much valuable information, his general knowledge of whales being very considerable. The scientific attainments of Dr. Rismuller are not appreciated in the New World as they should be. In a society whose one aim and object is the rapid accumulation of money, many things of this world that are of real importance and interest are scarcely noticed, that is at the time of their inception ; and so people go hurrying on, only to find too late that they had had a great man in their midst without their knowledge. If Dr. Rismuller had made a fortune rapidly out of his discoveries, people in America, Canada, and Newfoundland would have thought him a wonderfully "cute" fellow, and would have placed him on the pedestal of fame allotted to successful trust magnates and other human sharks, but as it is others have for the most part benefited by his genius, and he is still comparatively a poor man.

CHAPTER X

ACROSS NEWFOUNDLAND

BEFORE starting on my expedition into the interior it was necessary to return to Placentia, where I met my friend, John McGaw, and the three Newfoundlanders who had arranged to accompany me. Two of these, Bob Saunders and Sandy Butt, have already figured in these pages; but the third man, Frank Wells, I had only met once, although I knew him to be a hard worker and a good man for woods or canoe. John McGaw (a near neighbour of mine at Horsham) had expressed a wish to visit Newfoundland, and had undertaken to study geography, leaving all the arrangements in my hands. "He travels fastest who travels alone" is one of the truest proverbs, and I must confess that on most occasions I have had no wish for a companion. Now, however, I made the exception, and did not regret it. McGaw was a first-rate comrade, helping in every way—an excellent shot too—a good hand at whatever he turned to, whether in the line of carpentry, mapping, or photography.

After seeing the canoes and provisions on board we left Placentia in the *Glencoe* on 2nd September, and arrived at Pushthrough, in Hermitage Bay, on the following evening. Mountains rise from the shore of the south coast, and the scenery would be fine if the timber were less stunted, but exposed as it is to the southerly gales, the trees have not much chance to grow to any size. After leaving Fortune Bay there are only a few inhabitants along the coast. These are

194

THE DYING FLURRY OF THE BLUE WHALE

(*From Millais's " The Mammals of Great Britain and Ireland"*)

mostly concentrated at the cod-drying stations, such as St. Jacques, Harbour Breton, and Gaultois, all pretty little villages nestling under wooded hills. At Pushthrough we found lodging in a small grocer's shop, where McGaw and I had to sleep in one very small and damp bed, out of which we were in continuous danger of falling.

September 4 broke fine and clear, and with a rattling breeze astern we fairly raced up Baie d'Espoir (Bay Despair) for fifty miles in a small schooner which we had hired. As we advanced the scenery became more and more beautiful until we reached the exit of the Conn River and the telegraph station, where we were obliged to anchor in the middle of the bay on account of the shallowness of the water. The owner of the schooner having refused to proceed further, we were forced to load up our canoes in the middle of the bay and get aboard them in a good breeze, quite a ticklish business, and one for which none of us had much relish. However, this was safely accomplished, and we made for the shore at top speed. Once there all danger was past, and we paddled along happily to the head of the bay—a great sand-flat covered with goosegrass, and the home of thousands of Canada geese in spring. Just as we were about to enter the river a boat was seen chasing in our wake, so I stopped my canoe and was greeted by two men, one of whom— evidently a Micmac Indian—introduced himself as Joe Jeddore. Joe said that he could take me to see Mr. Leslie, the telegraph operator at Conn River, whom I was anxious to thank for certain inquiries he had undertaken on my behalf; so giving my canoe to Frank Wells, and telling him to make camp on the river, I entered the boat and was rowed for two miles to the telegraph station, where I met Mr. Leslie.

Mr. Leslie is the son of an English army doctor who had fought at Waterloo, and himself a man of good education and attainments; he had isolated himself in this out-of-the-way corner of the earth quite voluntarily. Bay Despair was indeed a lonely place when he first came to it and built the station twenty-five years ago. There were no inhabitants but the Micmac Indians, who dearly loved him for his honest dealings, and the wild geese which came in spring and the caribou in winter. He is a man who despises civilisation in all its ways. With poor pay as the operator of the telegraph station of the Anglo-American Company, he had nevertheless married twice, and supported a family of twenty-one souls. The nature of the man may be signified by his lament to me that Bay Despair was now getting "too crowded." He said there were now no less than thirty to forty souls, mostly in the employment of a saw-mill which had recently been started, so he was on the look-out for some place where a man could live in peace without being "hustled." His chief sorrow was the threatened extinction of the Anglo-American Company, which for so many years had been the only means of communication of the Newfoundland people with the outer world.

After a chat with Mr. and Mrs. Leslie, and a meal of cloudberries and cream, I started through the dark woods in the direction of camp, which I found on the banks of a small river coming in at the head of the bay.

No travellers or hunters ever come this way, our sole forerunners up the Baie d'Est waters being that old sportsman, General Dashwood, who has now passed on, Alexander Murray, and the ubiquitous Mr. Howley. General Dashwood and Mr. Howley had made the journey *via* the Baie d'Est system up to Pipestone Lake, and thence to Crooked

Lake, and so on to Noel Paul's Brook, and down the Exploits to civilisation. It was this route that I meant to take; but after reaching Mount Cormack, the centre of Newfoundland, I found the character of the country so uninteresting, the prospects of stag-hunting so poor, and the fact that the route had already been mapped by Howley, that I retreated a short distance and turned east over the unknown country at the headwaters of the Gander, and so worked on to my old hunting grounds and the east coast.

It is impossible to refer to travel in Central Newfoundland without mentioning the journey performed by W. E. Cormack in 1822. As the exploit of Cormack is but little known outside the knowledge of a few well-read Newfoundlanders, I may briefly narrate his experience.

W. E. Cormack was born at St. John's in 1796; he spent his school days in Scotland, and studied at Edinburgh and Glasgow Universities. Between the years 1819 and 1834 he added greatly to our knowledge of the flora of North America, being a good naturalist and a lover of nature. He also wrote papers on fish and fisheries.

In 1836 he went to Australia, and cultivated tobacco with success for two years; then to New Zealand, where he turned farmer. After this his restless spirit took him to California, where he engaged in mercantile and mining pursuits. After this he moved north, and established the Agricultural Society of British Columbia. A great lover of field sports, he numbered amongst his friends and correspondents such scientific and literary men as Sir W. Hooker and Professor Faraday. Though fond of writing, he left no literary works. He died at Victoria, British Columbia, in August 1871.

There is a great deal of truth in Cormack's sarcastic

introduction to the short account [1] of his remarkable journey across Newfoundland :—

"Early in the spring of 1822, being in Newfoundland, a far-famed country, in which I felt a most lively interest, and free from professional engagements, I determined upon exploring the interior of this island, a region almost totally unknown, and concerning which and its inhabitants, the Red Indians, who were supposed to occupy the whole of it, the most besotted conjectures were entertained, particularly by the chief delegated public authorities, to which quarter one was inclined to look for some proofs of a feeling of interest for the condition of the country, *through the means of which they obtained their bread.*"

To a great extent the same may be said in the year of grace 1905.

After a preliminary run to test the stability of the Indian Sylvester, he added one European to his party; those in authority in the island proved most unfriendly to Cormack. He says (p. 6): "It is necessary to mention that the chief Government authority was opposed to the project—and with which he was made acquainted—of obtaining a knowledge of the interior of the country. In consequence of this I was deprived of the services of the European who was, unfortunately for me, a stipendiary by local appointment, and I could not add to my party either by hiring or obtaining a volunteer." Notwithstanding this obstacle, Cormack started from Trinity Bay in September 1822.

When the explorer arrived at the centre of the island, his Indian wished to make for the south coast, but encouraged by promises, &c., he persevered on beside his master. He then

---

[1] "Narrative of a Journey across the Island of Newfoundland," by W. E. Cormack. The only one ever performed by a European. St. John's, 1873.

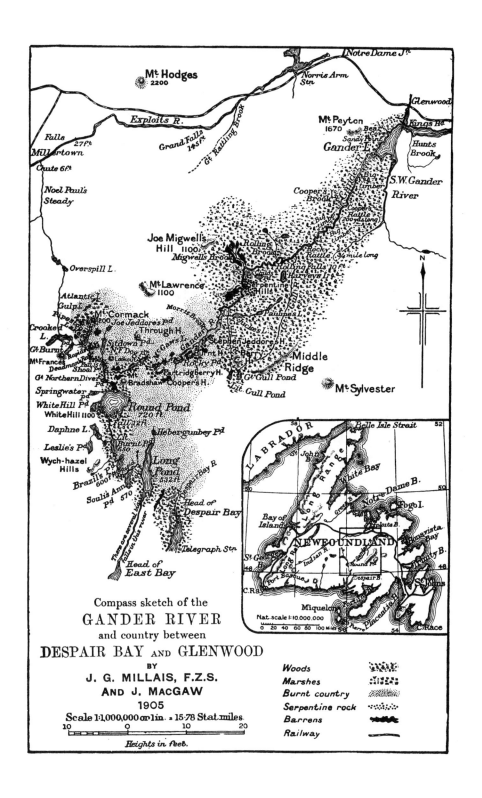

Compass sketch of the
GANDER RIVER
and country between
DESPAIR BAY AND GLENWOOD
BY
J. G. MILLAIS, F.Z.S.
AND J. MACGAW
1905
Scale 1:1,000,000 or 1 in. = 15·78 Stat.miles.

10   0   10   20

Heights in feet.

Woods
Marshes
Burnt country
Serpentine rock
Barrens
Railway

Nat. scale 1:10,000,000

0 20 40 60 80 100 Miles

HARBINGERS OF WINTER

met a single old mountaineer Indian, James John, from Labrador, who was friendly and helpful. The Red Indians or Beothicks were six or seven miles to the north at that season, whilst the Micmacs were at Bay Despair. On 2nd November Cormack brought his eventful journey to an end at St. George's Bay, on the west coast.

Since Cormack's day great strides have been made in the geological survey of the island by such able pioneers as Alexander Murray and James Howley, especially the latter, who, with a little assistance from the Government, has worked with untiring zeal for many seasons to fill up the gaps in the unwritten page; and yet there is still much of the interior which is unmapped and quite unknown, notably the wild regions between Crooked Lake and La Poile to the southeast from the White Bear River to the Victoria Lake.

On 5th September we commenced our journey into the interior, having been joined at daybreak by Joe Jeddore, the Micmac Indian, with six white packers whom Mr. Leslie had engaged for me. After going for about two miles up the river we took to the woods, the packers taking loads of about eighty pounds each, and marching ahead at a good rate. The necessity of employing these men became imperative, as it would have taken our four helpers at least three days to have transported all the outfit and canoes over the hills to Long Pond, a distance of six miles, and the first of the long chain of lakes and streams that stretch two-thirds of the way to the Red Indian Lake. From six in the morning till seven in the evening the men made three double journeys, eighteen miles in all, and worked untiringly. Our own men did two journeys, and at night we had brought all the stuff and canoes across the range and through the forest, and were comfortably camped on the shores of the big lake.

Long Pond is a large sheet of water, in character very similar to all other Newfoundland lakes, possessing a wide and stony beach, flanked by pines and deciduous trees.

In the forests are:—The white pine (*Pinus alba*), black spruce (*Pinus nigra*), red spruce (*Pinus rubra, Pinus balsamea, Pinus microcarpa*), white birch (*Betula populifolia*), black birch (*Betula lenta*); poplars, locally called "haps," such as *Populus trepida* and *Populus grandidentata*; maples (*Acer rubrum, Acer striatum*), mountain ash or dog-wood (*Sorbus Americana*), choke cherry (*Prunus borealis*), and small wild cherry (*Prunus Pensylvanica*), hazel and alder (*Alnus crispa*).

The whole of the interior is covered with that lovely flowering shrub, *Kalmia Glauca*.

Long Pond is a dangerous lake to cross. Being high and open, the wind rises rapidly, and a slight breeze will create such a "jabble" on the lee shore that canoeing must be undertaken with caution. Two years previously Joe had nearly lost his life in this lake. He was accompanying a white man on a short hunting trip, and on his return the lake "looked" easy to pass. To Joe's experienced eye, however, things seemed otherwise, and he advised waiting a day till it was calm. His master, however, was in a hurry, and decided to chance it, with the result that both boats were flooded as they approached the southern shore, and sank in about five feet of water. If the accident had occurred two minutes earlier, all on board must have been drowned.

Next day, accordingly, Joe shook his head when he spied little white waves breaking on the distant shore, so we remained till midday, afterwards making a start up shore to the narrowest crossing place, about a mile and a half wide, and the wind being slight, we paddled across in none too pleasant a sea. For my part I was glad when we landed with only a little water in the boats. At once we entered the Baie d'Est River, up which the men paddled, whilst McGaw and I walked ahead in the hope of finding deer, but only to find old summer spoor.

After a short portage we reached Soulis Ann Lake, where I caught some ouananiche for supper. During the night the wind and rain came on, and we were detained all the next day and till midday on the 8th, when the wind abating, we made a start along the lake. We were now in a "burnt" country, and found the surroundings far from beautiful. As far as the eye could reach from the lake shore to the bare mountain ridges was nothing but one gaunt sea of bare poles, the result of a great fire in 1893. Here and there the woods were recovering in the shape of short thickets of birch or scattered groups of spruce, firs, and larch, but the whole aspect was most mournful, and I longed to get on to "timber" where we might reasonably expect to kill a stag. At four we passed Soulis Ann Lake, and continued our journey up to Baie d'Est. The river here looked suitable for trout and ouananiche, so, getting out our rods, we fished for an hour and a half in two likely-looking pools, with great success. The ouananiche fought splendidly, but seldom reached a pound in weight, whilst the trout were a little larger. I killed three dozen, the largest a trout of two and a half pounds. In the evening we walked up the river, where the canoes met us, and took us to camp on a spot we named Sandy Point, on Brazil Pond. The sun set in a blaze of glory as we sat over the fire and ate our meal of fish and tea.

The morning of the 5th September was beautifully clear and sunny as we paddled merrily up Brazil Lake, until we reached the short river which connects it with Little Burnt

Lake. Here we took out our rods and fished, although the worst time of the day for such an operation, and soon had enough ouananiche to feed our men for another day. At the end of the Little Burnt Lake we again struck the Baie d'Est River, which was now become exceedingly rocky and difficult to negotiate. The stream being low, the river was nothing but a series of rocky levels, on which the men had to be most careful with the canoes. It was in such places that Joe exhibited his great superiority as a canoe man. Standing up in his boat, he poled it through rapids and past rocks in a way that excited our wonder and admiration. The less skilled white men were in the water all the time, hauling, guiding, and lifting, and Little Bob distinguished himself by falling out of his boat into the river. Consequently Joe was always about half a mile ahead of his companions, for whom he waited with a sort of patronising air. Sometimes they tried to copy his method, but with indifferent success, either through the poles breaking, or the stream, being too strong, would turn the heads of their canoes round and land them on a rock in mid-stream. However, as the red man passed up stream with skill, the white men made up for it with pluck and determination, and if they had a rough time occasionally, it was all accepted with a never-failing good nature that renders these simple people so acceptable to those who employ them.

At sunset we reached green timber again in the shape of Round Lake, the largest sheet of water in Central Newfoundland. It was shallow in many places, but, after going two miles, we put into a beautiful little bay, and camped in a forest of high trees. Fresh signs of deer were noticeable on the beach, and there was every prospect of seeing big game very soon. As we sat round the fire and spun yarns,

JOE JEDDORE

enjoying our meal of ducks, fish, and tea, we all felt very happy and comfortable. The roaring camp-fire of sticks crackled and shed its genial warmth. Out on the lake the water was like a sheet of glass, except in a little bay where a mother red-breasted merganser was teaching her young to dive. From the distance came the swan-like trump of the Canada geese, as they returned from berry-picking on the hills, and now and again we could hear the melancholy "who-eee" of the great northern divers as they settle for the night.

No pen could describe or brush convey any idea of that crimson sunset, or the flood of golden light that bathed the hills, the far-away islets, the tangled woods, and the glassy lake.

We are led by some invisible hand from the heat and turmoil of life to the beauty of space and the joys of distance, into the cool, green places where no man comes.

Soon the golden ball sinks beneath the horizon, to be succeeded by a short-lived twilight. The querulous loon is uttering low-voiced calls to his mate, and grey phantoms rise cloud-like in the evening mists, drifting away with clanking voices into a land of silence. It is the day's departure, and we turn to the incense of the larch smoke and the crackling blaze of the burning logs. Then one drops to sleep on a couch of scented "vars," amidst the lonely mountains of the northland, with the starlight overhead.

It may seem strange to the town dwellers that there are many men so constituted that the luxuries of civilisation have no attraction for them, but it is no mystery to those who have seen both sides of the picture. The outdoor man has by far the best of it, for he leads the life that God and Nature intended him to do. If his disappointments and difficulties are great, his joys are intense, and he feels that at any rate he has lived and known. One who has lived much in that great world, where there is no pretence, must feel chilled when he stands amid a gallery of cold faces and listens to the vapid talk of men and women in whose lives he cannot bear a part. In the wonders of the eternal forests those vast spaces are real and earnest, whilst the voices that speak to him are those of friends.

CHAPTER XI

THE MOUNT CORMACK REGION AND HISTORY OF THE NEWFOUNDLAND MICMACS

ROUND LAKE is another somewhat dangerous sheet of water to circumvent in light canoes, so we had to be careful next morning, as a fair breeze was blowing astern when we headed northwards along the western shore. I was in front with Joe, for we expected to see a stag at any moment, and fresh meat was now becoming a strong desideratum. About a quarter to nine Joe raised his finger and pointed ahead.

"There's the stag," he said, "an he's travellin' fast."

The telescope revealed a fair stag still in the velvet, walking with the smart, business-like step that means a good $5\frac{1}{2}$ miles an hour. He was going in the same direction as ourselves along the lake beaches, and I saw that we should have to make a considerable detour to head him and get the wind. Hard paddling was now the order of the day, so we put our backs into it and forged ahead to avoid a group of small islands that lay between us and the deer. In a quarter of an hour we were abreast of the stag. He never stopped or looked about. After another ten minutes we were about a quarter of a mile ahead, and decided to cut in on to the land and head the beast. During this manœuvre the stag quickened his pace, and looking up sharply, stood at gaze.

"Don't move a muscle," I said, as we stared each other out of countenance at a distance of 400 yards. The stag appeared satisfied and proceeded, and so were we. He was now out of sight, and we rushed the canoe in for a point where I knew our quarry would shortly come. McGaw, who was watching the stalk from the lake, said that immediately we disappeared the stag started at full gallop for the point where we met, much to my surprise, a moment later. I could just see his head and horns as he peeped at me from behind a tangle of fallen timber, and, knowing that no better chance would offer, fired at once. The bullet cut a wisp of hair from the stag's chin, and he made off up the shore at full speed. I now ran to the point and lay down, expecting him to stand before taking the woods. It was as I hoped, and he slowly swung round at 150 yards and gazed back before disappearing. The moment he stopped, I fired and broke his spine. He was dead before we got up to him. Pleasure was written in every countenance as the canoes assembled, for we had meat now to last us for a week at least, and meat means strength to man. The stag carried a pretty head of twenty-five points, but the horns were not large, so we did not take them.

The wind was rising fast, so, after loading the canoes with all the meat we could carry, we proceeded, with some difficulty, to the northern shore of the lake, where McGaw and I went ashore for a walk, the boats following us. Here we found three good outbreaks of raw petroleum. Something might be made of these wells, as well as the fine chrome iron deposits which we saw later at Pipestone, were it not for the difficulty of transport. At noon we entered a beautiful "steady," and, after halting for the midday meal, we journeyed on northwards up an unnamed small lake, which we called Northern Diver Lake, from the numerous birds of this species that frequented its waters. At one place we cornered four

McGaw Fishing

Portaging a Canoe, Dead Man's Rapids

birds of this species in a shallow of the river at its northern end, and, thinking that one might come up near the boats as they broke back for the lake, I took McGaw's gun in my hand. I had no sooner done so, than a large female almost sprang into Joe's canoe, and he, striking at it with the paddle, drove it to wing, when I easily shot it as it flew by. The specimen proved a beautiful one in full summer plumage, and was the largest I have seen. I think the American form of the great northern diver is larger than the European bird, of which I have shot many. Even where it is not hunted, it is always the same strong and cunning creature, and seldom gives man a chance of killing it.

Half a mile up a stiff bit of river brought us to a fine steady, which eventually led into Shoal Pond, where we camped for the night on a wooded island.

During the evening I had a long talk with Joe, who held out no prospect of seeing good stags after we should pass Pipestone Lake and Mount Cormack, which we hoped to reach in two days. Moreover, he said the country was barren and desolate to Noel Paul's Brook, and that we should reach civilisation too soon if we pursued that route. Moreover, the main features of this country had been mapped out by Howley, so we determined only to visit Mount Cormack, about whose geographical position I was doubtful, and from thence to return to Shoal Pond, where we were now camped, and afterwards to strike east over the unknown country towards Burnt Hill. Thence we could easily reach my old hunting-grounds on the Gander, and might expect to get some fine heads before passing down stream to Glenwood.

Accordingly we "cached" the greater part of our stores under a birch-bark "tilt," and proceeded on the following morning with such impedimenta as would last us for a week.

A fine-looking deer country to the right of Shoal Lake tempted us to put in a day there, and I ascended to the top of a hill, from whence a splendid view was obtained north as far as Cormack, east to Burnt Hill, and south to Mount Bradshaw over Round Lake. Away to the west we could see the White Mountains and great area of unknown land as yet unmapped, and unvisited even by Indians. McGaw ascended another ridge, and did some mapping. We saw numbers of female and small caribou, but no stags, these being still hidden in the dense woods.

The following day we continued our journey up stream, the river becoming more and more difficult as we proceeded. Shallow succeeded shallow until we reached a point known as Dead Man's Rapids, where it was necessary to portage everything for half a mile. Whilst McGaw and I walked ahead, a fine stag broke out of the woods close to Sandy Butt, and another was observed making across the river when we stopped for lunch. For this one I ran hard, trying to cut him off, but he rounded a bend out of sight at 400 yards before I could get my rifle to work. At 3 P.M. we reached a small unmarked lake which was so shallow that we could only crawl along. Then ensued another steady, and then a series of the worst rapids we had encountered. In fact, it was impossible to get the canoes through them, and so we carried round through the woods, finding ourselves at Pipestone Lake at five o'clock.

Here the country was all burnt, and swarming with doe caribou. Wherever we looked there were little parties dotted about. We stalked two lots in the hope of finding a stag for McGaw, but without success. One small party seemed to be lost in a brown study on the shores of the lake, so we thought we would have some fun with them, as the

HAULING OVER A BAD PLACE ON THE BAIE D'EST

WORKING UP THE BAIE D'EST RIVER

"There goes Four Hundred Dollars!"

canoes would shortly appear and scare them along the lake
shore towards us.   McGaw, Joe, and I accordingly took
stones in our hands, and played at being ancient Britons,
just like naughty schoolboys.   We lay in the caribou trail,
and, as soon as the canoe approached the deer near enough
for them to get the wind, there was a wild rattle of stones
and the game was rushing like a charge of cavalry down
upon us.   All the five deer almost trod upon us as we
raised ourselves on our knees and saluted the attack with
a volley of rocks.   One deer cleared Joe's head within a
few inches.   Of course we did not hit anything, but enjoyed
the consternation and the sport as much as if we had slain
a noble hart.

In the morning McGaw started for the end of the lake
As the sun was setting and the men were building camp,
more and more deer appeared.   McGaw pursued one lot
that appeared to have a stag amongst them, but no stag
was there when he had headed them, so we went to bed
without any damage having been done except to a portion
of my knickerbockers which had tried conclusions with some
sharp rocks.

In the morning McGaw started for the end of the lake
with the intention of taking the height of Mount Cormack,
whilst I hunted an area to the east of Sit Down Lake, and
gradually worked round to the foot of Sit Down Mountain,
which I ascended to make some observations.   During the
day we walked many miles, and encountered numbers of
doe caribou and a few young stags, but not one adult stag
was to be seen, a state of things I had quite expected.   Not
so Joe, who had declared that we should find plenty of
stags out in the open ground at this season, and could not
now account for their absence.   On questioning him closely,
I found that when he had been to Pipestone before, the

O

time was July and early August, a season at which the big stags do move out of the woods, drawing from the rivers to avoid the flies, and so the circumstances were easily explained. Late in August the stags again take to the woods and hardly ever show out except at early dawn, until the beginning of the rutting season (20th September), and often not as early as this.

As we were returning to camp we saw a wonderful thing. I call it wonderful, because few men, even professional trappers, have ever seen the beast—a veritable black fox, as black as ink. We were descending a low range of hills, when right in front of us, and, most unfortunately, dead down wind, appeared the rarity. He saw us as quickly as we saw him, and, like a flash, he whipped round, and, erecting his magnificent brush of black and white, darted over the skyline and was lost to view.

"There goes four hundred dollars!" said Joe sadly. "Ah, if we had only been fifty yards to the right, we should have been out of sight and under the wind, and I could have *tolled* him."

It was one of the most melancholy "ifs" I can remember in my hunting experience. The Indians have a "call" or "toll" for nearly every animal. They can bring a fox right up to within 20 yards by making a sibilant noise produced by sucking the back of the hand. Reynard takes it to be the cry of a hare in difficulties, and seldom fails to advance close to the sound. Stag caribou are "tolled" by grunting loudly in two different ways, and this vocal effort requires little skill or practice on the imitator's part, for the first beast I tried it on answered at once, and came grunting up close at hand.

The "herd" stag will quickly answer the caller and advance

MOUNT CORMACK, THE CENTRE OF NEWFOUNDLAND

MOUNT CORMACK FROM PIPESTONE LAKE

for a short distance, but the "travelling" stag will come very close if the calls are properly made at suitable intervals. By using the double grunt at short range, I have brought a stag to within five yards of the stone behind which I was concealed. Sometimes the Indians can attract an amorous stag by flicking a white handkerchief from side to side at the edge of a wood. The stag can see this at a considerable distance, and will sometimes come at full speed to the spot where the Indian lies concealed—I saw this done once in the following year; and geese can also be called, when they first arrive in the spring, by waving a white rag and imitating their "honking" call, but after the first fortnight they take little notice of the lure. A small white dog is also attractive to geese in the spring, and one Indian I know of has killed numbers of these birds by this method.

Beavers, when they have been undisturbed for long, are very curious in relation to strange sounds. They will come swimming out of their house even at the firing of a gun. The Indians usually call them with a hissing noise, or one produced by munching the lips. Another favourite "toll" is a sound made by tapping the trousers with the hand. The most successful beaver "caller" in Newfoundland is John Bernard, or Johnny "Bow-an'-arrow" as he is named by the Glenwood folk, who, when the season for the animals was "open," killed great numbers by making a sound that resembled the cutting of chips off a tree. It is said that the unfortunate rodents never fail to respond to this noise. John Bernard is the only Indian in the island who can produce this seductive note. Most of the Indians kill beaver by cutting down the "dam" and shooting the animals as they come out of their "lodge" and holes — an easy method. The Indian has no call for the lynx, but one or two of them can attract the otter by imitating its shrill whistle.

Shortly after the departure of the black fox, we saw a fine stag plunge into the Pipestone Lake and swim to the other side. It was interesting to see how carefully he chose his landing place. Instead of going directly to his point of landing, he swam about fifty yards first to one side and then to the other, so as to get the wind from the right quarter. He then stepped cautiously on to the beach, and galloped straight into the underbrush. A caribou stag in early September is no fool.

McGaw returned in the evening from Mount Cormack without having seen a stag, but with the knowledge that the mountain is wrongly marked on the map. For it stands right at the north point of Pipestone and only about one and a half miles distant from the lake, instead of some four or five miles due east, in which position it has been charted. As far as I know, no one has visited this mountain since Cormack was there in 1822, and so its position must have been marked, like a good many others, from mere hearsay. We also found a high mountain to the south-west, quite as high as Cormack, and which we named Mount Frances. There were, too, several new lakes to be seen from the top of Cormack and Sit Down Hill.

After taking the heights of these hills, for they can scarcely be designated as mountains, we left on the following day to return to Shoal Lake. At daybreak Saunders and Frank stood outside the camp and surveyed the heavens.

"Guess we're goin' to have *dirt* to-day," said Little Bob laconically.

"No, I think it's goin' to be *civil*," argued Frank, who

Reuben Lewis, Head Chief of the Newfoundland Micmacs

was an optimist of the most pronounced type. But Frank was wrong for once.

The word "civil" is used to express several meanings in Newfoundland. The expression, "It's a civil day," is too obvious to require explanation, but it is used in another curious way, to signify "gaining sense or knowledge of a thing." Thus Frank delivered himself one evening :—

"We'd an English captain here once that tried to shoot deer on the best army principles, an' I couldn't get him cured nohow. He'd get a small hill betwixt him and the stag, and then make rushes in full view of any other deer that might be about. When he'd come to de nex' mound he'd fall down flat like he had de stummick ache and peek round expectin' to see de stag, which by this time was travellin' up de country. Then he'd look round sour-like, and ses he, 'Dese caribou about de wildest deer I ever struck, and most difficult to hunt.' But by-and-by he see army tactics warn't no use, so he got *kind o' civilised*, and used to say Newfun'lan' 'ud make a fine training-ground for de British Army."

During the night the wind had shifted to the south, and September 14th was one of the worst days I ever remember. The rain descended in a perfect deluge, and we worried on in the teeth of a gale till 5 P.M., when, soaked to the skin in spite of our heavy sou'-westers, we arrived at the island like so many drowned rats. Two or three times during the day Joe wished us to put up, but I wished to press on as the time was getting short, and we were anxious to reach the stag country before the migration commenced. The white men never said a word, but toiled away with the canoes and at the portages with silent doggedness. In bad weather or with rough work the two temperaments, that of the white and the red man, are manifest. It may seem strange to those that do not know them that the Indian, who spends all his life in the woods, should dread bad weather and hard work. But so it is. He will always stay at home on a wet day, and fears to go abroad when changes of temperature are going on. Joe, excellent fellow as he was, cordially disliked getting wet, and the slightest chill or illness gave him most gloomy forebodings. Nearly all Indians are gluttons. Some can digest the enormous quantities of fat they eat, and others get indigestion and are a prey to melancholia. Joe was one of the latter, and when the results of a too generous diet of deer fat were manifest, he would come to us with a face of extreme woe.

"What's the matter, Joe?" we would say.

"Ah, I have a lump like a lead ball just here," pressing his diaphragm. "I am very bad. John Hans at Conn River died of just such a thing last winter, and Joe Brazil he——"

"Let's look at your tongue," I would say, with my best Harley Street manner. "Yes, to be sure, a case of Asiatic cholera; don't you think so, Jack?"

McGaw, thus appealed to, would at once ratify my diagnosis with a learned air, and go for the Burroughs & Wellcome case. Two azure globules of the most body-rending description were then inserted in Joe's mouth, and next day he would come up smiling.

On another occasion the results of a generous diet had a bad effect on poor Joe, and he was in considerable pain. The doctors put their heads together, and more by good luck than good management effected another speedy cure with some horrible compound whose name we could not read on the bottle. After this our fame was established.

"You could make much money down at Conn River,"

said Joe to me one day. "We have no doctor there but the priest. He knows lots, but he ain't got no medicines like yours, pore fellow."

When he became melancholy Joe was always pitying some one, either himself, the priest, the Government, or his wife. *A propos* of his wife, I asked him one day if his wife went with him trapping.

"No, not now; she came once, but she got to stay at home now to look after de apple-tree."

"Good gracious, what for?" I asked.

"Why, you see, I've got a fine apple-tree, the only one in Conn River, and the fall she was in with me the 'beach' boys got flinging stones, and smashed all my windows and took the apples."

"But surely you don't care for the apples more than your wife."

"Well, no, but I've got a pig—and what between watchin' that apple-tree and feedin' de pig on squid, she don't have no time to do nothin' else—pore woman."

It must not, however, be supposed that Joe was a melancholy individual; on the contrary, he was generally full of fun and laughter. He could see a joke as well as any man, and his skill in woodcraft was exceptional. He was as lithe and strong as a lynx, and could run over the marshes and hills like a deer, and climb like a monkey. He was most careful of stores and canoes, and when guiding was necessary he proved himself to be a genuine guide.

I had an example of this on the morning after we arrived at Shoal Lake Island, from where we were to start on the following day up the Dog Lake Brook into the unknown country. Joe had never been there before, and so he made it his business to go and find out the condition of the brook and its fitness or otherwise for canoes. He said nothing to me, but at four the next morning I detected him lighting his pipe by the fire. He slipped silently past my bed and, making his way to a canoe, paddled away swiftly into the darkness. At half-past eight Joe was sitting at breakfast with the others. He had *run* six miles up the river and back, twelve miles in all, and knew all about the stream. I liked that, because it showed a strict attention to business and proved that he had our interests at heart.

The heavy rains of the previous day had made it possible for the canoes to be dragged up the brook, but they required careful management, the men being in the water the whole time. McGaw and I walked on ahead, reaching Little Dog Lake about 4 P.M. Here we saw smoke curling up from the lake shore, and knew this must be made by the two Matthews boys, sons of Noel Matthews, a Micmac Indian who lived at Bay Despair, and whose hunting-ground we were now passing through. Accordingly I sent Joe to their camp to invite them to accompany us for a week or eight days, to help us to pack over the difficult country between the two watersheds. This they agreed to do, and so met us on the following morning by the brook side, where they at once took pack to help lighten the canoes.

The two Matthews boys were regular wild Indians of the woods. Martin, the eldest, was a youth of nineteen, with a perfectly expressionless face and an insatiable appetite. I have never seen a man eat so much in so short a time. A stag breast and ribs were a comfortable meal for him, and such trifles as cans of butter and milk seemed to disappear down his capacious throat as if by magic. We possessed some wonderful liquid called " St. Charles evaporated cream," and never fully understood its grandiloquent title until Martin got his fingers round a tin of it one day. All the odd pickings of the camp went mouthwards as soon as they were spied, and where food was concerned he was a veritable wolf. His brother Michael was little inferior in the knife-and-fork line, but he was of a more silent and retiring disposition. On the whole, I forgave their expensive tastes, as they worked well for us for eight days, carrying fairly heavy loads, and the labours of our men would have been much harder had it not been for their timely help. Each of the brothers possessed a starved-looking Labrador retriever, clever, amiable beasts, scarcely less hungry than their masters. Whilst this party were in camp everything eatable had to be deposited in the trees.

The following short account of the Micmacs since their landing to the present day may be of interest to Newfoundlanders, who at the present have little knowledge of their present numbers, movements, and habits.

The Micmac Indians, who are a branch of the Great Algonquin race of Eastern Canada, first arrived in Newfoundland about the middle of the eighteenth century. They were said to have been brought over to help to exterminate the unfortunate Beothicks. But though I have no respect for the early colonial administration of the island, I do not believe that this was the real reason of their coming, but that more readily explained causes contributed to their arrival. They had probably heard, perhaps from the Mountaineer Indians of the Labrador, who are themselves a branch of the Algonquins, of the excellent trapping and hunting to be found in the island, and had come for that purpose.[1] There is little

---

[1] It will be noted by the reader that Cormack, on his first journey in 1822, met a Mountaineer Indian, James John by name. The direct descendants of this Indian live in Bay Despair at the present day.

doubt that for years after their arrival they entertained a wholesome dread of the painted Beothicks, or Red Indians, and left them severely alone in their hunting-grounds about Red Indian Lake and to the northwards, themselves only occupying places on the coast-line and working into the interior by the Baie d'Est and Long Harbor and other routes.

The Micmac Indians in Newfoundland, according to Cormack (1822), amounted to 150 souls. These were dispersed in bands in the following places or districts, viz. St. George's Harbour and Great Codroy River on the west coast; White Bear Bay and Bay Despair on the south-west; Clode Sound in Bonavista Bay on the east coast; Gander Bay on the north-east coast; and a few at Bonne Bay and Bay of Islands on the north-west coast. At this time a few Mountaineer Indians from Labrador joined them, and even Esquimaux from Labrador sometimes visited the island.

Of the Micmacs there were twenty-seven to twenty-eight families, averaging five to each family. They all followed the same life, hunting and trapping in the interior. After October they repaired to the sea-coast, and bartered their furs for clothing, ammunition, tea, and rum.

During this period the Micmacs did not acknowledge a chief, but certain members in each village were treated with especial respect. They considered, and still do, that Cape Breton is their home. Cormack speaks of the extraordinary endurance of the Indians, and that in his day individual hunters of great stamina could actually run down a stag, a feat even now performed by the Mountaineer Indians of Labrador. This could be done in a single day. At first the stag easily outstrips its pursuer, but after a run of four or five miles it slows down and is eventually overtaken.

In 1822 the Micmacs were professedly Roman Catholics, with a dash of the Totem Pole thrown in. They blended their own particular ceremonies with the worship of God, and were besides that very superstitious. To-day they are all Roman Catholics, and show the greatest respect for their priest, who lives in Harbour Breton and visits Conn River twice a year for the purpose of holding the confessional, receiving subscriptions to the Church, and performing marriages. During these visits the Indians are very devout, and listen to their pastor with close attention. They are very generous with their money, and do whatever he tells them. At Christmas Joe Jeddore is high priest, and conducts the Sunday service.

It is a common saying in Newfoundland that the Indians are dying out, but the following notes given to me by Joe Jeddore and five other Indians speak for themselves. They are not dying out, but have left certain old stations owing to the pressure of the white man and the exhaustion of the hunting-grounds in the neighbourhood of the coast and railway. Consequently they have concentrated at the Conn River in Bay Despair, and make this their headquarters, from which they work the whole of the central portion of the main island, south of the Red Indian Lake. Altogether there are twenty-five families at Conn River to-day, consisting of about 125 souls. These, added to the few individuals in other parts of Newfoundland, make a total very similar to that given by Cormack in 1822. All the able-bodied men are hunters and trappers. They also do a little lumbering in the spring, and the routine of their lives is as follows. They live at home in their houses from February to April, eating dried fish, smoked caribou flesh, together with such civilised commodities as flour, bacon, tea, coffee, and sugar, which they either exchange for furs with the Gaultois and Pushthrough merchants or purchase with their fur money. In April some of them go logging, and sell their timber to the mills, mend their nets and traps, and do any odd work. During May, June, July, and part of August, they fish about the bays, creeks, and rivers, but never go to sea like the regular cod-men. Much of this fish is eaten; the rest is salted for the dogs and pigs.

In August the regular hunters take their packs on their backs, and walk to their "tilts" or birch-bark shelters in the interior. Here they have stores of food, ammunition, and traps laid by. Some few, like the Matthews and Benoits, proceed by boat. In August and September these Indians, who generally live in pairs and share results, kill four or five stags apiece. The hide they use for many purposes, and the flesh is dried in the fire smoke for winter use. But their principal quarry at this season is the black bear, of which they kill considerable numbers. Their methods are as follows. The hunter repairs at daybreak to the top of the highest mountain, and there waits the whole day till sunset, overlooking a wide area of burnt ground and blueberry patches. Sooner or later Bruin will appear, and the Indian stalks to within 30 yards, and shoots him with his double-barrelled muzzle-loader—the gun they all use. In 1903 Noel Matthews killed seven in September at Crooked Lake, and in 1904 Nicholas Jeddore slew nine in the same month near Burnt Hill. Bears are in consequence becoming scarce in Newfoundland. About 15th October the Indians set out their great circle of traps (each circle being a round of about 5 miles); most of these are the ordinary gins, but numbers are made for fox,

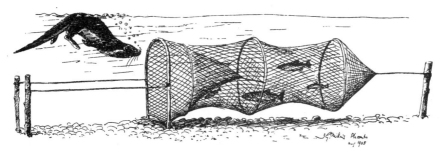

NET OTTER TRAP

Deadfall for Otter
made of spruce roots and stakes
by Joe Jeddore Sept. 28th 1905.
J. G. Millais

lynx, marten, and otter, out of forest materials, and are shown in my illustrations. The neatest of all is the wooden "dead-fall," set for the otter.

From October to February the whole of Central Newfoundland is covered with traps, and, as Joe remarked, a man could not go for twenty miles without having his dog killed or caught by the foot, unless he keeps the animal by his side.

At the end of October the hunters go out to their homes on the coast, and then start in again in November to visit their traps when the snow comes. They then re-set the traps, put fresh baits, and kill a couple of caribou on the way to the coast, their trained dogs hauling them. The traps are visited again and re-set in January or February, the dogs again hauling out one or two fat doe caribou to the coast. Work in the interior then closes for the year, though in February many of the Indians travel inland a day's journey to the main herd of the wintering caribou, and conduct a "surround." Caribou are in thousands near the south coast at this season. The Indians depart at daybreak, and after locating a herd of several hundreds in a valley they occupy all the main trails leading out of it, and send some one to move the deer. As soon as they are started the caribou rush for the passes, where the Indians lie concealed, and a considerable number are killed at short range with guns loaded with swan-shot. On the whole, the Indians are not wasteful in their methods, far less so than the white man, as every part of a deer is used, and they never kill one unless it is for some special purpose. I doubt if each individual hunter shoots more than ten stag and ten does in a season, and this is not an excessive number, since we know how abundant the deer are.

The following is an accurate list of the Indian trappers, and their respective hunting-grounds in Newfoundland :—

Frank Joe	Hunts	Burgeo country and Western Maelpeg.
Little Frank Benoit . .	„	Spruce Pond, NW. of Maelpeg.
Paul Benoit . . .	„	Crooked Lake.
Frank Benoit . . .	„	Crooked Lake.
Ned Pullet . . .	„	Long Pond, between two W. Maelpegs.
Noel Louis . . .	„	Western Maelpeg.
John Benoit . . .	„	Nimooch-wee-godie.
Frank MacDonald . .	„	Godoleik (W. of Conn).
Ben Benoit . . .	„	Island Pond, NW. of W. Maelpeg.
Noel Matthews } Martin and Michael } .	„	Crooked Lake.
Noel Jeddore } John Denny Jeddore } .	„	Sandy Pond.
Stephen Joe (stepbrother of Joe J.)	„	Burnt Hill and Podopėkgutch.
Joe Jeddore . . .	„	Burnt Hill and Upper Gander.
Nicholas Jeddore . .	„	Burnt Hill and Upper Gander.
John Bernard . . .	„	Middle Ridge and Glenwood.
John Stride . . .	„	Northern side of Sylvester.
Reuben Lewis . . .	„	Kagudeck.
Stephen Bernard . .	„	Sandy Pond and Shoe Hill Ridge.
Peter John	„	Eastern Maelpeg.
Micky John } Peter John } . . .	„	St. John's Pond.
John Hinx } Paddy Hinx } Johnny Hinx } . .	„	Wiskomonagodie, Eastern Partridge-berry Hills, S. of Maelpeg.
Mathew Burke } Johnny Benoit } . .	„	Tolt and Piper's Hill Brook.
John Barrington . .	„	Eastern side of Tolt.
Lewis John . . .	„	Eastern side of Tolt.
Len Joe	„	Grand Lake.
Ben, Abraham, and Noel Paul	„	Exploits River.
Matty Michel and son .	„	Bonne Bay.

The Micmacs now acknowledge a local chief, although they always refer all matters of extreme importance to the head chief, John Dennis, who lives near Sydney, Nova Scotia. In 1900, at the death of old Joe Bernard, Reuben Lewis was elected as a probationary chief of the Newfound-

TRAP FOR LYNX

To reach the bait it is necessary for the Lynx to place its
fore-paws on the trap

TRAP FOR FOX OR MARTEN

When set it is covered on the top with spruce

land Indians, and in June 1907 he will go in state with the principal men of Conn River to Sydney and be invested with the full right of chieftainship and the possession of the gold medal which is the badge of office. I have been invited to witness the ceremony, which is partly of a private nature, followed by public feasting, dancing, and the wearing of the old Indian dress, but, much to my regret, shall not be able to see it.

Reuben Lewis is a quiet unassuming bachelor of about forty years of age. He leads the same life as the other Indians, and is generally accompanied by his sister, Souly Ann, a lady of generous proportions. To him are referred all questions and disputes about territorial trapping areas, and he has the power to give decisions, which are always regarded as final.

Reuben Lewis is one of the few men who has been badly mauled by a black bear.[1] He was hunting some ten years ago with Noel Jeddore near Burnt Hill. Reuben fired at a large dog bear, and badly wounded it. After tracking for a short distance they saw the bear lying still, and Reuben went up to it, and gave it a kick to see if life was extinct; the bear, which was far from being dead, sprang up and seized the hunter by one leg, at the same time flinging his gun out of reach. Reuben lay as still as he could, but the bear chawed up both his legs and one hand, whilst Noel ran round trying to fire, but fearful of wounding his friend. At last Noel came so near that the bear dropped Reuben a second to growl at him, and whilst doing so he obtained

---

[1] I can only hear of one other authentic instance of a black bear attacking a man. About forty years ago a white man fired at a black bear on the shore near Bay de Nord. He wounded it badly, and then foolishly put down his gun and went in to kill it with an axe. The bear attacked him and bit him to death. Both combatants were found lying together.

a shot and dropped the bear dead. After some weeks in camp Reuben walked out to the coast and had completely recovered in three months.

The Micmacs live to a good old age, for old John Bernard, "doyen" of the community, is eighty-seven, and can see and walk almost as well as a man of thirty. Noel Matthews, whom I saw in Bay Despair, is another fine specimen. He accompanied Mr. Howley in several of his arduous journeys. He is seventy years of age, and is still the most skilled man in a canoe in the island. He goes "furring" and packing just as he has always done. Until recently another remarkable old man was Louis John, aged eighty-one, but he went in as usual in 1906, and dropped dead one day as he was lifting his load.

The curse of the Indian is cheap rum, and nearly all the young men drink hard when they get the opportunity. It is no uncommon thing for a trapper to make from 300 to 500 dollars in the course of a season's work, and to waste it all during a few days' debauch. This is all the more deplorable because very often white fur-traders encourage the Indians to drink as soon as they have concluded a deal, and cheat the unfortunate men if they once fall into their clutches. Many of the Indians, too, wander away with two or three bottles of rum in their pockets, and after being dead drunk lie out for days in the rain and snow, when severe chills are contracted, which are generally followed by consumption. Numbers die of phthisis and measles, and the mortality is high. It should be made a penal offence to sell rum to Indians. Yet the Indian, even when a habitual drinker, has marvellous self-control. The late chief, Joe Bernard, drank heavily until he was made chief, and then gave it up. The present chief, Reuben Lewis, was also of a Bacchanalian tendency,

Joe making an Otter Trap

Sunlight in the Forest

THE SOURCE OF THE GANDER

JOE TESTING THE WIND

until he received word from Sydney that he must abandon the habit on being elected, which he has done. It will give the reader some idea of the fearful mortality which prevails amongst these people from the above-mentioned causes, when it is stated that Steve Bernard, my hunter in 1906, was the sole survivor of eleven strong children. Drink, consumption, strains, measles, and carelessness had killed them all except Steve before they came to the age of twenty-one.

I am well aware that nothing one man can say, however true, will have the smallest effect on the Government of a country when that Government has to listen, as it always does, to the "Vox populi" and to regard it as the "Vox Dei." Such a voice, however, is often only the cry of cruelty and oppression. But at the same time I consider that the Indians have "rights"—rights which have come to them by custom and inheritance, just as much as to the white man, and that within reason these should be respected, before a tribe has been completely exterminated by war, disease, and rum. English and other Governments always become sentimental and kind-hearted when a race is nearly extinct, since then there is no fear of future political complications. But is not this the very essence of selfishness? and would it not be better to try and make the original owners of the soil our friends instead of our enemies, by treating them with a little consideration, a little common sense, and a little knowledge of their manifest weaknesses? By so doing we might show them that there is some force in the arguments of Christianity over the Totem Pole. The half-breed Micmacs of Newfoundland are the most amiable and law-abiding of the North American tribes, and it should be the duty of the Government to know more of these people, to understand their rights in the different trapping areas, to keep in close touch with their chief, and

*to enforce laws by which it will be a criminal offence to sell
them a single drop of liquor.*[1]

The sanctity of their trapping-grounds is considered
inviolate by the Micmacs. They live on fairly good terms
with the Newfoundlanders, but let another Indian or a
white man come into their trapping area for the purpose
of taking fur, and the amiable red man is at once trans-
formed into a demon of rage and jealousy. I only saw Joe
angry on one occasion, and that was when we were descending a rocky hill to the Gander, some distance above Rolling
Fall, when we found two lynx traps made during the
previous winter. Joe's eyes blazed, and he gave a grunt
of fierce dissatisfaction. When we got to camp he put down
my rifle carefully and disappeared into the woods, returning
some ten minutes afterwards with a face of thunder and
lightning.

"It is as I thought," he hissed; "they have killed *my*
beavers, and I will get even with the devils," only he did
not say devils. Then he proceeded to let loose his passion
on the white trappers who had for the first time ascended
the Gander, a province which Joe considered his exclusive
right, and poured such a torrent of threats and abuse on
their heads that I have seldom heard. I think that something will happen to the boats of those unfortunates next
time they move into the interior, if nothing worse occurs.

"Joe is a very good fellow," said Little Bob later, "but
I should not care to meet him alone in the winter if I had
a pack of 'fur' on my back," a sentiment in which both
Frank and Sandy cordially acquiesced. In fact the New-

---

[1] In British Columbia it is an offence punishable by severe penalty or imprisonment to sell liquor to Indians. Why should not this be done in Newfoundland?
Surely the people are as sensible and humane.

Four Photographs showing Various Methods of Spying

foundlanders generally regard the Indian with some fear and distrust. Indians either like you very much or they do not like you at all, and will leave you to starve in the woods. Personally I saw nothing to be alarmed at in Joe's attitude. "Furring" was his sole means of livelihood, and as he had first found the hunting-ground and could get no other if it were spoilt, he naturally was incensed at the incursion of white men whose business, he considered, was amongst the ships. "The coast is the white man's; the woods are ours," is the Micmacs' motto.

On 16th September we continued our journey eastwards, McGaw and I walking ahead as usual. At noon a broad sheet of water came into view, which from its shape and size I knew to be Dog Lake. After a cup of tea and a short rest, my friend and I set off into the country to try and procure some meat, which we had been without for two days. The ground was terribly swampy and broken, and the walking extremely arduous. After going for about three miles I ascended a larch tree and immediately spied a string of five doe caribou moving round the edge of a small copse. The wind was right, so we advanced rapidly upon them, and as McGaw under his licence was not allowed to kill a doe, I took the shot at 80 yards and dropped the best deer. Each of us then shouldered a haunch and made our way to camp with frequent stoppings for rest. Here the men soon turned up with the canoes, and we all had a glorious feast, the Matthews boys swallowing great chunks of flesh as if they had not eaten for a week. In the evening we got aboard, and paddled swiftly to the northern end of Dog Lake, from whence our long "pack" was to commence.

CHAPTER XII

DISCOVERY OF THE SOURCE OF THE GANDER AND
INCIDENTS OF STILL-HUNTING IN THE TIMBER

NOTHING in the universe is so attractive as the unknown. To the man of imagination it is the great magnet which draws him away to seek fresh worlds to conquer. There is in the very sound of the word that hidden mystery that "tinges the sober aspect of the present with colour of romance," and no one, however dull, is ever quite romance proof. In consequence, men rush wildly at the North Pole and after other unconquered fields, although the results achieved are often out of all proportion to the labour involved.

It may seem strange to the reader that there should still be unexplored districts in a small island like Newfoundland which has so long been a British colony, and yet it is a fact that out of a total area of 42,000 square miles, at least two-thirds of the country is still as little known as it was when John Cabot landed. The island has an entire length of 317 miles and a breadth of 315 miles; but, broadly speaking, all that is known of the interior is a five-mile strip from the coast where its population of 250,000 dwells, and the main waterways which have been principally mapped by Murray and Howley since the year 1870. The reason of this want of knowledge is easily explained. Horses cannot go far in because there is no grass except on a few of the more slow-moving rivers, and men can only carry on their backs supplies for a short journey. But the principal reason, at least it seems so to me, is that the Newfoundlander being purely a fisherman, and delighting only in the acquisition of the harvest of the sea, knows and cares little about possible farm lands. Moreover, he has always been unable to build light draught canoes of tough wood, because no wood capable of withstanding the rocks of the rivers is to be found in the island. He is also clumsy in the rivers, and unable to use a pole like the Indians. Perhaps he gets a few miles up an easy river in his punt, but on meeting with difficulties, such as the breaking of his soft wood boat, readily gives up the task. He has any amount of pluck, but no skill on the rivers. Though all at home at sea, he is all at sea at home.

The little bit of unknown we were about to enter had only been traversed by one man, a miner named Guzman, who crossed from Bay Despair in 1875, led by Nicholas Jeddore, Joe's father. Mr. Howley had ascended the Gander on foot, and had reached Burnt Hill, which we could now see about twenty miles to the east, and Alexander Murray had surveyed and marked Partridgeberry Hill, the highest mountain in Central Newfoundland, having reached it by packing across from Round Bond. The country between the Upper Gander and Dog Lake was unmapped and unknown, a space of about fifteen miles in a straight line left blank. Actually we found that this unknown area was about twenty-five miles broad. It really meant about forty miles of walking, as it was necessary to keep on the high ground to the south, so as to avoid the swamps. Our men therefore could rely on little help in the way of water during their thirty miles journey, for they must follow the valley route and carry everything on their backs for the greater part of the distance.

Accordingly I determined to divide the party. Taking the

three Indians and Saunders with McGaw and myself, we were to go right on to a spot where I knew there was good hunting on the Upper Gander. Then McGaw and I would go into camp alone for a week or ten days, and send the Indians and Saunders back towards Dog Lake to assist Sandy and Frank, who were meanwhile to get as far as possible. This theory seemed to be the best plan, as not only could we survey the easiest route for the packers and canoes to follow, but we should probably kill some deer on the way. The meat of these could be eaten by the men, and their position pointed out by Joe, who was first of all to accompany us.

We made an early start, and after going a mile or two, skirted to the south-east to avoid swamps. Here we noticed a small brook flowing eastwards, and being the first water travelling in this direction, we decided to follow it up to its source, which was found in a small still pool, and which we knew must be the source of the Gander. This little brook emptied into a pretty lake about two miles long which, having no name, I christened Lake McGaw. By existing maps the Gander stops under or to the eastwards of Burnt Hill, but as a matter of fact there is a continuous stream, albeit small in summer, through the small chain of lakes to within half a mile of Dog Lake.

After photographing our discovery we ascended rough ground through burnt timber and over rocks for two miles, and then found ourselves on the shoulder of Partridgeberry Hill. Joe was setting the pace, a "cracker" in spite of his 80-lb. pack, and being so "sassy" I suggested an ascent to the top of the mountain, from which point we could take observations and see the best line for future progress. No sooner said than done, though the two Indian boys and

Saunders lagged behind; we made the summit in half-an-hour. The day being fine, there was a magnificent view in every direction. All the main features of Central Newfoundland were plainly visible; Cormack, Sit Down, and Shoal Lake Look-out were easily distinguished to the north-west; Bradshaw Mountain, and even the hills across Round Pond, to the west; whilst to the north-east Joe Migwell's Mountain, and even Blue Hill, seventy miles away, was shining through the blue haze.

At our feet was one long valley stretching from Dog Lake to Burnt Hill, twelve or fourteen miles due east, where the main Gander forests commence. A long strip to the north-east was burnt timber, and this blackened forest extended to Great Rattling Brook, and so goes on to the railway at Badger's Brook.

Immediately beneath lay three lakes, McGaw's, Rocky Pond, and John Jeddore's Pond, each connected by the Gander flowing eastwards; behind us to the south were bare rolling hills, which fall to the south-east and rise again in the great forests of the Middle Ridge.

We did not stay long on the summit as it was cold, and we were anxious to get as far as possible the first day. So after taking some photographs and sketches we continued eastwards at a steady pace for four hours. Then we descended into a wood to "bile the kettle," and, having no meat, felt somewhat dissatisfied. Incidentally Martin annexed two-thirds of a large tin of butter (enough to last three healthy men for four days) and upset a can of milk into his tea. On resuming our tramp we all kept a sharp look-out for a stag, but sign of deer was scarce, the animals evidently not caring much for the open country at this season.

The sun was low when we at last came under the frowning

mass of Burnt Hill, and we flung ourselves wearily against some rocks for one of the usual "spells." Presently all rose to refresh on the delicious blueberries which were nearly as large as cherries, except Martin, who was too weary to crawl. As I turned to speak to him and point out a place where I thought we should camp for the night, he slowly raised one red finger and, pointing to the summit of the mountain, said, "I see fox."

It seemed that Martin had made a wonderful "spy," for to see a fox crawling along the mountain 700 feet above was little short of miraculous. The telescope, however, revealed a large doe caribou, and as I was about to take it from my eye it revealed another beast in the form of a large stag feeding about 100 yards below. We must have meat, but oh! that hill, when you have tramped twenty miles and are feeling tired, and twenty miles in Newfoundland is pretty stiff work.

Joe released from his pack was like a greyhound slipped from the leash, and the way he raced up Burnt Hill was a sight to see. I set my teeth, and followed him as fast as I could, but after a bit I slowed down and let him go on, for I knew he could not kill the stag with his axe. By-and-by we came within view of the highest ridge, and caution being necessary, Joe proceeded to behave himself with reason, and allowed me to search the ground with the glass. There was the doe, but the stag we could not see for a long time, but suspecting that he had fed on, we gained the crest and crept onwards. A bush in movement at first attracted our attention, and then the stag's horns came into view above it on the same level as ourselves. Consequently I decided to get above our quarry at the risk of moving the doe, which was now in full view. A short crawl brought me within 200 yards of the stag feeding quietly on the hill beneath me, so I sat up to take a quiet shot.

"What are you doing?" said Joe, who never took shots farther than forty yards; "we can get close in."

"I don't want to," I replied, for I was anxious to show him what the Mannlicher could do.

The bullet took the deer high up through the ribs, and he staggered a few yards with his head down. I then fired again and hit him close to the same place, when he pitched forwards a few yards and fell dead.

Joe said nothing, but shook his head and picked up the rifle, into the nozzle of which he tried to insert his little finger, but without success.

"So," he said, "if you offer to give me a rifle like that las' year I wu'n't say 'thank you,' but now I think him pretty good," and he walked off to bleed the stag. Its head was a very pretty one of twenty-seven points, but encumbered as we were with other things, it was impossible to carry it. Joe said that his brother, who would shortly hunt in the neighbourhood of Burnt Hill, would carry it out for me to the coast for five dollars, so I left the bargain in his hands.

As he was cutting off one of the haunches I happened to look down the hill to see if our men were still in sight, when I observed five caribou galloping along the base of the hill and coming in our direction. Three of them were undoubtedly stags, so I made all haste to cut them off, leaving Joe to skin and follow me. The wind being right, I easily headed the deer, which, in the fading light, looked much better than they really were. Two of the stags had pretty heads of about twenty points, but they were not the sort of animals I desired. Joe joined me in a few minutes, laden with ribs, breast, tongue, and a haunch. We made for the wood, over which a haze

of blue smoke hung, and we were soon at work with knife and
fork. It is wonderful what meat will do. We were all dog-
tired, but in half-an-hour after a good meal we were all in-
spirited and refreshed. Saunders had done wonders for a man
of fifty-nine. Of course he had carried his pack quite in the
wrong way, the 70 lbs. being all on the back of his neck
instead of being properly distributed. He had fallen twice
to the ground from sheer exhaustion, but his indomitable
spirit had carried him along where a more skilful and less
plucky individual would have lagged behind or given in.

After a good night, during which the men slept without
shelter by the fireside, we continued our journey down the
Gander, which was now developing into a good-sized brook
with several deep "steadies." In one of these Joe pointed
out a colony of beavers which had lived there unmolested for
the past six years. After walking steadily from 7 till 10 we
encountered the first large "droke" of birch, and far along in
the distance, to the east, could see the commencement of more
green woods. Signs of deer now became more frequent, and
we kept a sharp look-out. When packing, the usual plan is
to walk in line steadily for half-an-hour, and then to take a
short rest. During one of these "spells," as they are called,
Martin again made an excellent "spy," noticing the head
of a stag sticking out of a peat bog about 600 yards
above us.

It was now McGaw's turn for a shot, and as the wind was
right he got within 200 yards of the deer without difficulty.
Here Joe, who could not sit still and see another do a stalk,
joined us, and so getting some rocks in between ourselves
and the quarry we advanced to within 100 yards, where
a suitable spot to shoot from offered itself. My friend
then fired at the stag, which was now on his legs, feeding

DOG LAKE.

slowly along, and struck it through the ribs. Another shot was unnecessary, but he fired again for practice, and the stag, after running a few yards, fell dead.

This was McGaw's first trophy, which means much to the man who has shot it; so, after taking the head and neck skin, we cleaned the carcase and left it for the future consumption of our packers.

After the midday rest and meal we kept on until night-fall, when, finding a fine wood of birch, we made camp for the night, after going about fifteen miles. Close to camp was a large backwater, cut off from the main river by the finest beaver dam I have ever seen.

The amount of work which had been effected by these clever animals was tremendous. By the sides of the main pool were large timber roads, along which the beavers had dragged their birch logs, and then slid them down the muddy banks. Fully an acre had been cut down, and the remnants of their forays lay in all directions. Following up the main lake we discovered another small one, and at once detected the beavers' house on the other side. Whilst we looked and admired the ingenuity of the whole construction, two of the occupants suddenly appeared and commenced swimming slowly up and down. Both were adult animals, and did not seem at all shy as they came and surveyed us with cocked ears within thirty yards.

" There are about twenty live here," said Joe, "and I could catch them all when I like, if it warn't for de law." Which proves that the Indians do respect the game laws when they are just.

In the time of Cormack (1822) beaver were numerous all over the central part of the island; but constant molestation, both by white men and Indians, had made them so scarce that measures were taken for their protection a few years ago. This has done much good, and the beavers have not been trapped or shot to any extent. The close time, however, ends in October 1907, and it is certain that unless further restrictions are put on the killing of this interesting animal, the whole stock in the island will be rapidly wiped out.

The Newfoundland beavers subsist largely on the root of the water-lily, *Nymphea odorata*, called by the Indians " beaver root." They also eat the bark of the spruce and the small twigs of birch. Their habits are in all particulars the same as those of the Canadian beaver. There is one point which I should like to mention in connection with the building of the dams. Many authorities assert that the mud is carried in the paws and dumped down in the place required. The Indians in Newfoundland say that the mud is invariably carried in the mouth both for the dam and the " lodge "; that the beaver deposits it in place, and turning round quickly slides or smears his tail over this natural plaster, and thus makes it set. Sir Edmund Loder, who has closely watched his own beavers at Leonardslea building their dam, also tells me that the mud is carried in the mouth. One of the cleverest things the beaver does is the way in which it anchors many branches of birch in the water near the lodge or bank holes. When winter freezes the pond the beaver can then dive in from the holes under the ice and take such branches as it requires for food into its warm den, and there devours them.

One of the few superstitions of the Newfoundland Micmacs relates to the beaver. They say that these animals come up from the salt water and take up their abode in some small pond. For the first three years these new-comers are very wild, and it is impossible to trap, shoot, or call them. When they cannot catch a beaver they say "he has just come from the sea."

At daybreak Bob Saunders roused us with the news that a large stag was standing on the other side of the river, and that he appeared to have a very good head. I sprang from my bed, and, seizing my rifle, ran out in my "nighties." Yes, there he was, staring fixedly at the camp, and I sat down on the cold stones and let go, estimating the distance at 150 yards. The stag sprang away, and after going a short distance turned sharply to the right and crossed the river. During his passage I fired two more shots at him, both going just over his back by an inch or two. But an inch is a clean miss, and I had the mortification of seeing a fine head dash into the alders and pass away. I had not troubled to settle myself in a good shooting position, and so had missed a good beast.

At noon we struck the heavy timber, and the spoor of deer was seen in abundance on both sides of the river. As we were about to halt for tea a stag came out of the wood at about 170 yards, so I sat down and killed it as food for McGaw and myself. I may say in passing that every eatable part of this deer and the two others which we had previously killed was eaten by ourselves and the men during the next eight days. It was, in fact, fortunate that we had found and shot these three stags just at the points where they were wanted, for it made the work of the packers much easier. About twenty minutes after this incident I recognised my old camp of 1903 at the riverside. Here the men rested for the night, and then departed again up stream, leaving McGaw and myself to our own devices for a week.

During the first day McGaw went down stream for about three miles and watched some open stretches, seeing two good shootable stags, but in difficult positions. On the same day I travelled up stream to a good crossing place. Several deer came close to me, mostly does and young stags, and at 3 P.M. I saw a party of five crossing the river about 600 yards above me. It was interesting to watch their movements and to see their terror when they struck the spoor of the men who had travelled up the bank in the early morning. On getting the wind from the track they at once rushed pell-mell back into the river, where they stood staring for about a quarter of an hour. Then they tried to cross it again about 100 yards farther down, when a similar panic overtook them. After walking down the river for 400 yards, during which they tested the wind and retreated from the offensive taint three or four times, they came close to my position and I could examine them at leisure. The party consisted of two old does, a two-year old, and a five-year old stag, with eighteen points. One of the does carried a head with a large number of points—fifteen—this being the largest number I had seen.

McGaw and I had built our camp right in the open and commanding a view of a much-used lead, where I had seen two fine stags pass two years before. Our reindeer beds lay on the slope of the hill, and it was decided that whoever was first awake at dawn should watch this lead. At daybreak I was awakened by a violent shaking and found my companion busily engaged in detaching me from the arms of Morpheus.

"There's a big stag making for the lead," was McGaw's first ejaculation, an announcement which needed no further explanation than to sit up and seize our rifles.

"Go on, old chap," I said; "you saw the beast first, and must take first shot. Distance, 320 yards."

It was a long and difficult chance with hazy light, but it was our only one, as the wind was blowing directly from

A Simple Snare for the Varying Hare

A humane form of trap which should be adopted in Great Britain

us to the stag, which looked to be a splendid one. McGaw aimed carefully and fired, and the stag only raised his head sharply. Then I fired. My bullet evidently struck a stone just under the deer's brisket, and, causing some particles to touch the stag, frightened it. As it galloped away my companion fired again without effect, and immediately afterwards, as the animal dashed up to the forest, I let go my second shot, which fortunately broke the beast's neck. This was the only long shot I fired during the trip, and I felt much elated at bringing it off. When we got up to the fallen one, we were much surprised to find that it was not dead, although its neck was actually broken by the bullet, so I shot it through the heart to end matters at once. The head proved to be one of the largest I have seen in Newfoundland, the horns being long (40 inches) and massive, but with very few points— nineteen. This being the first good trophy we had secured, we returned to breakfast in great spirits, as we were now in the real home of the stags, and I hoped my friend would secure such another during the next few days.

Camping and hunting alone or with a companion offers no great hardship or difficulty in Newfoundland, and but for the trouble of cutting logs, washing dishes, and lighting the early morning fire, it is much the same as if your men were with you. We had, however, chosen a shocking site on a steep slope, and our fire was continually tumbling down the hill into the river and throwing its heat, when we wanted it, in the wrong direction.

This day, 21st September, proved to be a very enjoyable one. We spent the morning in photographing and sketching, &c., and then, taking some provisions, started down the river for the rest of the day.

After proceeding a mile, the rain, which had been threaten-

ing, came down in torrents, so we retreated into a birch droke
at the riverside, where we lit a fire and kept watch alternately
up and down the river. At about 2.30 I saw a stag skirting
the timber in a bend of the river some 600 yards away ; the
wind could not have been worse, and appeared to blow directly
from us to the spot whence the animal was slowly moving
along with its head down. As he did not seem to "get" us,
I resolved on a sharp run in—the only action possible, for
in another minute the stag would turn up into the woods and
be lost for good. The rocks were wet and slippery, but we
raced along, keeping an eye fixed on the stag the whole time.
Once he raised his head and looked about, and we sank into
the soaking grass and bush ; and then on again at the risk of
breaking our legs for another 300 yards. As we approached
the stag, which was on the other side of the river at a sharp
bend, I saw how it was that he had not received our wind—
a broad ride of low forest here intersected the high trees and
formed a sort of air-chute from the west, which, meeting
another wind and our scent winding down the river from the
north-west, bore it outwards and upwards before it reached
the stag. We were now within 100 yards, so McGaw sat
down and fired, as the head was a good one. The first bullet
went over the animal's back, but had the effect of driving the
deer out of the wood into the open. A second shot seemed
more successful, as I saw the stag wince and a moment after
come rushing for the river, which it endeavoured to cross.
Here McGaw fired three more shots without effect, as he had
become a bit excited and had emptied his magazine. But
no more were necessary, as the noble beast, throwing up his
head, plunged madly about for a few moments and rolled over
dead in the stream.

My friend was now full of joy, as he feared he had missed

LONGHORNED STAG SHOT BY THE AUTHOR ON THE UPPER GANDER,
SEPTEMBER 1905

his mark, and, hastily stripping off his coat, went into the river to remove the head. He brought ashore a good, massive set of horns, wild in appearance, but not large in frame. The evening was drawing on, so we returned to camp and killed our stags over again around the blazing fire. During the next few days the weather was still and hot, and deer move about but little at such times. Under cover of the night many stags crossed from the dense forest of the south to the "loose" timber on the north bank, as I could see by the fresh spoor each morning. We saw a couple of stags every day, but nothing with a head good enough to tempt one to take a shot.

On the night of the 24th the men came with the canoes, having had an arduous journey of eight days since leaving Dog Lake. They had received some help on the three lakes, but the river itself had proved nothing but a series of shallows and rocky benches, in which it was unsafe to drag the canoes, so they had had to pack nearly the whole distance. Martin Matthews and his brother had worked well and were of great assistance in portaging the outfit; in fact without their timely help the packers would have been three days longer on the road.

As he had now only one more stag to kill under the terms of his licence and was also anxious to catch a steamer for home early in October, my friend now departed for Glenwood, about 60 miles down the river. He was to stop either at Serpentine Hill or Migwell's Brook, and I felt sure he would kill a good one at one of these places. As a matter of fact he saw five stags the first day at Serpentine Hill and killed the best one, a twenty-eight pointer, and so returned to civilisation, having thoroughly enjoyed his tramp.

It is a curious thing how the habits and movements of

Q

wild animals will change with different seasons. In 1903, when I hunted on the Gander, all the big stags were constantly to be seen standing out on the river or crossing it during the morning or evening. By 20th September they were ready to move out, collect does and travel south with them. I explain this by the fact that the winter of 1902–3 had been an exceptionally mild one and the stags had early come into fine condition. Now in 1905 a different state of affairs prevailed. The winter of 1904–5 had been one of the severest on record, and when the spring came, the deer were reduced to the most wretched condition. As a rule they can get at the caribou moss in April by scraping in the snow with their feet, but in this season the frost continued to pack the snow into a hard block which could not be penetrated, and the deer were forced to subsist on the "maldow," a bearded moss which hangs in the fir-trees and which is only capable of supporting life. The result was a very backward season, in which the animals, with few exceptions, grew poor heads and were in no condition. In consequence the rut was deferred for a period of nearly three weeks, an almost unheard-of event in Newfoundland, and the big stags were still keeping closely to the timber as late as 25th September.

I saw, therefore, if I was to obtain a first-class head or two, I must adopt a different method of hunting, and search for the bearers of antlers amongst the timber itself. Now to hunt the caribou stag in its home of dense woods, such as stretches on the south bank of the Gander from Burnt Hill to the Gander Lake, was quite out of the question, owing to its great density, and the fact that deer would hear the advent of man before he could catch a glimpse of one of them. Some thousands of stags inhabit this great forest,

GRALLOCHING

CAMP SCENE ON THE UPPER GANDER

and a few cross the river every night to feed amongst the
loose timber situated on the north bank, as well as to lie
up where the trees are not so closely packed as on the
south side.

It was, therefore, necessary to become a "still-hunter,"
and to seek the stag by slow and careful manœuvres in the
semi-open forest to the north. Numerous tall larches are
scattered throughout this country, and from the topmost
branches of these, small openings in the woods and various
glades can be spied at intervals; so during the next eight
days Joe and I spent our time alternately creeping slowly
up-wind about the forest in moccasins, and spying likely
bits of country from the tree-tops. This is by far the most
entertaining and difficult method of hunting the caribou. It
is quite distinct from river-hunting, which I have already
described, and which requires patience, quickness, and straight
shooting, sometimes at long range; or open-ground stalking,
which is easy; or waiting on trails at migration time, which
is scarcely sport at all. Once in the timber, with its eddying
winds, its intense stillness, and its abundance of noisy débris,
the caribou stag becomes a high-class beast of the chase,
and almost as difficult to kill as the wapiti or the red stag
under similar circumstances. With the trees around to help
the sight, sound, and olfactory nerves, he seems to gain
unusual perception, especially during the short season prior
to the taking of wives. The crack of a stick, the slightest
movement, or the puff of the tainted atmosphere, and he is
off full gallop without further inquiry. Those who have only
seen the caribou stag under conditions of the "rut" or the
blind movement of migration, are in no sense qualified to
speak of him as a beast of the chase, as it only takes in one
point of view. In the wood he is a different animal altogether,

and an object worthy of the hunter's skill. In Canada I have heard old hunters say that, next to the moose, the caribou is the most difficult animal to kill in timber, and here in Newfoundland the same animal that any boy could slay in the last week of October will not be shot in mid-September by tenderfeet with hobnailed boots.

The day after McGaw left I moved camp a mile down stream to a large birch droke, and saw a fine stag just as we were building the lean-to. By running in I got within 200 yards, and had just time to put the glass upon his head, and see that he was not good enough. Next morning we were early astir, and whilst preparing for the day's hunt, I sent Joe up a high larch-tree at the back of the camp to view the ground. He had departed about five minutes, when I saw him again descending the tree, so I knew he had seen something. A moment afterwards he ran up to say that a stag with very fine horns had just appeared for a second as it fed along among the trees about 400 yards away. As the wind was right, coming from the north, we circled away from the camp to marshy ground, to make less noise, and so advanced through the trees in the direction which Joe indicated.

"It was just there he was," whispered my companion, as he pointed to the blackened spoor caused by the impress of the cutting hoofs. We stood perfectly still for five minutes, as the wind had dropped, and showed signs of being shifty, and then, hearing nothing, moved cautiously forward in circles on to a high stony mound from which a better view could be obtained. We were just leaving this, when I happened to glance behind me, and at once detected a small snow-white spot amongst the trees. Almost immediately it disappeared, and I knew that it must be the stag coming back on its own spoor. A retreat was therefore necessary, as the wind was swirling about in a disheartening fashion, so we ran as noise-lessly as possible for a short distance on our back tracks, and I then saw the stag walking slowly forward amongst the trees with his ears set at an attentive cock. He had obtained a puff from our tracks and was going to examine them. Suddenly he stopped and started, so I sat down immediately with my back against Joe's shoulders. At this moment his fears seemed to be realised, and he swung round to gallop across the open space about 10 yards broad. As he did so, I fired and broke his back, giving a second shot as he tried to recover. This stag carried a beautiful set of antlers with thirty-four points, and was by far the best I secured in 1905. The bays were exceptionally fine and the beam very long (46 inches) and very broad in the centre. What made it to me a fine trophy was its wild nature, as it had extra points sticking out of the main beam just above the bays. The whole head seemed to carry a little forest of antlers all the way up the horns, making it very attractive. Like so many caribou heads, it had, however, only one good brow; the other, though long, being of the scraggy order. I went to camp for my camera, but it came on to rain hard, so after skinning off the head, we had to return to camp, and waited till it became clearer.

"Kesculah" (the closing shower), said Joe, surveying the heavens as we made a start into the country, and kept working the timber steadily till sunset. We had many more "Kesculahs" that day, and, having tramped about 10 miles towards Great Rattling Brook, sat down to rest on the edge of a great open barren surrounded by dense timber. "A good place to watch," suggested Joe, so we made a fire and were refreshing ourselves with tea and meat when a stag appeared on the edge of the woods behind us. He was a very big fellow, but his horns were wretched, and, like all bad heads, he wandered up close at hand, giving me time to make some sketches at 30 yards distance.

Shortly after this incident I was standing half undressed in front of the fire, drying my soaking clothes, when Joe, who was, as usual, "up a tree," pointed to the north with his long red finger. Something was flashing in and out of the trees, a deer for certain, but of what sort I could not make out, even with the help of the glass.

"Dat him for sure; he's going fast and lookin' for de does."

Joe was right, for we presently had a good but momentary glimpse of an immense stag rapidly passing along the edge of the timber with his nose on the ground. I bundled on some clothes and we made off at our best speed across the marsh to head him. We had not gone far, however, when we both plunged in up to our waists in the bog. To extricate ourselves was a moment's work, but a few yards farther a similar disaster overtook us, Joe going in up to his armpits, from which uncomfortable position I had to haul him. We now found ourselves in a perfect maze of bogs, and after vainly endeavouring to find a passage through, we were forced to retreat by following our own spoor back. Now we made a fresh start only to encounter a further series of bog holes and treacherous swamps, through which, after some careful manœuvring, we eventually found a passage.

Meanwhile the stag was rapidly advancing across our front at a "running" walk, so we had to put on all steam to head him. He was almost opposite to us and about 350 yards distance, when he must have caught a glimpse of our movements as we sought to place some bushes between us. He stopped short at once and stared at us, and we sank to the ground and lay perfectly still. It was bitterly cold, and

STAG'S HEAD WITH FINE BROW SHOVEL SHOT NEAR
MIGWELL'S BROOK, SEPTEMBER 1905

we were wet to the skin, and there that wretched animal kept us for fully a quarter of an hour without moving. I began to shiver, and my teeth to chatter, but still he kept his neck stiff and straight. At last, after what seemed an age, he moved on a few yards and we raced for the bushes. Here, another staring match ensued, till Joe, losing patience, said, "I don't think that stag quite make us out. He think we's another stag, so I 'toll' him."

The Indian thereupon commenced an appalling series of loud grunts, enough, as I thought, to scare every deer out of the country; but not so our amorous friend, who at once replied with similar noises, and trotted up to within 150 yards. The sun had set, so I could not see his horns properly, but Joe said they were better than those I had obtained in the morning, so, getting a good rest, I fired, and struck the stag in the middle of the chest. He galloped off madly, so fast that I felt sure the shot was fatal, and did not fire again. After going about 50 yards he tripped over a hummock and fell dead.

"As big a stag as I see," pronounced Joe, as we gazed on the fallen one; but his head, which appeared big in the evening light, although a fair one, was disappointing, and I had to reckon it amongst the mistakes every hunter makes in dealing with these deer.

After cutting off the head and recovering our kettles and clothes, we made for camp, a distance of seven or eight miles. Most of this was tough walking, where alders slashed you in the face and unseen holes and swamps met you at every step, but we accomplished it in the semi-darkness without mishap, and so got home after a hard though most enjoyable day.

All the half-wooded country on the north bank, between

my camp and Little Gull River as far as Great Rattling Brook, was full of deer, principally consisting of big stags, mostly old fellows "going back." On 26th September I saw eight stags, either by spying from high trees or still-hunting in the timber. Four of these got the wind or heard us and there was no chance of seeing their heads, and three proved to be old fellows whose days of good horn growth had vanished.

Just as we turned to come home in the evening we found ourselves in a series of little stony hills close to the river. The wind blew directly in our faces, and in rounding one of these little mounds we suddenly came upon a very large stag with his head down in a hole of moss. His eyes were completely obscured, and so he had neither seen nor smelt us. It was very interesting to survey a big stag, for he was a very large fellow, within 15 yards, without his being aware of our presence. He bore an extraordinary head, not on account of its size, but on account of its smallness. A complete caribou head was there with double brows, good bays, and tops, but the whole was not larger than that carried by a good three-year-old. I stood regarding it with interest, whilst Joe whispered, "That's a curiosity head and you must shoot it," which I did after some hesitation.

If the reader is interested in horns he must be struck by the curious disparity this head bears to the long-horned specimen which I had killed during the past week. In fact, amongst the Newfoundland caribou I have shot every type of horn that is supposed to exist amongst the various so-called sub-species which inhabit Western British Columbia and Alaska. Forms of horns alone are by no means a sure test of species or sub-species, although it is well to bear in mind that every local race of deer has a certain general type of its own.

CHAPTER XIII

WORK AND SPORT IN THE UPPER REACHES OF THE GANDER AND GULL RIVERS

DURING the night we were serenaded by a lynx, which kept up an unearthly caterwaul at intervals. It had doubtless smelt the meat and was calling to its partner.

Nearly all white men as well as the Indians say that there were no lynxes in Newfoundland fifteen years ago, and that they came to the island about this time from Labrador by means of the ice bridge at the straits of Belleisle. It is also said that as the lynx entered so the wolves departed. But I do not think that this view is correct, for as long ago as 1622 Captain Whitbourne noted the presence of "leopards" in the island and subsequent writers also mention the "wild cats."

Doubtless they were very scarce until recent years, but now they are the most abundant of all the carnivora in the island, and do much damage to the game.[1] They live to a large extent on the small varying hare and grouse, seldom touching carrion until forced to do so by extreme hunger. Everywhere one sees their tracks on the sandy shores of the lakes, and at night and early morning I have often heard their screaming caterwaul. He is a sly silent beast is *A-bak-sigan*, the shadow, and his retiring habits hide him from the gaze of man. Of all animals he is the easiest

---

[1] I have little doubt that the great increase in the number of lynxes is due to the introduction of the small varying hare, which furnishes a good supply of food at all seasons. Animals which are well fed always breed more regularly and have large families than those which are only just able to support life.

to trap, the best method being that employed by the Indians, of which I give a sketch. A good Indian trapper will kill from 50 to 100 in one season. I have never seen the lynx, but I have seen the tragedy of the little hare's death written on the snow as plainly as if I had been there to witness it. Here is where the lynx suddenly stopped in his prowling walk; here is where he crouched on seeing the unfortunate "rabbit"; and again that is where he leaped after his prey in immense bounds, rapidly overtaking the scurrying form. The scattered earth and leaves with crimson patches and tufts of hair on the frozen snow show where the death took place, and the tracks of the lynx now walking slowly indicate where he has borne his victim to the side of a bush where more tufts of hair, two leg bones, and a skull and eyes, exhibit the last stage of the tragedy.

No doubt lynxes kill a few very young caribou fawns, but only those that are lying hidden in the undergrowth apart from their mothers.

The day following that on which I had killed the two big stags was a typical day's still-hunting, and its various incidents will serve to show something of the nature of this particular form of the chase and its excitements, so I take leave to copy it directly from my diary as it was written.

Wednesday, 27th September.—We moved camp this morning three miles down the river to the mouth of Little Gull River, where we left Bob to build a camp in the angle of the two streams. It was a beautiful autumn morning, clear and still, with the golden leaves showering from the bushes into the river. We had left camp in the darkness, and so saw the day break in all that pellucid clearness which is a never-failing source of wonder and enjoyment to the lover of Nature. Round about were the wood thrushes,

Thirty-four Pointer with Irregular Horns Shot near Little
Gull River, September 1905

trying with the advent of their new clothes to reconstruct the songs of spring-time, and lilting sweetly among the bushes. Occasionally a flock of crossbills passed overhead with their clinking cry, or a solitary pine grossbeak chanted a low melody from the top of some spruce. Even the last of the brilliant yellow-and-green wood warblers had not vanished, and still chased the flies in sheltered nooks.

Everything in the air bespoke autumn. The slight night frosts had imparted an activity and a potency to all things. The delicious scent of the spruce or fir boughs over one's head, or the odours of the wood fire that blazes up merrily, are all more intense and satisfactory as the season advances, and we sit round the blazing logs with appetites sharpened by weeks of pure air and healthful exercise. This is Life —and I am enjoying it. We have found the stags too; we are even camped in the "Sanctuary," where no man comes, and that, though selfish, is none the less delightful.

A party of jays rose from the river bank as we launched the canoe, for they had already found some of the spoils of yesterday, and were taking their share, carrying off the meat in large mouthfuls, or bearing it in their feet to some rotten pine in the forest where the winter stores were hidden, from which retreat they uttered their mellifluous whistle. Rain and wind had been prevalent for the past few days, but to-day a clear sky and a glow in the east gave promise of a fine day, certainly the worst weather for still-hunting, but pleasant for man, who likes to sit and gaze into the distance.

We walked noiselessly to our first spy-tree, an old larch about 50 feet high, and up this Joe climbed like a monkey, whilst I pottered about and gazed in admiration at an immense dropped horn I had discovered. On this horn were no fewer than twenty-six points, and others had already been eaten away by does during the previous winter.   Ah, if only I could see the grand fellow who bore that trophy! he must have been a veritable fifty-pointer.   Whilst Joe spied I beat the ground carefully in circles in the immediate neighbourhood, in the hope of discovering the other horn of the pair; but I did not find it, although I discovered two other splendid horns (both right antlers), one bearing twenty points, the other twenty-one.   That stags of forty, forty-two, and fifty points had each shed their antlers within 200 yards of one another in 1903, for they were all two years old, was somewhat remarkable, but it shows what magnificent heads are still hidden in the forest of the Upper Gander.

In ten minutes Joe descended, having only seen three does and a small stag, so we proceeded to a high mound of sandstone rock which commanded a splendid view of the whole of the open forest to the north.   Much of it was so hidden that there might be dozens of stags there without our seeing them, as the whole place was covered with fresh tracks and droppings.   The best chance was to wait and view a moving stag, as such an one is quickly picked up by experienced eyes as it flashes in and out amongst the trees, even a couple of miles away.

"I think stags goin' to be very quiet to-day, boss," remarked Joe, as he shut up the glass.   "It's goin' to be too fine"—a prognostication that was not fulfilled, for at intervals we kept viewing deer the whole day.   We had not long to wait when Joe made an excellent spy, seeing a stag moving through the trees fully a mile away.   He was heading due west, and travelling from thicket to thicket over very broken and hilly ground.   "We must run," said Joe, and run we did, until we were both exhausted.   Down into holes, through alder swamps, then up little sandy hills, through little thickets, then on to hard moss ground, then

Walter L. Cobb, Photo.

Returning to camp after a good day

through two streams, and then up a tree, to see how the game was progressing.

"Not far enough yet," said Joe, so on we went, making great casts down-wind, and watching from every available point. He might pass close to us or behind us at any moment, so thick was the timber in places, but at "cutting-off" stags, Joe was my superior and seldom made a mistake, so I left it entirely in his hands. At last he said, "He gone by unless he stop somewhere up-wind," a sound piece of judgment, which we now acted upon by moving across against the wind. We had not proceeded far when Joe, who was in front, suddenly stopped and drew back slowly, so I knew he had seen the quarry. I crept forward and saw a large stag lying on a steep mound above a brook, about 100 yards away, and, whilst observing his horns, which were poor, a loud crash of antlers resounded in the forest about 60 yards to the right, and there was the sound of war and turmoil. The fighters were in a thick place, but, as the wind was blowing well, I crept in on my hands and knees, and got within 30 yards of two five-year-old stags, who were doing a little bit of preliminary practice. They were not fighting seriously, but boxing, to try their strength, and I obtained a splendid view of their manœuvres at close range. They seem to spar in much the same manner as red deer, always whipping round quickly to gain the advantage of the hill whenever one or other obtained the push. After watching them for ten minutes, and whilst making a sketch, one of the combatants gave his antagonist a good blow in the side which caused the latter to retreat precipitously on to the top of myself. I was too intent on my work for the moment to see what was happening, and looked up to find a great beast staring me in the face within five yards. I rose to get out of his way, deeming a closer acquaintance undesirable, when he dashed round with a loud "whoup" of fear, and, taking the other stags along with him, stood for a moment on the hill and then galloped off to the north.

We had not left the hill two minutes when we encountered another large stag—a regular old patriarch he looked, with thin, wretched horns. He was moving westwards, so we let him go by without disturbance. At midday we found two more stags by slow still-hunting. These were also undesirable old fellows, and about three another big fellow heard or smelt us as we passed along, and galloped off in great terror. About four we passed several does, and then saw the usual snow-white neck of a large stag as it lay on the edge of a small barren. What was my surprise to see, on raising the telescope, that the beast was a "hummel,"[1] or hornless stag, certainly a rarity, but one we did not appreciate. It was getting late, so we turned homewards down-wind, still hunting carefully as we went along. It was getting nearly dark when I saw the stern of a large stag move round a belt of firs about 200 yards to our left, and at once left Joe and crept after the animal. The horns of the stag were swaying from side to side as they always do when a well-antlered deer moves along with his head down, so I had hopes of securing another good head. Presently the stag turned sideways, and I sat up and allowed him to see me, as I wanted him to raise his head. The result was not satisfactory—a well-formed twenty-five pointer, but not class enough, so he was allowed to trot away to his friends.

So home to camp at seven, without having fired my rifle and having seen nine warrantable stags.

During the next three days we continued our still-hunting, and were successful in finding a good many deer, but no

---

[1] Hummels are much rarer amongst caribou than red deer. Joe had only seen two in his life before the present example.

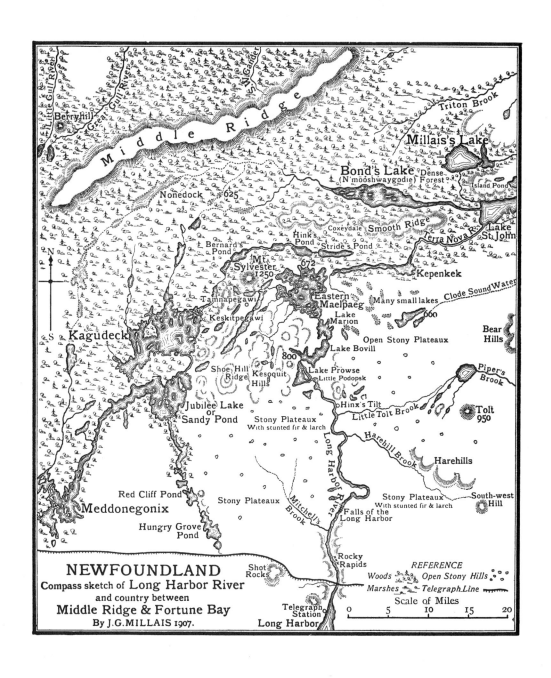

NEWFOUNDLAND
Compass sketch of Long Harbor River
and country between
Middle Ridge & Fortune Bay
By J.G.MILLAIS 1907.

Little Gull River
Great Gull River
Berryhill
N. Gander
Triton Brook
Middle Ridge
Millais's Lake
Nonedock
625
Bond's Lake
(N'mooshwaygodie) Dense Forest
Island Pond
Lake St. John
Coxeydale Smooth Ridge
Terra Nova R.
Hink's Pond
Bernard's Pond
Stride's Pond
Mt Sylvester 1250
672
Kepenkek
Tamnapegawi
Eastern Maelpaeg
Many small lakes
Clode Sound Water
660
Keskitpegawi
Lake Marion
Bear Hills
Kagudeck
Open Stony Plateaux
Lake Bovill
Piper's Brook
Shoe Hill Ridge
Kesoquit Hills
800
Lake Prowse
Little Podopsk
Tolt 950
Jubilee Lake or Sandy Pond
Stony Plateaux
With stunted fir & larch
Hinx's Tilt
Little Tolt Brook
Harehill Brook
Harehills
Red Cliff Pond
Stony Plateaux
Long Harbor River
South-west Hill
Meddonegonix
Hungry Grove Pond
Stony Plateaux
Mitchell's Brook
Stony Plateaux
With stunted fir & larch
Falls of the Long Harbor
Shot Rocks
Rocky Rapids
Telegraph Station
Long Harbor

REFERENCE
Woods   Open Stony Hills
Marshes   Telegraph Line
Scale of Miles
0   5   10   15   20

heads worth shooting. On 30th September I moved camp to Serpentine Hill, and on the following day killed two fine stags, one of which carried a very pretty head.

Serpentine Hill or Hills are a long chain of rocky hills about ten miles long on the south bank of the Gander. They are only slightly wooded, and afford a magnificent view of the whole of the sparsely wooded flats and smaller sandy hills on the north bank. By ascending a short distance you can see deer moving anywhere within a radius of two miles, and so the position of a camp in such a spot is simply ideal. At daybreak Joe had gone to spy, and awoke me with the news that a stag with very good horns was feeding about a mile away on the other side of the river. I jumped out of bed, pulled on my boots, and we ran to the canoe quickly and crossed the river. Here we found ourselves in a large swamp, which extended for a mile to the hard ground and forest, where the stag had been spied. Through the marsh we continued to run until I suddenly felt quite exhausted and unable to proceed farther. It had not occurred to me that a cup of tea and a few biscuits would have been a good thing on which to commence the day, and now I felt faint and almost unable to proceed. We crawled on slowly for a few hundred yards, and then Joe pointed out the "open," where he had seen the stag with two does. After waiting a few minutes one of the does came into view, so we sat down, expecting to see his lordship at any moment. Since he did not appear, I sent Joe to climb a tree to my left, and lay down to rest and await eventualities. Joe had hardly left me when I saw both the stag and the other doe come through the short timber to my right. I therefore recalled the Indian and worked into a good shooting position. The stag was a small one, but seemed to carry nicely-shaped antlers, so, when he passed across my front

at 100 yards, I fired, and struck him right through the heart.
Joe soon skinned off the head, and we returned to camp
slowly, where a good hot breakfast soon put me to rights
again. *Mem.:* Do not in future run over swamps in the
early morning without first having taken some food. It
is not wise.

After breakfast we ascended the mountain where we had
discovered a good spying-place, and so settled ourselves
for a long look. Five or six deer were already in sight
in spite of our having run over a good part of the ground.
It was, however, my turn to find a good beast, for, with the
aid of the telescope, I just caught a glimpse of him as he
glinted in and out of a great belt of spruce fully a mile and
a half away. The white neck of a big caribou stag is quite
conspicuous at a great distance, and even at this long range
I could see that the bays were large and thick.

So once again we were down the hill, over the river and
running northwards across swamp and barren for a point
ahead of the amorous traveller. First we encounter a doe
and a fawn, then two young stags, and then Joe, after a
tree spy, marked what he thought must be the big fellow
I had seen. It was a good-sized beast in truth that he
had seen moving in front of us, but on heading him I saw
at once that it was not "my" stag, as his bays were almost
absent. He came sauntering along, so I thought I would
try a little amateur "tolling." To my surprise the stag at
once responded, and came grunting up close to our shelter and
would hardly go away. We left him, and hurried on thinking
that the big stag must either have passed by us or still be
to the north-east and heading west, in which case we might
see him. But work which way we liked, there was no sign
of the deer for an hour at any rate, when Joe ascended a
high larch on the edge of dense forest, and tried to survey

the country to the east. He remained up in the branches for ten minutes, and then descended. Just as his feet touched the ground, I heard an unusual noise of some sort. Joe stood rigid, and asked me if I had heard anything, to which I replied that I thought I had detected a low grunt. We stood listening intently, when over his shoulder I saw a great stag walking slowly towards us out of the timber. We crouched low at once, and he came on, giving me an easy shot at 50 yards, the sort of chance which could not be missed. The stag ran fully 100 yards after receiving the bullet through the heart, and then turned a somersault and fell dead. I rushed up to the fallen one, which I felt sure was an exceptional head, but was much disappointed to find that this was not the case. The deer itself was the largest I had ever seen, but the tops of the horns, which had been thrown back as the animal came towards me and were in consequence out of view, were exceedingly poor. We took a haunch, the shank skins for moccasins, and the head, and were back in camp at one.

The following day Joe and I were following a wooded stream up towards Great Rattling Brook, ten miles to the north, when I saw a large doe feeding on dead alder leaves, and stood to watch her. She picked each leaf off daintily, and kept looking up the brook as if waiting for another deer to appear. We naturally inferred that there must be a stag with her at this season, and so sat down and waited for fully an hour without hearing a bush shake or a stick crack.

" I think we go on," said Joe at last, and we rose to proceed, at the same time showing ourselves to the doe. There was a loud crash close by, and I could just see the white stern of a big stag as it sprang from the bank into the stream and dashed away. Running forward, I found a clearing, and had a good sight of the stag, which I saw at

R

once had splendid brows. So I snapped at him as his back showed up for a moment and missed. After running 30 yards farther he turned sideways to recross the stream in which I was myself standing to gain a better view, and so presented for a moment a good broadside. My second shot was quite successful, as it broke the stag's neck, and caused him to fall with a great splash into the brook.

This was the second best and the last head I secured during the expedition. The brows and bays were all that could be desired—in fact these parts were quite perfect, but the tops were short and somewhat spindly. However, I was glad to have secured three fine specimens in nine heads, and that is as many good heads as any hunter can expect to shoot unless he strikes new ground and meets with a large number of stags in an exceptional year, as I had done in 1903, and did afterwards in 1906.

In all the lakes lying adjacent to the Gander the dusky mallard (*Anas obscurus*) was plentiful at this season. This species, similar in habits to the common mallard (*Anas boschas*) is widely distributed through North America and Canada east of a line formed by the Rocky Mountains. North of a line drawn from the St. Lawrence to the Rockies the "black duck," as it is generally called, is numerous in all the prairie pools and in the lakes and muskegs of the great north as far as the Arctic Ocean. In New England it is known as the dusky duck, in the Southern States as black mallard, in Florida and Mexico as the black English duck, and it is the *Mahkudasheed* of the Canadian Indians. A dull bird of black and brown it looks at a distance, but when handled the bright orange legs, green bill, and metallic blue and green speculum give it a certain beauty of colour. Males and females are very similar in appearance. They spend the winter in the Southern States, and arrive in pairs in Canada and Newfoundland in

BELLEORAM

BELLEORAM BREAKWATER AND VIEW OF THE IRON SKULL

April, where they at once seek for nesting sites. The nest is formed of pine needles, twigs and leaves, and in all their breeding habits and general mode of life they are exactly similar to the common wild duck.

During the following eight days I experienced a great deal of hard walking to determine the course and position of Little Gull River, Great Rattling Brook, and the lakes and hills adjacent to them. I found several new lakes in the valley between Serpentine Hills and the Middle Ridge. I also found the correct trend of Great Gull River, and its eventual convergence and course parallel to Little Gull River, and many other points which are of interest to geographers and surveyors, and which may seem somewhat dull to the general reader. Joe and I must have walked over 100 miles in the time, and I was somewhat weary when we reached Rolling Falls on the 9th of October. During all this tramping, in which I attended solely to claims of geographical interest, I saw many stags and does, but not one of sufficient calibre to tempt me to contravene the close season. I admit it is curious, but it is nevertheless a fact.

On the 10th we made good progress down the river, which was very low and dangerous. We passed the Rocky Rapids in safety, but, in trying to run a small rapid just below, had a narrow escape from being drowned. Joe, who was in front and carrying a light load, successfully passed between the two rocks, where the stream though fast looked safe enough; but when Saunders and I attempted to run it, we found our canoe wedged in between an unseen rock and one of the larger ones, and with a wall of rushing water higher than the canoe racing by on either side. Seeing the danger, we both drove our paddles on to the rock, and exerted all our strength to lift the canoe. At first it scarcely moved and the water poured over us, half-filling the boat, and then the force of the stream made itself felt, and gradually bore us onwards and outwards to safety into a small rapid. It was a ticklish moment, and I felt much relieved at only getting a ducking. When low the Gander is a dangerous river even to those who know it, and the traveller if nervous will do well to walk down stream. The way is long, but the beach is safe.

On the 10th we were detained by a gale, snowstorms from the east, and on the 11th much the same conditions prevailed ; yet we made a start and reached the Gander Lake in the evening, after as hard a day's paddling as I can remember. Here on the lake, thirty-three miles long, we met the full fury of the north-east, and had to go into camp for two days, although only fourteen miles from Glenwood, which we reached in safety on October 14th, and so ended my third expedition in the wilds of Newfoundland.

Joe was going to walk away back to his "tilt" up in the mountains near Burnt Hill, a distance of eighty miles, and, as I had not allowed him to carry a gun on our trip, McGaw and I thought that as he had served us well we would make him a present of one to help him to obtain supplies on his way. His joy on receiving the new muzzle-loader was great, and the woods about the Glenwood saw-mill were soon echoing with a series of loud reports. Having tried his gun, which he pronounced as good, he purchased some commodities and came to say "Good-bye," as I had arranged that the steamer would take him to the far side of the Glenwood Lake, thus saving about fifteen miles bad walking. . "See here, boss, next time you come to Newfoundland we'll go partners together. You can do all the shootin', and I will trap, and we'll make lots of dollars." It did not occur to his simple mind that I did not want to make a few dollars out of his local knowledge, but he meant it as a compliment, and I took it as such.

"Good-bye, boss; you come again, an' if I shoot a fifty-pointer, I keep him for you," and the red man shouldered a seventy-pound pack, lifted his gun, and drifted slowly down the road out of sight.

Glenwood has grown considerably since I was there in 1903. They have been busy at the saw-mills, and had made no fewer than seven million planks in 1905, and houses had sprung up on all hands. Only that unique institution the Reid Newfoundland Railroad went on as usual. The primitive rolling stock and the problematical road bed were still there, serving as a highway for numerous goats. Now goats are clever creatures, and, though they used the track as their path through the woods, they had also discovered the safest thoroughfare. Certainly there was reason why the trains could not overrun a goat, but there was no reason why the goats, like Mark Twain's cow, should not come aboard and bite the passengers.

We had quite a safe and uneventful journey to St. John's. At Terra-Nova some trifle occurred to cause a delay of two hours. At Whitburn we ran off the track, and ploughed up the permanent way for about 200 yards. This *contre-temps* occurred close to the station, so section men got to work and put us on again. Then at Avondale the cylinder head or something blew off the engine, and we had time to do a little berry-picking and make sarcastic remarks. However, we reached St. John's within a day of the advertised time, which is considered pretty good travelling in Newfoundland.

CHAPTER XIV

TO MOUNT SYLVESTER WITH THE MICMAC INDIANS

It was not my intention to visit Newfoundland in 1906, but a variety of circumstances caused an alteration of plans, and so September 18th found me speeding west again in the old *Corean*, bound for St. John's. By a careful study of the habits and movements of the Newfoundland caribou, I had gradually formed a theory that nearly all the great body of the deer which summered in the sanctuary between Round Pond in the centre and Terra-Nova and Glenwood in the east, moved southward about the end of October, *with converging trails*, and that these roads met somewhere in the neighbourhood of Mount Sylvester, where, Joe Jeddore had informed me, the country became high, rocky, and open. It is well known to the Fortune Bay men that the main body of the deer appear in great numbers in the open country immediately to the north of Fortune Bay about 20th November, by which date all the adult stags are hornless. It was therefore a fair assumption that if I could find both the breeding parties, as well as see the beginning of the big "trek" as it left the woods and emerged into the open country at some point near Sylvester, I should probably encounter the stags *before they had dropped their horns*, and in such numbers as travellers seldom see. This was proved to be correct, for, although the season was an unusually late one, I did find the ideal hunting-ground and the stags in all their pride of possession.

Having told Joe that I should not come in 1906, he had therefore made other plans to go trapping with his brother Nicholas. Nevertheless, he was good enough to delay his trip for several days, to make sure that I could obtain the services of one Steve Bernard, who alone knew part of the Sylvester country, and another excellent Indian, John Hinx, whose hunting-ground lay to the east in the neighbourhood of the Eastern Maelpeg. These two men were to meet me at the Long Harbor telegraph office on 3rd October.

Another cogent reason for adopting this route into the interior was that I wished to ascend and map the Long Harbor River, the largest unknown stream in Newfoundland. No white man had ever passed up its waters, so that it held some fascination for me. Mr. Howley, of course, had been to Mount Sylvester, but he had reached it through the Bay de Nord River and its chain of large lakes, and he had not had time to survey the waters or country to the east, or to do more than roughly indicate the position of the Maelpeg, with its sinuous bays and hundred islands. All the district north of Long Harbor telegraph station was practically unknown, except the immediate neighbourhood of the coast, where a few Fortune Bay men go in annually for a short distance to kill deer in the late fall.

After two days spent in St. John's to collect provisions and canoes from Mr. Blair, I took the train to Placentia, where one finds the *Glencoe* ready to steam along the southern coast. At the station I met the Premier, Sir Robert Bond, who asked me to sit with him, and we had a chat for three hours until we reached Whitburn, near which place he has a comfortable home, to which he retires from the cares of office every Saturday to Monday.

Sir Robert Bond is much interested in birds and mammals,

and has been a hunter in his day. At present he is very anxious to introduce capercailzie and black grouse into the island, and I hope in the near future to send him birds and eggs for the experiment.[1] If once they could be started, I feel certain that these splendid game birds would do well in Newfoundland, for both in summer and winter there is an abundance of the foods on which they thrive. The winters, too, are not more severe than those of their native Norway.

The *Glencoe* had been to the bottom of Hermitage Bay since I sailed on her last year, but she seemed none the worse for the ducking, except that the cabin doors would not shut; and one very proper old lady seemed to be much shocked by the fact that she could see the other passengers dressing. Captain Drake knew every submerged rock on the south coast but one, and that one he unfortunately struck on 6th June, off Ramea, and punctured the bottom of his ship. The sea poured in so quickly that there was nothing left but to beach her, which was done in dense fog. The pumps were kept working, but she settled down. Wrecking apparatus was, however, soon on the spot, when the *Glencoe* was raised, and reached St. John's on the 17th of the same month, when she was docked and repaired. Much sympathy was expressed for Captain Drake, who spends his life taking risks, and seems to be always on the bridge day and night. No one, in fact, could run a steamer in summer on the south coast in the way he does, so it is a satisfaction to all Newfoundlanders that he retains his position with the complete confidence of the public.

---

[1] By the time these lines are published the introduction of capercailzie and black grouse to Newfoundland will be an accomplished fact. Forty birds were procured by me in Norway through the agency of Mr. Lindesay, and it is hoped they will reach Newfoundland in safety. The Newfoundland Government, in bearing all the expenses, have shown a proper appreciation of the wants of local sportsmen, and all lovers of nature will wish the experiment success.

On 30th September we reached Belleoram in Fortune Bay without incident. Belleoram is like all villages of the southern outports, a delightful little sleepy hollow, nestling under stony hills and dense spruce woods. A dreamy *dolce far niente* atmosphere, suffused with the ever-present odour of drying cod, pervades the place, for it is a sort of backwash of civilisation, where the one event is the coming and going of the steamer, and the one topic of conversation the price of fish. The day was Sunday, and the good people, in clothes of funereal black, were trooping into the little wooden church. None, however, stared rudely at the stranger, but with a courteous smile the good folk wished me good morning. They will stop and talk too, with a charming lack of self-consciousness, which is one of the pleasantest traits in the Newfoundland character.

The evening brought Mr. Ryan, with his little schooner, from Long Harbor, and we sat down for a good talk on the prospects of the expedition.

Philip Ryan is a somewhat remarkable character. For forty years he has been in the service of the Anglo-American Telegraph Company, and, as his work does not entail any arduous duties, he can spend his time in farming, sport, and in doing a little trade with the Indians. He is one of the only two men whom the Indians trust and have regular dealings with, and his fairness and kindness to these nomadic people have earned for him a reputation which is only shared by Mr. Leslie[1] of Baie d'Espoir. It is no slur on his intelligence to say that he invariably gets the worst of a bargain, for he is of that rare kind which does not count success by the acquisition of money, but rather that he may do unto others

[1] Mr. Leslie has now left Newfoundland for good, and has settled in Nova Scotia.

as he would be done by. If there were more pioneers in our colonies of the stamp of Mr. Leslie and Philip Ryan, we should not hear so much of the treachery of the savage races, nor the quarrels of the native and incoming white man, for the deceit and sharp practice of traders always bring in its train the bottle and the white man's curse. To give an instance of Mr. Ryan's methods, it is enough to say that whenever he is absent from home, the key of his house is left under the door for any wandering Indian to find. The traveller may open and help himself to what he likes, taking flour, sugar, bacon, and tobacco. He lights a fire, stops in the house as long as he likes, and may not be there for another year; and yet the owner never loses so much as a darning-needle, nor does the Indian fail to render to him an accurate account of the things he has taken, and to pay for them in the skins of foxes and otters. I wonder in how many Hudson Bay stores such a state of things would be possible, and yet the managers of these posts have only themselves to blame for the loss of confidence.

Ryan's temperament is of the mercurial Irish variety un-dulled by the lapse of years; he is sixty, and the hard knocks of life, of which he has had more than his full share, have not impaired his joyous disposition. His strength and activity are extraordinary. It was blowing a good breeze. " Here," he shouted one day, as we were returning to Belleoram, "climb up to the top of that, and we'll hoist the flag of the Cariboo." Steve looked up sadly to the thin and swaying topmast, and mumbled something about not wishing to die just then. " Matty "—to the other Indian—"you're a man; shin up like a good chap." But Matty shook his head and looked sheepish.

"God bless my soul!" ejaculated the old fellow, springing

THE NEWFOUNDLAND WILLOW GROUSE.

Lagopus lagopus allent.

up, "you boys have no grit nowadays." So, throwing off
his sea-boots, he seized the line in his teeth, and clambered
up to giddy heights without a stop.

Long Harbor Office, where Ryan lives, is forty miles from
Belleoram, and it took us all day to reach our destination.
In darkness we cast anchor beside a little island. A row of
half a mile brought us to shore, where two Indians, Micky
John and Paddy Hinx, rose to greet us. They told us that
Steve Bernard and John Hinx were both on their way, the
former from Bay Despair, and the latter from his "tilt" up
to the north-east, to meet me; that I should be able to
start in two days, though no two Indians could get up the
Long Harbor River. This was rather serious news, as I
had hoped to do my trip with two Indians; however, the
difficulty was solved by the arrival on the following day of
Matty Burke and Johnny Benoit, who agreed to come with
me for seven days, and to help Bernard and Hinx with
the boats until the worst of the rapids were passed.

On 2nd October came Steve Bernard, looking considerably
the worse for wear, as the result of one of the inevitable
"sprees" which preludes such trips into the "country." But
the walk of forty-five miles had sobered him, and he was
in that frame of mind which brings a chastened spirit and
a desire for work, having wasted all his money at the shrine
of Bacchus.

Steve is the sole survivor of eleven children born to
old Joe Bernard, late chief of the Newfoundland Micmacs,
all of whom have died from the bottle, consumption, or
strains, the three principal causes which decimate the red
men. He is twenty-eight years old, as strong as a bull, and
good-natured to the highest degree. When he was not
singing mournful Indian dirges and Gregorian chants, he was

generally laughing or chaffing John Hinx or the others, and I found him an excellent guide and hunter in his own province. Like all the Indians he loved deer hunting, and soon became proficient with the telescope. His capacity for carrying heavy weights was extraordinary. "I like to take those," he said one day, making a grab at my coat, rifle, telescope and camera, which I had set aside for my own small pack, when crossing a mountain range, and flinging them on the top of his hundred-pound pack, "and when we come to the brook, you climb on top, sir." This I did by way of experiment, and the great weight seemed to trouble him as little as a fifty-pound pack would harass a white man. In the rivers he was not the equal of Jeddore, Matty Burke, or John Hinx, but the Indian nature is nothing if not acquisitive, for in a few days he worked his pole with considerable skill and untiring patience.

I spent the remainder of the day in placing my provisions in linen bags, and making all ready for a rough and watery trip, and on the morning of 3rd October, accompanied by Steve Bernard, Matty Burke, and Johnny Benoit, we made a start up the river.

Matty Burke is a half-bred Frenchman of about thirty-three. In the river he was invaluable, and very skilful with the pole. Ashore he was a splendid camp man, being a good cook and excellent woodman, as all the Indians are. In appearance he was a picturesque ruffian of the old *coureur-de-bois* type, and would have made an excellent stage villain at the Adelphi. At first he seemed to be of a somewhat suspicious nature, and was always watching me out of the corners of his eyes, but this soon wore off, and he became the gayest of the party when his buoyant Gallic nature asserted itself.

"Those very bad men, them St. Pierre policemen," said Matty suddenly, one evening, and evidently expecting me to acquiesce, for the stage villain's eyes flashed, and he was burning under the injustice of some fancied wrong.

"What did they do to you?"

"Enough—for I would kill them all could I do so. They are bad men, and take me to prison when I made not the row. Las' summer I go in a brig to St. Pierre, and one night in the café we had good times—about thirty of us—English, French, American, and Newfun'lan' fishermen. I was drunk—yes—very drunk—yet I commence not the row. Bimeby a feller pull out his knife, so I go for the door, and tumble on the wooden steps. As I come out a policeman come in, and we fall together into the street. Then the devil he grab me, and say I must go to the prison house with him, which I not like, and so resist him much. He take me by the arm, so I hit him with all my strength between the eyes, and he drop like a shot stag. Just then I try to run, but my legs are no use, when four more policemen come up and put iron things on my hands; but I fight hard and bite two of them all over, so that we are all covered with blood. Then they are too strong for me, and they put me in a cold stone house where I cannot get out, though I tried hard. In the morning I say to the man that lock the door, 'I give you four dollars if you let me out,' but he only laugh and say I must see de magistrate. Dat feller makes me pay ten dollars, all I had. The cunning rascal, he puts it in his pocket to get drunk with no doubt. It was all too bad. I done nothing, and not commence the row." Simple Matty, he could not understand that getting blind drunk and half-killing a gendarme was not the best way to behave in a foreign port.

"You should a got jailed in Harbour Breton,"[1] remarked Steve, with a sly twinkle in his eye. "That's the place to enjoy yourself. Nicholas Jeddore he got put in prison there —two falls ago—for setting de woods afire. He said he's never had so many Christmas dinners afore, an' all the people were wonderful kind. All day he could go about wherever he liked, and used to fish and make little canoes for de children. An' at night all he had to do was to go and report himself, and sleep in the most comfortable bed he'd ever seen. He was quite sorry to go home, and said next time things were rough he's goin' to ask to be took back."

Johnny Benoit was of quite a different type, a visionary boy of eighteen, with great, big, dreamy black eyes. He had the sort of expression that sees "God in clouds, and hears Him in the wind." He was very good-looking, but did not like work, partly because one of his arms was half paralysed through rolling logs when he was too young, and partly because he had fallen over a precipice two years previously and been half-killed. But he was a nice, amiable creature, and with his dislike for labour, quaint thoughts, and sweet far-away expression, would have made a successful minor poet at home.

The first few miles of the river were easy, so I worked in the big canoe, and we made good progress with our poles. Towards evening, however, the stream became shallow and rocky, and we had a taste of what the Long Harbor River was like—endless falls, boiling runs, and sudden "drops" where lifts were necessary. At sunset we reached a very bad place above a birchy island, where a portage of everything for half a mile landed us on a high shelf of rocks, where we made

[1] The Government prison on the south coast.

NEWFOUNDLAND MICMACS

HOW TO CARRY A HEAD TO CAMP

camp for the night. As we sat at supper a shout in the woods announced the advent of Johnny Hinx, who arrived tired and cheerful after a thirty-five mile walk from his "tilt."

John Hinx, a typical half-breed of an English father and Indian mother, is one of the most experienced men in the island. He has been all over the south and central portions, and has made his living by trapping and log-cutting since he was ten years of age, and is now fifty, though in appearance he might have passed for thirty-five. He became my cook and camp man, but was, nevertheless, an excellent hunter, and always accompanied Steve and me on our tramps after deer, when his sharp eyes were sometimes responsible for some outlying stag which we had overlooked. He possessed a great knowledge of the deer and their movements, and what he did not know of otters and otter-trapping was not of much account. He was tall and good-looking, spoke broken English, and, being fearful of being misunderstood, was at first somewhat reticent, but as time wore on he would chatter as freely as Steve, and entertain us with tales of flood and forest that always had some interesting point. One night he told me a story that was in itself an object-lesson, as illustrating the reasons why the red man hates and distrusts the white.

When John Hinx was eighteen he was the sole support of a widowed mother and a sister in Baie d'Espoir, so he hired himself to the boss of a mill in Gambo for a year at twenty dollars a month. In the spring he cut logs, in summer he cooked daily for a large camp of thirty men, and in the fall he shot deer and carried them on his back to camp. The year went by, and he demanded his money, wishing to return home, but after promises of increased wages he was induced to stop another nine months, and to work harder than ever; always, too, with the thought of how pleased his mother would be when she saw her son again with plenty of money in his pocket. At last the time came when he would stay no longer, so he demanded his wages, and prepared to travel. What was his consternation when the mill manager said he was quite unable to pay him a cent, and that he must wait until better times. The excuse given was that two cargoes of lumber had been lost in transit to St. John's (these Hinx ascertained afterwards had safely reached St. John's, and been sold at a good price). Weary, dispirited, and without food or money, the poor Indian set out in the dead of winter to cross the island, from Gambo to Conn River, nine days' hard walking. The snow fell unceasingly, the deer were all away to the south, and with ragged clothes, and madness in his brain, he tramped the long trail like some hungry wolf ranging the winter forests. More dead than alive he reached his mother's home at last. Thirty years have gone by since those days, but the bitterness of it all still remained in the Indian trapper's heart, and I should not like to be that cheat of the Gambo mill if John Hinx were to meet him alone in the woods one day. It is possible that the account might be settled.

The night of 3rd October was the coldest I have experienced in the island. Fifteen degrees of frost were registered, and everything — eggs, butter, &c. — was frozen solid; but on the following morning a bright sun, playing on the jewelled leaves and grasses, caused a thaw, and the Indians were able to make fair headway in the worst river I have seen in Newfoundland. It is a very bad stream, where Indians have to get overboard and haul the canoe by main force through the cold water, but this they had to do the whole of 4th October, and the three following days. Yet with wonderful patience and good nature they worried on at their task, whilst Johnny Benoit, who was little use in the river, and I marched ahead over the bare open hills of sand and stone, and looked for mythical willow grouse. The Indians were dying for fresh meat, and I did my best to find game of some sort, and the only luck I achieved was on 5th October, when I encountered a covey of six grouse, all of which I killed by blowing their heads off with bullets from the Mannlicher. Fortunately they were very tame, and only flew a short distance after I had killed the first two, when the remainder sat on a rock and stared within ten yards before meeting their fate.

Until recently the willow grouse (*Lagopus terra-novæ*) was very abundant in Newfoundland, and his cheery call, so like that of our own grouse, could be heard at all seasons in the barrens near the coast. In October the sportsmen of St. John's are accustomed to go for a few days' shooting to the barrens about Placentia, St. Mary's Bay—in fact, to all the accessible parts of the south coast—and to hunt in company with some local guide and a brace or two of pointers and setters. Until 1903 excellent sport was to be had, as many as twenty and even thirty brace being killed in a day; but of recent years a great diminution has taken place amongst the birds, for now eight to ten brace would be considered a good bag in the best places. Many reasons have been assigned for this depreciation in the stock, but none of them seem to explain matters satisfactorily. In fact, everything is in favour of the grouse, since predatory animals, their chief foes, are becoming very scarce, and no one molests the birds during the breeding season. Over-shooting will not give the correct answer, because the grouse are now just as sparsely distributed through the immense tracts of unshot ground, where formerly they were exceedingly abundant, as in the places where the gunners go.   Mr. Leslie[1] attributes the scarcity of grouse in the interior to forest fires, and has several times seen coveys overwhelmed and stupefied by the smoke.   Certainly in the course of my travels in the central parts of the island, I have seen but two coveys of grouse and one covey of the rare Newfoundland ptarmigan (*Lagopus Leachii*).   Only in the barrens between the upper parts of the Long Harbor and Mount Sylvester have I seen a fair stock of grouse.   I think that a series of cold and wet summers following in succession have had much to do with the inadequate supply of birds.

The habits of the Newfoundland willow grouse are identical with the Dal Ripa of Norway, which are too well known to need any description.   These western birds are, however, much tamer, but are similar in their migratory habits, or, it would be more correct to say, local movements.   At times they fly in large bodies from one district to another, and often visit the outer islands on the east coast, some far from land, such as the Groais Islands.

The Newfoundland ptarmigan (*Lagopus Leachii*) is now becoming a somewhat scarce and local species.   It exists in most of the mountains near the coast in Hermitage Bay, on the Iron Skull in Fortune Bay, and in the Long Range Mountains and hills between Victoria and Red Indian Lakes. It is slightly smaller than the European species, but its habits are similar.

On this day the river became so impossible just above a large waterfall, that we had to resort to a portage of one

---

[1] Mr. Leslie has seen caribou in winter digging out the moss, and followed by a crowd of willow grouse.   As soon as the deer vacated the holes the birds dived in to get at the partridge-berries.

MICMAC INDIANS PACKING

John Hinx and Steve Bernard are seen carrying over 120 lbs. a-piece, and yet how jolly they look. With such a weight they will tramp all day.

and a half miles to clear the worst of the rocks. In consequence, our progress was very slow—sometimes not more than four or five miles per diem were made.

On the upper part of the Long Harbor River I noticed considerable quantities of a coarse native wild hay, of such a quality, too, that ponies would thrive upon it during the summer months. On the Gander it is found in abundance for the first twenty miles, but disappears immediately above "Rolling Falls," where the country becomes more high and exposed. It is also found in quantities in the Gould Valley (Conception Bay), and about Colinet (St. Mary's Bay), whilst the people of the west coast bring down boat-loads every autumn from Codroy, Fischel's, Robinson's, St. George's, and the Humber Rivers. I have seen a few horses on the Gander in very good condition through living on this native hay, and there is no reason why pony-raising should not be a profitable industry amongst the people of the south and west coast, *if they would only import and breed the right kind of pony*. A few of these animals are bred on the west coast— poor weedy beasts, which are destined to transportation for life in the Cape Breton coal mines, and all they are fitted for. But a better class of horse is needed, one something of the rough nature of the Welsh pony or the Norwegian carriole pony, which could live hard, stand snow and bad times, possess some pace, and pick up quickly in the spring and summer on native grass and plants.

The prospect of a better river in a day or two soon put us in good spirits. The worst was over, said John, and we should only encounter two more days of rough water before finding "steadies" and the inevitable chain of lakes which intersect the summit of the plateaux. All night long the Indians sat up in their stuffy little "tilt," alternately eating, stitching fresh moccasins, and chattering in their mellifluous dialect. Sometimes they slept an hour or two, and then rose again to replenish the fires and roast bits of grouse. The next day, however, heralded in a deluge, with equinoctial gales which lasted all day. I went out for several miles on to a high stony country, and found deer plentiful, seeing two old stags and fifty-four does. We crossed the river twice, which took Steve to his waist as he ferried me over, and returned in the evening soaked to the skin by the drenching rain.

The next day was fine, so we started for the north again, encountering numerous rapids and small waterfalls, but in the evening some welcome "steadies" appeared, and we paddled up these until we reached the first of the chain of little lakes known to the Indians as "Podopsk." October 10th saw the last of our struggles with the river, when at midday we arrived at a fine lake which has no title, and which I have named "Lake Prowse," after the Judge. It is a fair-sized sheet of water, about two and a half miles long, in the shape of an equilateral triangle. The left bank is clothed in heavy woods, almost the first we had seen since leaving Long Harbor, and a single large island, a mile long, exists on the east side. Fortunately, there was only a gentle breeze at our backs, so we made good time over the open waters, and, after hauling up over heavy rapids at the north end, finished our canoe journey for a time. Here Matty Burke and Johnny Benoit left us for their trapping-grounds in the neighbour-hood of the "Tolt" Mountain, about thirty miles to the south-east. They promised to help us down the river at the beginning of November.

My plan was now to "cache" the greater part of my provisions under the two canoes, and to carry as much as possible away to the west over the range known to the

Indians as the *Kesoquit* Hills, and to make my outside camps in a droke of woods amongst these mountains, and another still farther to the west in another droke on Shoe Hill Ridge, in the centre of Steve's trapping-ground. Steve had told me that the latter position commanded wide views for miles, which embraced an area to the north from Maelpeg to Mount Sylvester, and along which the main body of travelling deer came every fall. Both these camps would also be central for making expeditions into the unknown territory to the north-east and west.

CHAPTER XV

OPEN-GROUND HUNTING ON THE SHOE HILL AND KESOQUIT RIDGES

THE whole character of the country from Fortune Bay to Mount Sylvester is different from that of any other part of the island which I have seen, except the immediate neighbourhood of Partridgeberry Hill, in Central Newfoundland. The landscape is open, with rolling hills stretching away to the distant horizon. Here and there are little rocky eminences, locally designated as "knaps," from which miles of country may be easily spied. Marshes are few and small, and the whole ground is covered with reindeer moss, with a few blueberry patches. Sometimes one sees a sprinkling of scattered larches from seven to ten feet high, whilst tiny spruce forests, of some dwarf variety which never exceeds three and a half feet in height, cover many of the summits of the ridges. At a distance these little spruce woods look like grass or moss, and they are of such small stature that a passage between them looks easy; but if you are so unfortunate as to find your way into their midst, nothing remains but retreat, or a short cut to the nearest hard ground, for the deceptive bush is a mass of interlaced boughs of great strength, which makes progression extremely arduous, and at times impossible. No Indian walks through "tufts," as these dwarf forests are called, unless he is forced to do so, and the employment of Steve, who knows every deer and rabbit path in Shoe Hill and Kesoquit, was the means of avoiding much arduous labour.

THE MIDDAY SLEEP ON THE LAKE EDGE

DURING THE RUT THE HERD STAG REMAINS FOR MANY HOURS EACH DAY
IN THIS CURIOUS ATTITUDE

On the whole, the walking in this district was the best I have ever seen in any country where big game are to be found. During three weeks' hunting I never had wet feet, although only shod in ordinary shooting boots. Nor did I ever feel tired, although we had some long days and protracted runs to cut off travelling stags.

After an excellent dinner, and having deposited all our spare stores under the canoes, the Indians shouldered two huge packs of about 100 lbs. each, and we started up the Kesoquit Hills. The summit of the range was about 400 feet above the river, and from this point we obtained a splendid view in all directions except the north. The Tolt and the three hills above Long Harbor were plainly visible, and on this day, one of exceptional brightness, the rugged headland above Belleoram, known as the Iron Skull, was plainly visible. As we "took a spell" I worked the glass for some time, and only found a few small deer. The absence of stags was explained by Steve by the fact that the ground was too full of "tufts," which deer dislike as much as man.

Then came a walk over an ideal hunting-ground of great rolling corries, intersected by little lakes and marshes, which brought us to the only wood in the district south of the Maelpeg. It is known as Kesoquit "droke." Here for many years has been the hunting quarters of the Johns,[1] although it is now abandoned by them, and only the rough log "tilt" being used as a rest-house by Steve Bernard and Micky John on their travels to and fro. The place was a perfect one for a camp, as the wood was full of dry sticks, and there was a small lake at one side. Here one only had to run a few yards to the west where a fine view of one of the

---

[1] The Johns are an old family of Mountaineer Indians which came originally from Labrador.

best valleys for deer in Newfoundland spreads itself out for miles.

Along these valleys and hills deer were constantly passing, and during the rutting season a company or two were generally in view at any time of day from our look-out. Close to the camp was the greater part of a doe which Micky John had killed in the previous week, so I spent the next day in walking to the Great Maelpeg Lake, and following the course of two other unnamed lakes, which connect this large sheet of water with Prowse's Lake, and doing some mapping. We saw several stags, with herds of does numbering from five to twelve individuals, and they were all very tame and unsophisticated, as the wind was strong. In the evening it commenced to rain in the usual Newfoundland fashion, and we were glad to spread my waterproof sheet over the leaky "tilt" and so make things snug. For three days abominable weather, accompanied by damp fog, continued, so there was nothing to do but sit at home and wait for the weather to improve. On the 15th it cleared up, and we received a visit from Micky John and a little boy of nine—his nephew, named Steve John—who were on their way to Sambadesta (St. John's Lake), where they meant to spend the fall trapping "wood-cats" (martens). Between them they had a broken gun, no tent-sheet, and about enough provisions to last, with a stretch, a fortnight. They arrived soaked to the skin, but in nowise discouraged, for the disposition of these nomads is nothing if not hopeful, and they would talk of no other subject but the pile of skins they hoped to gather. With them came Johnny Hinx, my John's youngest son, a boy of eighteen, a splendidly set-up young fellow, happy in the possession of two hungry-looking dogs and a gun as long as himself.

We all broke camp on the morning of the 16th, each

party going in a different direction. For three hours we held due west over the top of the Shoe Hill Range, finally dropping down to a snug droke where I intended to make my main hunting camp. The day was very fine, and I saw two very large stags, with poor heads, and again in the evening two more, each with his band of does. All these I approached and examined at close range to observe their movements for some time. Nearly every company had a "watch" doe, which did not feed, but kept gazing in different directions all the time. The big stag at this season takes little notice of man even if he sees him, and if you grunt at him, he will come running in your direction to answer your challenge, but he invariably stops at some distance, as if loath to leave his wives, towards whom he frequently glances, whereas an "unattached" stag—that is, one travelling and on the look-out for fresh does —will not only answer your call, but will come right up to within a few yards of your position. I proved this many times during this fall, and was so successful in "tolling" two of these travelling stags, that I had to heave rocks at them to keep them off.

Immediately the leading doe gives the signal of alarm, the stag is the first to appreciate its true import. The does are full of curiosity, and wish to stop and gaze at the strange individual; but the stag knows only too well what the danger is, so he bends his neck, rounds up his harem, and rattles them off at full gallop whether they wish it or not. During these preliminary evolutions the young stag, which usually hangs on the outskirts of every troop, tries to do a little love-making on his own account by running away with some of the fair ones. The speed and activity of the master-stag are then worth seeing. He rushes madly at the rash youngster, who is always just too quick for him, and so they race over the hills in a ding-dong chase, until the big fellow finds he has achieved a moral victory.

The country to the west, known as Shoe Hill, forms itself into a great basin, in the centre of which was a lake, which I have named Shoe Hill Lake. On all sides of this piece of water the ground, which is quite open and stony, like Norwegian reindeer country, rises to several hundred feet, except to the west, where the land falls abruptly to the big lake, known in Howley's map as "Jubilee" Lake, and to the Indians as "Sandy Pond." Seated on the ridge, about one mile to the west of Shoe Hill droke, we could survey the whole of this vast amphitheatre, and during the next few days I found there many a fine stag with his attendant wives. By watching from various points with the telescope, I could pick up three stags to one that the Indians could see, even with their sharp eyes, so that Steve acknowledged the superiority of the glass and was industrious in learning its use. I found that on sitting down to spy, far the best plan was to survey the whole of the lake edges and then to take every small marsh in turn in the vicinity of the water. The reasons for the deer halting and resting at midday on the shores is explained by the fact that they travel all night from some distant point and are stopped by any large sheet of water, which they do not like to cross at night. At dawn the does begin feeding on the moss, and as the sun warms all things, they lie down and rest for several hours, or stand motionless with drooping ears. In spite of their size, it is not always easy to detect them, so well do their brown coats harmonise with stones. Often a herd remains in the same spot for several days if undisturbed.

It was some days before I found a stag with a fine head. I was watching a restless old fellow trying to move his

JOHN HINX AND A LARGE THIRTY-FIVE POINTER

harem from the lake edge, a proceeding they seemed to resent, being both warm and comfortable. But a four-year-old had just gone by and had made the master jealous and uneasy, so he went gently poking one fair lady after another with his long, spindly horns, and as fast as he got one up and moved to another, the disturbed one treated him to a look of contempt and lay down again. He gave it up at last, and scratched his head with his hind foot as much as to say, "It's no use arguing with the women."

"I tink those haliboo" (deer), said John, pointing his finger towards a lot of white spots that looked like stones two miles away on the ridge above Sandy Pond. The glass was upon them, and proved that the Indian was right. Fifteen does all asleep, and one great stag, with massive horns, lying in the middle.

It was just like a stalk in Scotland. We ascended the hill, and again took a look at the herd. The stag alone was awake now, and, with his head up, was looking about in an uneasy manner. What a noble fellow, and certainly the largest framed head I had yet seen. If only both his brows were as good as the one great shovel I saw on the left horn, he must be everything a hunter could desire. But alas, as he turned to me I saw the common hook that did duty for the left brow, and knew he was deficient in one respect.

However, the head was a great massive one, and I meant to kill him if possible, so we hurried on to get nearer in case the wind should drop. When within 600 yards of the ridge on which the deer lay, we encountered one of those awful little forests of tufts, through which it was absolutely necessary to force one's way, unless we were prepared for a mile circuit. It was only about 300 yards broad, but held us in its octopus

arms every yard of the way till we arrived breathless and
bathed in perspiration on the other side.   After this we took
a short spell to get cool, and then, again circling round more
isolated patches of spruce, we decided that the deer were
now up-wind and immediately below us.   So down we went,
keeping a sharp look-out.

Being in front, I soon detected the horns of the stag as
he moved along, keeping the does together.   They were all
passing slowly to the west, most of the does feeding, and
would cross our front about 150 yards to the left.   Being
on the sky-line it was now necessary for us to crawl some
distance without being seen, when we found that the only
cover consisted of a belt of spruce fully three feet high,
over which the shot must be taken.   Slowly the does, led
by an old, hornless female, came walking up the hill, stopping
at intervals to crop the moss and gaze about, and after what
seemed an age, the great stag, with lowered head, came
"nosing" along on their tracks.   I raised myself to look over
the spruce, when one of the does saw me, and began moving
about with bristling stern, a sure sign of danger.   The others
at once took the hint and gave a preliminary rush.   On
standing again, the stag was completely surrounded by does at
a distance of 100 yards, so I could not shoot until the whole
company were again on the move.   It was not long before
they strung out prior to leaving for good, when I fired from
the shoulder, standing up, and struck the stag high in the
neck, but without breaking it.   He shook his head and spun
round once or twice, and then dashed off after the retreating
herd.   For one moment he gave me a broadside, when I
fired again and dropped him stone dead, with a bullet at the
side of the skull.   The horns of this stag were better than
I had at first supposed them to be.   They were as massive

as any that can be found in the island, and the whole head would have been an extraordinary one but for the hooky point that did duty for the right brow.

After taking off the head, we rested and had dinner in the rain above *Walnamkiak* (Jubilee Lake), where Steve had his trapping tilt, and then, moving eastward, it cleared up, and Steve made a splendid spy, fully two and a half miles away, of a big herd of deer, with two large stags. Although we had been marching since daybreak, none of us were tired, so we at once set off over ground full of rocks and moss towards the lake of *Keskitpegawi*, where Steve had seen the game. If you want to be successful in Newfoundland, or anywhere else for that matter, you must not mind walking, even if it often leads to no result. In this case the stags were both old beasts with poor horns; one of them had broken his right antler in the centre of the beam, and was the first of nine stags which I afterwards saw similarly disfigured. In Scotland adult red stags only fight occasionally, whereas the reindeer males all fight whenever the opportunity occurs, and their horns being more brittle than those of red deer, wapiti, or moose, they are often devoid of points or pieces of the horns at the end of the rutting season. Nearly every adult stag had a point or two knocked off by the end of October, and one stag that I observed on 3rd November had both horns broken off close to the burr.

After remaining for some days at Shoe Hill, we decided to go on a three days' tramp to Mount Sylvester, to ascend the mountain and to hunt for fresh ground. The Indians were quite as interested at the prospect of visiting Sylvester as myself, as neither of them had been there, and both regarded the hill with a certain superstitious veneration. It is a saying amongst them that he who visits Sylvester *for the first time*[1] and leaves a present there, in the little black cave near the top, will obtain his desire—whatever it may be. In this dark retreat dwells the spirit of the mountain, who takes no heed of rich or poor, and receives with favour the gift, however trifling, provided it is given with reverence. As the visitors to Sylvester, red or white, number about half a dozen, the fortunate people in Newfoundland are reduced to a negligible quantity. However, the superstition is firmly imprinted in the Indian mind, and they would resent as an affront the attitude of any one who doubted the efficacy of the spirit's power.[2]

The distance to the mountain from our camp was about seven miles, and as it was a bright warm day with a fresh breeze from the west, the Indians made light of their heavy packs, and stepped along as fast as I cared to walk. Three miles to the north we skirted the lake of Keskitpegawi, where we passed two fine herds of caribou resting on the lake edge, and, continuing our journey, were about to take dinner on the bridge of land that separates this lake from Tamnapegawi, when I saw a big stag standing up on a knoll close to the last-named sheet of water. Leaving John Hinx to light a fire and prepare dinner, Steve and I made a wide circuit of half a mile and then dropped down a gentle slope covered with small spruce to within 300 yards of the herd. Here I had a good look at the stag's head, which, though not large, seemed well furnished with points. After a long survey I decided to let him go, so sent Steve to move the deer, whilst I ensconced myself in an angle of the lake along which I felt certain the stag must pass.

---

[1] Subsequent visits and presents are said to be of no use.

[2] As far as I could ascertain, Mount Sylvester is the only place in Newfoundland about which the Micmacs have any superstitions.

I CALLED THIS STAG TO WITHIN TEN YARDS OF THE CAMERA

THE LOVE CHASE

Thus I hoped to obtain a good photograph, as both the light and the wind were favourable. I had hardly got into position when the does got up and raced past me, and then, seeing the stag about to follow, I saw his horns facing me for the first time. As he came on he looked better and better, so at last I put down the camera and picked up the rifle, not a moment too soon, when I killed him with a shot as he went by. He proved to be a good thirty-nine pointer, with thick, though somewhat short horns.

After dinner we entered a different country to the bare stony ridges of Shoe Hill. Now it was all rolling hills, with small forests on either flank, and numerous little ponds and marshes, perfect early autumn deer ground. By-and-by I saw a big stag chasing two or three does out of one of these woods, and by a judicious cross cut caught him with the camera at twenty yards as he pursued his restless wives.

This stalking with a camera is great fun. You have many failures, and a few successes, whilst the best chance always occurs on a rainy day or when the camera has been left in camp. One evening, about a fortnight after this, I saw a small calf on a stony ridge above a lake. As it kept looking back into a deep hollow, I knew the mother and probably others were there. It was blowing hard, so Steve and I got within five yards of the calf just as it threw up its tail and dashed off down-wind. Now, the mother and a great heavy stag who was her companion had just caught a glimpse of the white flag when it was raised, and so started to pursue the path followed by the calf. Steve and I lay behind a large boulder directly in their path, so that the pair actually passed our station at a distance of three yards—a unique opportunity for a picture which could not be taken. As it was, I threw my hat on to the stag's back, where it rested a moment, to his complete consternation. Sometimes I "tolled" travelling stags, and photographed them within a short distance; but most of these were failures, as they were generally taken in the early morning. However, I got one or two successes, as well as taking a fine stag within a few yards as he lay asleep. If you have patience, are a skilled stalker, and are favoured by a strong wind, you can do what you like with the stag, *provided he is alone.*[1]

We were now within two miles of Sylvester, and had ascended a wooded hill and looked over when a lovely scene burst upon our view. A deep valley, crowned with heavy timber on each side, lay before us. At the base was a huge marsh two miles in length, whilst beyond it, Sylvester, in all its beauty, sprang directly out of the earth in one great cone. The lower slopes were densely wooded, but within 300 feet of the summit it was quite bare, and precipitous on the south side. The sun was setting and flooded the whole landscape with gold, disclosing three large companies of caribou, each governed by a master-stag. It was a scene that I shall always remember; one that the hunter sees in his dreams but seldom experiences, and which will live in the memory when my hunting days are past.

Our prayers for a calm day to ascend Sylvester were answered, and we were up before daybreak, on one of the finest days I can remember. There was just a touch of

[1] Speaking of the extraordinary tameness of single deer when carefully approached, Cormack says (p. 32): "A single deer on the plain, when there are no others near to sound the alarm, may be approached and knocked down by a blow on the head with an axe or tomahawk from a dexterous hunter. We happened to see a solitary stag amusing himself by rubbing his antlers against a larch-tree on a plain; my Indian, treading lightly, approached him from behind, and struck him on the head with his axe, but did not knock him down; he of course galloped off."

ASLEEP

frost, and as the sun rose I was out on a point of rock surveying the herds of deer far below our camp, and watching the golden light steal up the green and slate slopes of the mountain. We made an early start, as it was two miles to the base of the mountain. Whilst travelling I had already spied and rejected the three master-stags we had seen the night before. Whilst crossing the great marsh I saw two stags fighting on the side of Sylvester, but they retired into the wood, and we lost sight of them.

Near the north end of the marsh, and just at the base of the mountain, were situated the most remarkable deer trails I have seen in Newfoundland. These roads all debouched from one main road as wide and deep as a Devonshire lane. This path, we found, came right over the eastern shoulder of Mount Sylvester, and was the main "fall" trail which is trodden by tens of thousands of hurrying feet every November. W. Cormack, who was the first man to discover Sylvester, which he named after his faithful Indian follower, bore testimony to the abundance of deer trails at this point, and doubtless there is little alteration since the days when he wrote (1822). The path led upwards over the mountain for several hundred feet, and then branched to the left, where the side of the hill was cut into shallow chasms about 30 feet deep, in which grew spruces and vars. The ascent now became steep, and for the last 400 feet the mountain was bare, or covered with small Alpine flora. Near the top we visited the little black cave where the "spirit" of the mountain dwelt, and each of us deposited our offering in the shape of coins and cartridges.

Steve's wish was grossly material, and went no farther than a suit of new clothes; I naturally desired a fifty-pointer;

T

whilst John was distinctly romantic, and went as far as to hope for a new wife on whom he had already fixed his affections somewhere down in Baie d'Espoir. Steve's wish was realised, and mine too, in a measure, for the kindly ghost, although he did not actually produce a fifty-pointer, gave me what was probably the best head in Central Newfoundland, whilst from the last accounts I heard of John, he was making the running at such a terrific pace that no girl, however fastidious, was likely to withstand him.

The view from the top of this beautiful mountain is one of the best in Newfoundland. It was a clear day, and we could see nearly seventy miles in every direction. It seems as if a line had been drawn across the island, clearly cutting off all the forest and marsh country to the north and west from the bare and open stony hills of the south. To the north and north-west was the long line of the Middle Ridge clothed in a great sea of dense woods which stretch without a break from Burnt Hill on the Gander to Glenwood, Terra-Nova, and Cloete Sound to the east. Here and there dark patches of the highest woods crop up round St. John's Lake and N'Moochwaygodie (Bond's Lake), a large pond about five miles to the west of St. John's Lake, and the last unvisited and unmapped lake of any size in Eastern Newfoundland. About fifteen miles to the north-east are two ranges of low hills, known to the Indians as Smooth Ridge and Burnt Hills, and leading up to these and connected also with Kagudeck is a brook which passes through three small lakes which I have named Steve Bernard's, John Hinx's, and John Stride's Ponds, the last-named being the hunting-ground of the trapper of that name. Due east, in the open country, is the large lake known to the Indians as the (Eastern) Maelpeg (the lake of many indentations). It has never been properly surveyed,

DAWN—A SUCCESSFUL SNAP-SHOT AT 6 A.M., OCTOBER 30, 1906

A GOOD HEAD

as Mr. Howley had not time to do this on his short visit to
Sylvester, and it would take a man three weeks to mark
all its sinuous bays and hundred islands. To the south-east
were the lakes of Keskitpegawi, Tamnapegawi,[1] and another
small one about a mile long, whilst close under the mountain
were three other ponds of moderate size. Kagudeck, where
Reuben Lewis hunts, is a large lake surrounded by heavy
woods, and is situated about five miles to the west, and by
means of the Bay de Nord waters it would not be difficult
to ascend from Fortune Bay to this lake, and so on to Smooth
Ridge, where the head waters of the Terra-Nova rise, and
so pass eastwards down St. John's Lake and Mollygojack
to the sea.

I remained for some hours on the summit, enjoying the
lovely view and sketching in the various features of the
landscape. Tiny little spots of white and brown away at
the base of the mountain to the north showed two companies
of deer, each with a big stag, restlessly wandering from one
forest to another. About 2 P.M. we grew chilly from inaction,
and so descended to the woods and had an excellent dinner.
In the evening we again crossed the big marsh towards our
camp, and spent some time in watching a stag chasing a
doe in and out of the woods. He seemed to carry a fine
head, but when at last I obtained a good view with the
glass, the result was disappointing. From our camp I spied
the big herd which had settled by a small lake about a mile
to the west. This was the largest herd of breeding deer—
eighteen does and one big stag with a bad head—I had
seen; but a newcomer had joined them since the morning,
and I was anxious to inspect him at close quarters. The
stag which had lately arrived was quite hornless—in fact a

---

[1] I have retained the Indian names for these waters.

"hummel," or "nott," as these hornless stags are called in Newfoundland. He was an immense beast, quite the largest stag I saw on this trip, and did not appear to have a vestige of horn or even the knobs which denote the presence of pedicles. In Scotland the "hummel" is generally the master of any horned stag, and few can withstand him; but in this case the hornless stag hung around for more than two hours, watching an opportunity to dash off with some of the does, but without success, for the horned master seemed to inspire him with considerable fear. Next morning he had gone.

The perfect Indian summer continued as we started on our return journey to Shoe Hill Ridge. It was a hot day, and the men seemed to feel their heavy packs for the first time. We had passed several small troops of deer, and were making our way over the land bridge between Keskitpegawi and Tamnapegawi, having almost reached the spot where we had left the head of the thirty-nine pointer, when Steve, who was in front at the moment, suddenly stopped, looked up, and said, "Haliboo—steks—haskajit" (Deer, a stag, a very big one).

I looked, but could see nothing but some horns sticking out of a small forest of dwarf spruces about 200 yards away. Thinking that Steve was playing some joke because the horns were lying on one side, like those of a dead stag, I sat down and pretended to have been taken in, laughing the while. But Steve was serious, and the glass showed at once that the horns were of great size, and, by their colour, like those worn by a living deer. We left the packs and crept within 100 yards. The stag was either dead or dog-tired and fast asleep, for nothing moved when I whistled. I now made a mistake and went up to within 50 yards, always a foolish thing to do, as the close proximity of

GREAT DEER ROAD NEAR MOUNT SYLVESTER

THE SUMMIT OF MOUNT SYLVESTER, SHOWING THE
LITTLE BLACK CAVE

man is apt to scare a deer when it is lying down, especially an old stag. We waited half-an-hour, but the stag refused to move, then at last he lifted his horns and showed the whole of his bays, tops and brows, after a perfect chorus of whistles and grunts on our part. What a head! It must be the best in Newfoundland, such middle palms as neither I nor the Indians had ever seen before. I blessed the Sylvester spook and sat down on Steve's knee—a second error—and prepared to take the shot, for I could not see over the "tufts" without some such support.

If nothing will move a stolid deer, the snapping of a stick is nearly always effectual. John pulled over a rotten branch, and the stag at once sprang to his feet and bolted at full speed. I fired and missed handsomely, but stood up and prepared for a second shot, as I felt sure he would stand before his final departure. It was as I thought. The noble fellow sprang round to take a last look, at about 120 yards, and had scarcely stopped when, concentrating all my forces to be steady, I pressed the trigger and planted a bullet through the lungs. There was a satisfactory "plunk," the forty-five pointer reeled, threw up his head, and then fell to the ground quite dead.

How we rushed up to survey our prize, what mutual congratulations passed, what encomiums were lavished on the Spirit of the Mountain, and what a talk we had on big heads, I leave the reader to imagine. Neither the Indians nor myself had seen such wonderful middle palms—twenty-two large points on the two.

The sun was shining brilliantly, so I managed to take some excellent photographs, and the day being still young, we sat and skinned the head and enjoyed an excellent dinner, after which the Indians skinned and cleaned the

shanks for moccasins. About one o'clock we resumed our
journey, John carrying the big head, and Steve the thirty-
nine pointer, which we now recovered. Exceptional luck
had favoured us on this little trip to Sylvester, but more
good fortune was in store before the evening closed
in. About 3 P.M. I spied a large company of deer, with
a very big master-stag, which after some discussion we
decided to spare. Then we ran right on the top of a
fine stag with three does, about two miles from Shoe Hill
and close to the southern end of Keskitpegawi, and whilst
I was watching these, Steve spied no fewer than three
scattered companies upon a hill to the east, about two miles
away. One troop was exactly on the sky-line, and with the
aid of the glass I could see that it contained an exceptionally
fine stag with splendid tops. Evening was closing in, and
the walk would take us at least five miles out of our way
from camp, wherefore I sent John on the road home, and
with Steve relieved of his pack, made all speed for the hills.
The walking here was splendid—a great deal better than
the principal streets of Montreal—so we made good time, in
spite of a considerable circuit to gain the wind, and to avoid
scattered deer which appeared in all directions.

When we arrived at the ridge and looked for our deer
they had moved, so we worked up-wind for some distance
before we struck them travelling over the sky-line towards
Kesoquit. Two of the does looked scared and kept running
a few yards, so they may have caught a glimpse of us
as we ascended the hill, but the stag was very active and
would not let them run, and thus played into our hands. The
country, however, was perfectly bare and open, and I could
not, even after much running and manoeuvring, get nearer
than 200 yards, at which distance the master-stag offered me

MASSIVE THIRTY-FIVE POINTER SHOT NEAR JUBILEE LAKE,
OCTOBER 1906

MOUNT SYLVESTER

a broadside. I tried to get nearer and nearly lost my chance, as the leading does ran and he prepared to follow. Seeing that it was a case of now or never, I lay down, and taking the 200 yards sight very full, pulled, and heard the bullet strike. The stag ran a few yards after the herd and then stopped, when a second bullet, hitting him high in the neck, dropped him on the spot. In the evening and on the sky-line his horns had appeared to be exceptional, but on closer inspection they proved to be very good, but not so good as I had hoped. Yet to kill two first-class heads in one day in Newfoundland is a feat I had not previously achieved, and the days when such an event happens are rare indeed.

After gralloching, we left the stag where it fell, recovering the head some days afterwards, for Steve had his load and the big head to take to camp, where we arrived in the darkness. John had, however, made a roaring fire, and we sat long, talking over the events of this eventful day.

Since the beginning of things, man has had three dominant passions : to make love, to go to war, and to hunt wild beasts. Whilst time is teaching us that the second of these is not always an unmixed blessing nor an advantage, although we must ever be prepared for it, the first and third will remain with us until the crack of doom. There is a quiet satisfaction in the soul of the hunter who successfully overcomes the beasts of the chase, which not all the arguments of dilettanti and cognoscenti can influence. The healthy life, the excitement, and the freedom from care, once tasted, appeal with ever-increasing force to men—I mean strong men, who have seen all sides of life—for it contains the *essentials* of happy existence, and man, whatever he may be, will always follow the primal laws till the end of the chapter.

CHAPTER XVI

WANDERINGS ABOUT LAKE MAELPEG AND MOUNT SYLVESTER

DURING the following week four or five companies of deer with their attendant stags were seen daily, but the last week of the month signalised the close of the rutting season, and partial abandonment of the does by the stags. In some cases two or three master-stags could be seen with the herds, and these, though still looking at each other with jealous eyes, did not come to actual blows. One day at the north-eastern end of Keskitpegawi, my favourite hunting-ground, I saw three companies within half a mile of one another, and as I was watching a good thirty-pointer, he suddenly left his does and walked off in the direction of another troop. I followed quickly, hoping to see a grand battle, but was disappointed. The travelling stag commenced feeding as soon as he reached the fresh deer, and the master-stag, a very big fellow with fine double brows, took very little notice of him, except to give a few savage grunts of disapproval. After careful consideration, I decided to shoot this stag if I could get within shot. It proved to be a somewhat difficult stalk, as it was snowing hard and the does were scattered about in every direction on a perfectly open savannah. The wind, however, was blowing strong, and one can take liberties under such circumstances. Accordingly Steve and I crept in swiftly through the middle of the scattered does, and relied on their temporary confusion to effect a rapid advance. Whilst doing so, the Indian suddenly

A Great Stag.

observed a fresh stag advancing from the north along the lake shore, and accordingly we lay flat right in the midst of the deer, which were by this time very uneasy. I could not use the glass, but a temporary clearing gave us a glimpse of the newcomer's head, which was large but not remarkable. At this point we obtained some slight cover from a few "tufts," so, running swiftly forward whilst the does bunched together and stared at us, I got within 150 yards of the master-stag, and laid him low with a bullet behind the shoulder.

At the shot five more deer appeared on a knoll about 150 yards to the left, amongst which was a three-year-old stag. This the Indians desired me to shoot, for the purpose of making wading-boots to be used in descending the river. Accordingly I lay down again, and was successful in striking the deer through the heart, at which he ran about sixty yards and then fell.

There were some big stumps of dry wood here, so we all set to work at once, John skinning the three-year-old stag, Steve taking off the head of the big stag, and I lighting a fire and cooking dinner. The place was very exposed and the snow falling thickly, so it was some time before we finished our tasks. The young stag was in prime condition, so we took a haunch and the breast as well as his skin, and thus heavily laden returned to camp. In the evening I admired the skill with which the Indians fashioned their long boots. First of all the skin is cleaned, then Steve, making his knife as sharp as a razor, shaved off all the hair. The two pairs of boots were then cut into shape, and afterwards sewn tightly with thread made from the sinews of the deer's back. A seamed-over stitch is used, and very tightly clinched. John Hinx was engaged meanwhile in making a deep trough out of a log of "var." In this he placed about an armful of "var" bark, carefully broken into fine pieces with the fingers. Boiling water was then poured into the trough, and the "boots" left to soak for twelve hours. After this they were taken out, well scraped, and put out to dry. They are then finished and perfectly soft, strong, and watertight. It is curious that no skin but that of three-year-old stag is ever used for this purpose. A large stag's skin is too thick, and a doe's skin too weak.

"What beautiful socks those are of yours," I said to Steve.

"Yes," he answered, "but Indian women cannot make socks like white women. I get as many pairs of socks as I like for nothing from the Bay de Nord white women, every time I pass that place—and dinners too."

"How is that?" I queried.

"Well," said Steve, "I saved a man's life last winter, and I tell you story if you like."

To this I readily assented, and he began :—

"Last January it was very cold, and Micky John and me were in the middle of the country, about forty miles north of Bay de Nord, looking for some deer to sell to the wood-camps near the salt water. Micky had gone out, and I came back to tilt about midday, having killed a *pisage* (young doe). Our tilt was in a little droke by the side of a small brook, and as I go in, I see tracks of a bear or a man on the other side of the brook going north. When Micky came into camp about an hour later, I say to him, 'What for you cross the brook and go north, Micky?' For I know there weren't no bears about at that time of year, and I thought it queer that Micky should go across the stream, as it was broad and difficult to cross. But Micky say he had gone west, and those were not his tracks. So

THIRTY-NINE POINTER SHOT NEAR LAKE TAMNAPEGAWI,
OCTOBER 1906

SIDE VIEW OF THE SAME

I was curious, as no Indians were about in our country, and white men never come in so far, especially in the winter. We crossed the brook, and I see at once that the track was a white man's, as he wore boots, that he was running, and that he warn't carrying no load, cos his footin' was light on the snow. 'That feller's lost sure,' says I to Micky, 'and we must find him before night or he'll be dead.'

"I takes my tomahawk and some rum and meat and we flies along the track, for the man was scared and going fast. The footing goes in big circles, and now and again we see where the feller had fell down and bite at the snow, so he was about done and going mad.

"'Hurry up, Micky,' said I, 'or we'll be too late.' It was cold enough for frost-bite even with two pairs of mits, and when night came on, if a man fall and couldn't get up, he'd very soon die. But Micky was kind o' scared and say to me, 'What if he jump on us and try to kill us; when a man's mad with fear he do most anything.' But I show him the handle of my tomahawk, and meant to stun the feller if he try any tricks.

"The strength of that white man was considerable, for Micky and I had to run like deer on our rackets to gain ground, but by-and-by we see he was slowin' and fallin' oftener. Presently I sees his head poking out from behind a bush, so I shouts to him, and he rushes up to me and grabs me round the legs. Micky wanted me to hit him, but I knew he was only mad with joy. His name was Michael Fannell, and he said he thought he was going home. So he was— nearly.

"He was so done, with his boots and clothing all tore to pieces, that Mick and I had to carry him on our backs five miles to the tilt, but once there we rubbed him with rum, dressed him in our spare clothes, and soon had him asleep and comfortable.

"Three days afterwards we came with our man to a place about twenty miles above the Bay de Nord Mill, and there we meets a great company of men comin' to look for Michael Fannell. When they sees us they sets up a shout and runs to meet us, and the way those people carried on was somethin' terrible. Next day we came into Bay de Nord, and the whole people came out to meet us. Every bell in the place was ringin', every one who had a gun fired it off, and every woman in the place was cryin' and kissin' Michael Fannell.

"'Micky,' says I to my partner, 'there's something wrong about all this.'

"'What way?' says he.

"'Why,' says I, 'all those kisses ought to be for us, and nar a one comin' our way.' It wasn't right some way—so when a big feller says to me, 'What would you done if you'd found him dead?' 'Oh,' I says, 'I'd a brought out a piece of him any way—his head perhaps.'[1]

"Then all the women yell and run away. But they was kind anyhow, and told us that me and Micky would never want a good dinner or a pair of socks as long as we were coming to the Bay de Nord."

Foxes are fairly numerous about these hills, and every evening and morning we could hear their "yapping" as they called to each other. One carcase of a stag near the camp was almost finished by foxes and eagles. The eagles

[1] An Indian is fond of saying something gruesome just to see what the effect will be. These Newfoundland Micmacs do not like to be thought the savages many of the fisher folk consider them to be. This story of the rescue of Michael Fannell is known everywhere in Fortune Bay.

SIDE VIEW OF THE FORTY-FIVE POINTER

were here all day, but the more cunning quadrupeds only sneaked to their meal in the shadows.

The red fox of Newfoundland can hardly be said to differ from that of the adjoining continent, although American naturalists like to regard it as a separate sub-species under the name of *Vulpes deletrix* (Bangs). It is certainly smaller, as we should expect an island form to be, but that its colour is paler and less rusty I do not agree. I have compared skins from Newfoundland with those of Canada, and can find no difference in the size of the feet, which is supposed to be the chief character of the *V. deletrix*. "The cross-fox," "the patch fox," "the silver fox," "the mountaineer fox," and "the black fox" are all melanic varieties of varying intensity of the common red fox, *Vulpes fulvus* (Desmarest). A collection of Newfoundland skins exhibits all degrees of colour from the jet black fox with white end to its tail, which is by far the rarest and most valuable phase, to the true red fox. Of course the true type is the commonest; then comes the "patch," which may be said to occur as one in every six specimens. In every twenty there is a "cross" or a "mountaineer," and in every hundred a good "silver." The Indians say they get one genuine "black fox" in a lifetime. Noel Matthews obtained 380 dollars for a good skin of this rare variety, and this may be said to be the top price obtained by the trapper.

The habits of the Newfoundland foxes are very similar to those of the mainland, so little need be said beyond noting a few points of interest which I have not seen stated in other natural histories. These island foxes are practically omnivorous. They will eat any sort of fresh meat and carrion, but do not as a rule attack the carcases of deer until the first severe frosts set in. During the summer they live largely on trout, which they catch with great skill, by watching the shallows and darting in on the basking fish. Sometimes they hunt in pairs and drive the fish to each other. In the autumn they live on blueberries to a great extent, and will also eat other fruits. The Indians have told me that they are the deadly foe of the "weasel" (ermine), and that they kill and eat these little mustelids whenever they come across them. No Indian will touch the carcase of a caribou which a fox has once visited, owing to the practice the animal has of urinating upon whatever food he has found and wishes to revisit. The urine of the fox is very pungent, and its evil smell doubtless keeps off other predatory animals.

Foxes like to frequent high stony ground. Here they always have one or more lairs to which they retire in rough weather. In such places grouse are generally to be found, and I have often noticed piles of fresh-water mussels on exposed eminences, where they have doubtless been carried and opened by foxes.

Foxes have a remarkable sense of hearing, the Indians calling them from a distance of 200 yards simply by sucking the back of the hand in imitation of a vole or distressed hare. When the Indian desires to trap foxes in a new ground he always repairs to the highest point, and, looking down on the landscape, selects for his first traps the narrow spits of land dividing two large lakes. Foxes always pass to and fro along such natural bridges, and almost invariably to one side of the numerous deer paths, as they do not like to walk in damp places if they can help it.

My friend, Mr. John McGaw, witnessed an interesting exhibition of the playfulness of this animal shortly after he left me on my third journey. He was stalking two stags on Serpentine Hills, near the Gander, when he noticed one of the stags staring stupidly and backing away from some object

STEVE BERNARD AND THE FORTY-FIVE POINTER

which kept leaping up from the ground at its side. On approaching to within eighty yards of the deer, he saw that the curious object was a young fox engaged in an attempt to make the larger animal have a game with him. The fox repeatedly sprang into the air, snapping at the deer's side, and then, as these manœuvres were resented by the stag lowering its head to strike, it rushed round to the other side to repeat the performance. The nimble game went on for several minutes, Reynard apparently enjoying the fun of chaffing his clumsy friend, who did not appear to appreciate the joke in the slightest degree. Sometimes it bounded forward as if to seize the stag's nose, and then as quickly sprang backwards, standing just out of reach in the most provoking manner. My readers will be glad to hear that this merry little fellow retreated in safety.

Every day I went hunting either in Shoe Hill, Kesoquit, Maelpeg, or along Keskitpegawi. Deer were in abundance, generally in mixed companies or single stags that had finished the rut. On 30th October I saw nine big stags and 115 does and small deer, but nothing of importance. Except for two small gales with rain, the weather was delightful, and I enjoyed the experience of seeing an abundance of game and good heads all in the open country where a man can use his glass without hindrance. On 31st October the big migration set in from the north, and I saw no fewer than fourteen big stags and 145 does. These all came from the forest to the east of Sylvester, so I sent Steve to Kesoquit for more supplies, and went north with John to meet the deer and build a fresh camp. On 31st November a terrific gale with heavy rain burst upon us from the east, and for three days we endured considerable discomfort from the shifting winds. The water sometimes poured in under our flimsy sheet, and a tent would have been most welcome, but as we had no such luxury we had to make the best of a bad job, and built enormous fires, which were often moved to suit the wind. The camp, too, was a miserable one, much exposed, with the whole ground covered with rocks, so that I was at last forced to strike camp in a perfect deluge and make for Kesoquit. Indians, as I have said before, simply loathe travelling in such weather, but in this case they were quite cheerful, for a walk to Kesoquit meant warmth, shelter, and the various good things which had been "cached" there in the tilt.

As we marched through the rain and the mist on 4th November, I saw a single doe passing below us up the main valley. Her ghost-like form was soon followed by another and yet another, so we halted for a moment to see if anything better was to follow. Yes, here he comes, a noble fellow with long antlers. We watched him as he threaded his way through a small marsh about 200 yards to our left. We were about to rise and resume our journey when Steve sprang to his feet with the usual exclamation, "Haskajit" (a very big one), and peering through the mist I saw such a vision of horns as I knew could only belong to one of these mighty ones of the earth. It took us not a moment to run down the hill and strike in on a line where the two stags were passing, but—as bad luck would have it—the long-horned fellow came directly towards us and forced an immediate subsidence to the ground on our part. Here we lay as he walked by with mincing steps, whilst the big one whose horns looked enormous in the haze, walked quickly across the marsh at about 150 yards. There was no chance but to take the shot offered, so I aligned the sights as carefully as possible and fired. The bullet went over his back, and he at once dashed off at full speed. There was now only a faint blur to aim at, but by

EXAMPLE OF THE LIGHT-COLOURED VARIETY OF NEWFOUNDLAND CARIBOU, SHOT OCTOBER 1906 ON THE HILLS NEAR LAKE TAMNAPEGAWI

the greatest of luck I hit the deer right through the heart with my second shot.

"Very good," said Steve, "you kill him," although I was unaware that my shot had taken effect. We ran forward, and for a time could see nothing of our quarry, though Steve was positive I had hit him, until, going forward, we saw the antlers of the dying stag swaying to and fro on the top of a knoll. He was a noble thirty-five pointer, with large horns, only spoilt by the usual hook brow on the right antler.

This closed my hunting for the year, and perhaps for ever in Newfoundland. I had killed six splendid heads, four of which were of exceptional beauty, and my collection of caribou heads was now complete. This season had surpassed all my previous expeditions, both in the way of success, and in the enjoyment of finding and stalking deer in an open country where no white man had ever hunted before. Others will doubtless come after me, and for them I can only wish the good luck that attended me; but I trust that they will employ the Indians who accompanied me, and whose lawful hunting-grounds lie within this area of the country.

On 6th November we met Matty Burke and Johnny Benoit, and all packed up and carried the outfit and heads to the canoes on Prowse's Lake. From this point to John Hinx's tilt the stream was fairly easy, but for the next four days the Indians had to display all their skill in preventing the canoes from upsetting in the boiling torrent of the Long Harbor River. Several times they packed everything for a mile or two, but negotiated most of the worst rapids by "lining" down them, whilst one man kept the nose of the canoe straight with a long spruce pole. On 10th November we reached Ryan's, and the end of our canoe journey.

I will not trouble the reader with the difficulties I

experienced in getting to St. John's at this late season of the year, beyond briefly stating that after packing my heads in Belleoram I had again to recross Fortune Bay in Mr. Ryan's boat. Having missed the weekly steamer, there was nothing for it but to boat and walk across the country. After a heavy gale, we had to run for shelter into Anderson's Cove, but next day made Bay d'Argent. Here I said good-bye to my genial Irish friend, and taking the two Indians, marched for eighteen miles across the Peninsula to Bain Harbour in Placentia Bay. None of the inhabitants would or could convey me across the bay, as the weather was vile, but after beating about half the night I induced an old ruffian and his two sons to essay the passage in his lumber schooner for twenty dollars. The night was awful, blowing smoke from the south-east, and half-a-dozen times the skipper wanted to turn back, but by various inducements I got him to hold on till daylight. The seas washed over us, the cabin was so filthy, and smelt so abominably of bilge water and rotten fish, that it made me ill, and it was with great joy I hailed the welcome harbour of Placentia on the following evening after seventeen hours' misery. Here I caught the train, and next day the steamer for England.

The attendant discomforts of travel in out-of-the-way places are things to be taken philosophically by the hunter, and, in looking back on my days in Newfoundland, they seem few and easily forgotten, whilst the happy ones are numerous and deeply fixed in my mind.

How strange is England's ignorance of her colonies, and of none so great as that relating to Newfoundland. Those that give her a passing thought consider her people a mixture between French Canadians and Red Indians, who live in a climate that is a hybrid between the North Pole and a

Rough Water on the Long Harbor River

London fog. Instead of that, the traveller who goes to seek will find a happy people of the good old English stock, men to whom the Flag of England and respect for the King are no mere idle terms, but are a living ideal, which the lapse of centuries has not palled. There, too, you will find none of the pushful arrogance that often comes with new-found strength. Newfoundland has had some hard knocks from the ignorance of Downing Street, and her Governors, who are in the best position to know, have often been treated with scant respect; but withal, she does not fling herself into hysterics and talk of independence, but quietly awaits the day when England shall be governed by men who do not "only England know," but have the interests of the whole Empire at heart. I do not know much about politics, but I have travelled much in British colonies, yet it seems to me that until we have members of Parliament whose minds circulate a little farther than the village pump and their own small interests, we shall never know our own people or appreciate their ambitions.

One really clever man, Mr. Chamberlain, does not belong to that school. Whether his views about tariff reform and colonial preference are sound I will not discuss, but, right or wrong, he is a great man because he has done all that one man could do to lay bare our national self-sufficiency and the folly of neglecting "the cry of the children" when they call.

Then, too, Newfoundland is not a land of fog and icebergs. It has a fairly severe winter, but its late summer and autumn are certainly finer than Scotland.

"Over there is a sense of freedom we know not here. There is the great sun, the wide horizon, the dancing rivers, and the woods of ever-changing beauty. There is the blazing noon, with its manifold sights and moods of Nature—the

white-headed eagle, and the osprey lost in cloud of spray ;
the American goshawk chasing the belted kingfisher ; the
rattle of the great woodpecker ; the 'plop' of the beaver ;
the splash of the leaping fish, and a hundred more. There
is the evening of changing lights, when from the darkening
forest steps the great white-necked stag. There, too, those
exquisite nights of twinkling starlight, when you lie and toast
your toes at the blazing logs whilst the men spin yarns, and
the horned owl shrieks. It is the Spirit of the Wilderness
that calls, and the man who has not known has not lived."

CHAPTER XVII

THE NEWFOUNDLAND CARIBOU

FIRST of all I must warn my readers that this chapter is intended solely for the hunter and the naturalist, and that the general reader will peruse it at his own peril.

The name "caribou" is a native Indian word derived from the words "maccarib" or "maccaribo," and not from the French Canadian *quarré bœuf* (that is, a square ox), an origin assigned to it by Sir John Richardson, who wrote the first clear account of the American races of this deer. Lescarbot, in his *Nouvelle France* (1609), first mentions the caribou, whilst its existence seems to have been unknown to the earlier travellers, such as Cabot, Cartier, and Roberval.

Space will not permit me to enter into a discussion of the various local races of the reindeer or caribou found in Europe, Asia, and America, nor to argue on the vexed question whether the whole race should be regarded as one species, or a number of sub-species, of which the Norwegian reindeer is the parent form. Without doubt both views of the case are correct in their own way, whether zoologists belong to the camp of the "splitters" or the "lumpers"; but what I do consider a very great mistake is the separation by American and English naturalists of the two great races known respectively as the "Woodland" and "the Barren-land," and the assignation to each of different habits, a state of things which has led to the formation of sub-species such as *T. R. Stonei* and *T. R. Osborni*, local races assigned to the Woodland group, yet possessing habits practically identical with true *T. rangifer* of Norway, and *T. R. arcticus* of the Barren-lands. This is nothing more or less than confusion worse confounded, and based on an ignorance of the habits and movements of the various (so-called) sub-species. A close study of the wild races of Europe, Asia, and America has convinced me that nearly all reindeer spend a certain number of months every year in the timber (when they can find such shelter), and a certain time in the open grounds. In parts of Arctic America the Mackenzie herds, and in Finmark the Northern European herds, live for nearly six months in forests, only repairing to the open tundra or mountain wastes in autumn and winter, and again returning to the forest belts in spring. The same may be said of most of the other local races, whether so-called Barren-ground or Woodland.

In this work I have endeavoured to show, although it does not seem to be known to naturalists, that the Newfoundland caribou, which have always been known as a typical Woodland race, does precisely the same thing, and leaves the timber in October, returning to it again in the following April. Of course I do not mean to dogmatise and say that all the Newfoundland caribou thus travel, for during these great migrations there are large numbers which do not leave the woods at all, but are more or less stationary, whilst the main body passes through their midst. It is a curious fact in animal life, but no more strange than the habits of thrushes and blackbirds which remain in our gardens at all seasons, even in the autumn, while vast numbers of the same species are passing overhead for southern climes.

No doubt the reason of these movements of reindeer to open ground is that which prompts the inspiration of migration

FORTY-EIGHT POINT HEAD IN THE POSSESSION OF SIR R. G. REID

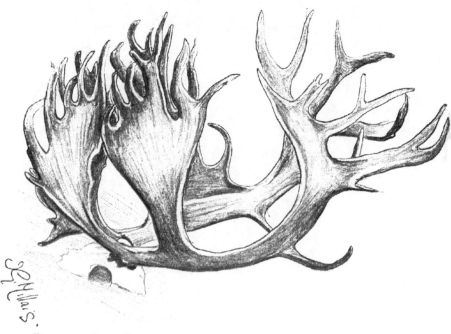

FORTY-NINE POINT HORNS PICKED UP ON THE GANDER, 1906, BY HESKETH PRICHARD

amongst all mammals and birds, namely, the absence of a proper food supply for great numbers. When the winter sets in the frost is more intense in forests, and the snow deeper. This causes a "trek" to some area where the wind blows the snow from the exposed ridges, and renders the moss easier to obtain. For converse reasons and the laws of greater protection, the deer return to the woods in spring. I think, therefore, that when the general habits of the American caribou are better known, and their migrations and horn growths, &c., better understood, we shall do away with several of these hastily constructed species, as well as the erroneous titles of Woodland and Barren-ground, which are quite inapplicable.

The Newfoundland caribou (*Tarandus rangifer* or *Tarandus rangifer terræ-novæ*, Bangs, whichever the reader may prefer to call it) stands about 48 inches at the shoulder (I have measured one 52 inches), 6 feet 8 inches in length, and weighs from 300 to 400 lbs. By the end of September most of the males have white necks and beards, but I have seen a few that were grey all over the neck. The ears and throat mane are always white, but the face and cheeks are generally grizzled, and are seldom, even in the darkest examples, as black as those of Eastern Canada. Sometimes a dark line of hair runs down the back of the neck, and there is always a black or dark brown bunch of hair on the upper surface of the tail. The upper parts of the body are dark or pale brown, but in this respect they are very variable, being almost pure white over the whole of the body in the light variety of this race. These white examples are found in nearly all local races of reindeer. The various names of the different ages of both sexes are thus recognised by the Newfoundland Micmacs :—

Very big stag, with a Roman nose = *Wach-tu-wich-hu-nema;* very big stag = *Haskagit;* very dark stag, with brown on the legs = *Wis-o-blich;* big white stag = *Wap-tu-quit;* black stag = *Mach-tad-u-git;* stag = *stecks;* stag with a wide head = *Pus-um-wat;* very old stag (sees nothing, has no teeth) = *Vis-o-blich;* almost full grown stag = *Bis-um-wat;* good-sized stag (*i.e.* staggie) = *Glon-an-nais;* pricket = *Frusanch;* deer = *Haliboo;* barren doe = *Sigum-tis;* doe, with calf = *no-sutk, Hal-a-gu-duk;* young doe = *Pis-age;* calf = *Tg-e-adu;* small fawn = *Ne-gudu, Punetquhin;* fourteen months' old calf = *susanch.*

In 1906 I made the interesting discovery, which is, I think, new to zoologists, namely, that the caribou stag sometimes possesses a sac containing hair in the throat skin. On October 20th I killed a very large stag near Shoe Hill, and whilst removing the neck skin my knife slipped and disclosed a very curious sac about five inches long and two broad; this contained growing hair on the inner skin, and the cavity was full of a mass of compressed hair soaking in a watery mucus. This skin bag was situated in a thin vellum of the inner skin in the region of the upper throat. The Indians call this little bag "Piduateh," and the few white men who know of its existence the "Toler" (*i.e.* crier or bell), so that it may have some close affinity to the long throat appendage found on the moose and known as the "bell." In the case of the caribou, the hair sac is internal with hair growing inwards, whilst in the moose the ornament is a long piece of hardened skin covered with hair, which hangs from the centre of the throat. The Indians told me that this sac is only found in one in fifty caribou, generally in the males, and that it is sometimes found in the inside skin of the cheek. The existence of this curious attachment has not been previously noticed. It seems to be useless, and can possess none of the functions of a gland.

The horns of the old stags are dropped between the 30th of October and the 20th November. Often the males cast their horns according to their years, the eldest first, and the youngest last. Many five-year-old stags keep them on until Christmas, but it is extremely rare to see a stag with good horns after the 1st of December. Unlike the red deer and wapiti, the new horns do not begin to grow at once, the tops of the pedicles being bare for some time before the new growth starts. In fact, Newfoundland stags only show an excrescence of a few inches in March; after this the horns develop rapidly. The horns of the males are hard to the tips on the 1st of September, and are rubbed clean between the 7th and the 12th of that month. At first they are pure white, but change in a few days to a beautiful chestnut colour. In Newfoundland it is said that this colour is obtained by the deer threshing its antlers against the alder bushes, which exude a reddish brown sap, a view which cannot be substantiated, because 80 per cent. of the stags rub clean on dwarf spruce and larch trees,[1] in whose neighbourhood there are no alders. But where alders are found they are very fond of swinging the antlers from side to side amongst them to clear whatever shreds of velvet may remain. As the horns dry, the stags repair at midday to high sandy " knaps " in the vicinity of their summer resorts and lie in the sun. The Indians say that they always go soon after to some stream, and there, gazing into Nature's looking-glass, see whether their ornaments are of the correct colour. If this view prove unsatisfactory they go to give them

---

[1] Some colour is doubtless derived by rubbing on the bark of trees, since it is easy to stain bleached antlers by dipping them in the boiling bark of var or spruce.

a further polish on the alders, and obtain the desired effect. This pretty superstition is not an Indian one, and may be found in many old books on hunting in England and the Continent, and the tale must have been received by the red men from the early English colonists.

The caribou does a great part of his horn-cleaning with the hoofs of his hind feet. In fact all deer with which I am acquainted use the hoof largely in freeing the horns of the velvet that clings to the coronets and other parts which are difficult to rub on trees. I have seen both wild and tame reindeer thus engaged, and the foot often get so involved in the antlers that you wonder how it will again become free. But they have a delicate sense of touch, and the most minute particles of velvet are thus removed, whilst there is no instance on record of the reindeer stag having entangled itself in its own horns.

As in the case of other deer, the best horns are carried by stags of from six to twelve years of age. The average horns do not bear more than twenty points, and have one fair brow shovel, and a hook for the corresponding ornament on the other horn. A good many have twenty-five points, whilst a good head generally has thirty points and over. Points are not all sufficient, but nearly every first-class head I have seen has borne thirty-five points or more. The ambition of every hunter in Newfoundland is to kill a forty-pointer, and a few achieve this distinction. I think that any hunter of experience who goes far enough afield and works hard in the second season ought to see eighty adult stags, and one amongst them will be a forty-pointer or even more.

Horns bearing more than forty-two points are extremely rare, yet every year one or two are killed. I have seen

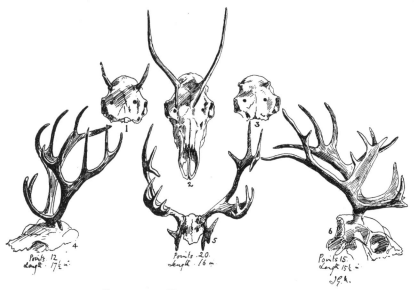

SKULL AND HORNS OF FEMALE CARIBOU

1, 2, Usual Types.   3, Hornless Female with Pedicles still present.   4, 6, Fine
Types from Specimens shot by the Author.   5, Twenty-pointer shot by
Matty Burke near the Tolt.

FORTY-EIGHT POINTER SHOT NEAR THE BUNGALOW,
GRAND LAKE, 1906

three carrying forty-eight points, and one of my own and a pair of dropped horns in the possession of Mr. H. Prichard have forty-nine, but I have never yet seen a Newfoundland fifty-pointer, although I am quite convinced that three or four heads with this large number of points have been killed within recent years. In 1905 and 1906 I picked up three horns on which are twenty-five, twenty-six, and twenty-six points respectively. Any of these may have belonged to a fifty-pointer, but as in no case did I find the corresponding antler, the case must remain in doubt. The following notes of big heads I have collected at various times, though it must be remembered that nearly every Indian and white man exaggerates both the size of the head as well as the number of points, so the reader can accept the evidence or reject it as hearsay as he pleases.

Micky John, an Indian, told me in 1906 that he knew of a pair of dropped antlers near the Gander which had fifty-three points; he had seen and counted them twice. In 1904 Nicholas Jeddore shot a fifty-point head, and sold it to a Mr. Taylor, a surveyor in St. John's. Joe Bernard, late chief of the Micmacs, and Peter John had each seen one fifty-pointer during their lives.

Very few Newfoundland horns exceed 39 inches in length. The general character is rather short and thick, with more massive brows and bays—that is middle palms—than those of other local races. If they have a manifest weakness it is in the "tops," which are often poor and thin, and a head which carries good double brows, bays, and tops is indeed a great rarity.

I have killed several over 40 inches in length, and in 1905 one of 46 inches, and this was the longest I had noticed in any public or private collection until the autumn of

1906,[1] when I saw a wonderful head in the possession of the Hon. J. D. Ryan, of St. John's. By some oversight I had not my steel tape with me, but should say that it is at least 51 inches long and 45 inches span between the tops. The brows and bays were poor, and it is not a remarkable head in other respects, but it is probably the longest and widest Newfoundland head in existence. The deer which carried these horns was killed by Matty Burke, a half-breed Indian, near the Tolt in October 1904. So far as I can ascertain the three Newfoundland heads best for all round qualities are as follows: The forty-five pointer killed by myself near Mount Sylvester in October 1906, and the forty-eight pointer shot by a railway man near Spruce Brook in 1905, and now in the possession of Sir R. G. Reid, at Montreal. Mr. Selous, who is a caribou expert, and has seen both examples, says there is little to choose between them. Sir R. G. Reid's head has better brow points than my forty-five pointer, but, in other respects, my specimen is the finer. The third example is a forty-eight pointer with magnificent bays. It was killed on the hills near Grand Lake by an American sportsman hunting from the " Bungalow " in 1906. I give an illustration of this head from a photograph sent to me by Mr. Whitaker. It is curious that General Dashwood, who had so much experience in Newfoundland, never killed a remarkable head; but such is the case, for I have seen all the heads collected by him, and, though he possessed many fine examples up to thirty-nine points, there is not one which might be called extraordinary. In St. John's, too, we should expect to find some remarkable specimens, but, beyond the

---

[1] In this year I obtained a head of 46½ inches. Rowland Ward in his horn measurements gives two Newfoundland heads of over 46 inches, but I do not think that they are correctly measured, as I have seen both of them.

head belonging to Mr. Ryan, a very large example possessed by the Hon. John Harvey, and a good forty-seven pointer in the possession of the Reid Newfoundland Company, I have not seen anything exceptional. This absence of fine deer-heads in the capital of the island can be accounted for by the fact that the great fire destroyed most of the best trophies, whilst travelling Americans give large prices for any head of remarkable beauty. My friend, Mr. Hesketh Prichard, picked up on the Gander in 1906 a very fine pair of horns with forty-nine points. These are very short, but possess magnificent brows.

Horns in which the bays are placed low down and close to the brows, as in Norwegian reindeer, are very rare, and I have only seen two examples, whilst equally scarce are horns which carry supernumerary points in the centre of the beam between the bays and the tops, of which I give two figures. Dwarf, or what we may term withered, heads are also somewhat unusual, and are usually carried by very large stags. Hornless stags, too, are not so rare as they are supposed to be.

For the purpose of comparison with other local races of reindeer, I give the measurements of the twelve best specimens of Newfoundland caribou which I have obtained in the island. In all scientific accounts dealing with the measurements of reindeer horns, no notice is taken of the size of the large brow shovel, a matter of great importance in determining the respective merits of individual heads. Mere length of horn is not everything in judging the qualifications of deer-heads, whilst in this species in particular we must consider beam, span, number of points,[1]

---

[1] The points of reindeer are difficult to count. No point should be included that does not fulfil the old watch-guard or powder-horn test, unless it may be a clean

symmetry, weight, and size of the large brow, a feature which adds so much to the general character.

Length on Outer Curve.	Circumference above Bay.	Breadth of Large Brow on Anterior Margin from Base to Top Front Point.	Widest Inside.	Points.	Locality.
46½	5½	14	31	45	Tamnapegawi Lake, 1906.
46	6	14	30	35	Upper Gander, 1905.
43	7	16¼	35	36	Shoe Hill Ridge, 1906.
42	6	16½	34	44	Upper Gander, 1903.
42	5½	15	31	31	Kesoquit Hills, 1906.
40	5	15½	32	38	Upper Gander, 1905 (picked up).
40	5¼	15½	39	25	Upper Gander, 1905.
38	5½	15	28	35	Upper Gander, 1903.
38	5½	18	31	35	Millais's Lake, 1902.
37½	6¾	17½	33	32	Migwell's Brook, 1905.
36	7	16½	29	49	Upper Gander, near Little Gull, 1903.
36	6½	13½	38	32	Kesoquit Hills, 1906.

Adult females measure from 36 to 40 inches at the shoulder, and weigh from 200 to 300 lbs. The hair of the head is dark brown, with white or grizzled crown and white nose, ears white, and neck grey, with a short white or grey beard extending from the throat to the chest. Upper parts dark brown with a row of very large spots or blotches of very pale brown on the flank. The legs, too, have more brown and black than the males. Black hairs are found on the upper part of the tail, whilst the rump, inner parts of the thighs, and under parts are white.

The horns of the females, when they possess them, are dropped as late as the end of April, and are, in consequence, later in development than those of the males. It is unusual

blunt snag at least half an inch from the main horn. The Germans count everything as a point upon which a torn piece of paper will rest, but we regard as "offers" all small excrescences that do not fulfil the old British conditions. For instance, Captain Cartwright's famous "seventy-two point" Labrador head, which I have recently traced, and on which he counted every offer, has in reality fifty-three points.

LICHEN EATEN BY CARIBOU

MALDOW OR BEARDED MOSS, A FAVOURITE WINTER FOOD
OF CARIBOU

THE NEWFOUNDLAND CARIBOU 319

to see their horns clean until 1st October. The usual type of horn is a long thin snag of some 15 to 20 inches, with a short, straight brow of 1 to 2 inches. Some, however, have six or seven points and a few ten to twelve points. A greater number of points than twelve is rare, the largest number I have myself seen on live deer being heads of twelve, thirteen, and fifteen points. The best head I know of is that of a female shot by Matty Burke near the Tolt in 1904. It bears twenty points, and is now in the possession of Mr. Philip Ryan at Long Harbor. Joe Jeddore told me that his brother Nicholas killed a female caribou in 1905 whose horns carried twenty-eight small points. He was to have sent the head to me, but the skull was eaten by dogs.

Quite 8 per cent. of the female Newfoundland caribou carry no external horns,[1] and yet I have never seen the skull of a hornless female that did not possess small pedicles. This is a somewhat interesting point, as it shows that there is a tendency amongst the females of that island race to lose their horns. It is remarkable, too, because all Norwegian female reindeer possess horns of some kind, and the Esquimaux of Labrador say they never see hornless females. Of the Eastern Canadian race, breeding females about Abitibi are frequently hornless, but Mr. Selous tells me that those of the Yukon in Northern British Columbia are all horned.

Calves are born in the woods in May, and have no natural enemies except the lynx, which kills a few in the early days of their existence. The mothers are very affectionate and suckle the young until September, when they are weaned. It is not unusual, however, to see a calf sucking

[1] My calculations are based on some notes I took of female caribou seen in open country, when I could easily examine them with the glass, in 1906. Out of 300 females, 1 had eleven points; 1, ten; 3, eight; 25, six or seven; 246, four or more points; and 24 had no horns.

the mother as long as she can give milk. At two years of age they will receive the stag. Without doubt they bear calves very regularly for more than twenty years, as the red-deer hinds do, and the percentage of barren does is very small. Instances of twins are rare, as are also pure white varieties. I saw a nearly white doe on the Gander in 1905, and in the spring of 1904 Steve Bernard shot a young doe, near Long Harbor, that was pure white all over, with pink and white hoofs.

The Indians say that in extreme old age the stags become both blind and deaf, and that they occasionally come across these old patriarchs whose horns are reduced to thin spires with a hardly perceptible brow. On this point they have an interesting superstition which is fully believed in. They say that when stags become very old they go down to the salt water and disappear in the sea, where they at once turn into large whales (Pudup) or into small whales (Halibuge or Muspage). The origin of this, I find, comes from the home of the Micmacs, Sydney, Cape Breton, where one day a hunter followed three moose along the shore for some distance, and then found the tracks entered the sea. Immediately afterwards he saw three large whales spouting off shore, and his simple mind connected the two facts. I explained the possibilities of the circumstance, but the Indians held firmly to their views, instancing that, conversely, stags often came out of the sea on to the land again. John Hinx gave several examples of this, and stated that his grandfather, Joe Paul, had once shot three stags near Conn River, whose stomach was "full of shrimps." The other Indians at once confirmed these tales. After this it was useless to argue.

The principal food of the caribou at all seasons is the

common reindeer moss (*Cladonia rangiferina*), of which there seems to be a large and a small variety. They also eat two other lichens, *Stereocaulon paschale*, and *Bryopogon jubatum*. The long-bearded tree moss, known to the Newfoundlander as "maldow," is a favourite food in winter. In the autumn the adults also eat blueberries,[1] the withered leaves of alder and birch, whilst the females and young are very partial to the small shoots of larch, on which I have seen them feeding exclusively. The females chew the points of every old horn they come across. With such a wonderful feast spread by Nature, the caribou would suffer no hardship at any season were it not for the sudden frosts following on thaws—at such times the winter rain freezes as it falls, and encrusts the ground and trees with a hard mass of ice, through which the deer are unable to break.

These ice storms are known in Newfoundland as the "Glitter," and are the cause of all the sudden local movements on the part of the deer during winter. The most remarkable instance occurred in the first week in December 1898—one of the severest winters ever experienced in the island. Tens of thousands of caribou were collected in the neighbourhood of the woods and open country just south of Sylvester, and extending to the Tolt in the east and the Long Harbor River as the western boundary. A glitter came on suddenly, and the whole of these deer moved in a single night to the west at full speed. Several of the Indians saw the trails made by the mass of deer, and described them to me as at least ten miles wide, with few intervals in between. Only one man saw the great trek. His name is Joe Rigg, and

---

[1] The stomach of a stag I killed in 1906 was half-full of blueberries. These it must have swallowed as the berries lay on the ground amongst the *C. rangiferina*. I do not think that they eat the berries off the bushes.

X

he is the game-warden of Long Harbor country. I had the good fortune to meet him in 1906. Joe had gone in to shoot a couple of deer about ten miles north of Mr. Ryan's house, and described the night as the most wonderful he had ever seen. As far as the eye could reach there were "millions and millions of caribou," and he stood in astonishment the whole day as the pageant rolled by. Putting aside Rigg's pardonable exaggeration, the deer seen by him must have constituted a half of the stock in the whole island, perhaps a hundred thousand, and the sight must have been a remarkable one. These deer moved west without a stop till they came to Conn River, where dozens were killed in the streets of the village. From thence they held on, and dispersed themselves from this point westward as far as Burgeo for the rest of the winter.

When reindeer are caught in isolated positions, such as small islands and ranges of mountains, by one of these sudden frosts following a thaw, and there is no chance of escaping to less exposed places, the whole stock die of starvation. Such a calamity occurred on the Upper Laerdal mountains in 1892, and on several islands in the north of Hudson's Bay some years ago, and I could name other instances.

Purely local movements, brought on by sudden meteorological conditions, must not be confounded with the annual migrations which take place in nearly all parts of the island at two distinct seasons, and which I shall now endeavour to describe.

Caribou, like other species of deer which occur in large numbers, are in the habit of changing their habitats. In the case of moose these changes of range are generally gradual, extending over a period of several years, whilst the reindeer may suddenly desert a district in which they have lived for years for no apparent reason.[1]

Twenty years ago the main winter abode of the Newfoundland caribou stretched from Bay Despair to La Poile, whilst a certain number, nearly all small deer, spent this season until the spring in the high country, just below the forest belt, stretching from Terra-Nova and Cloete Sound to St. John's Lake. It is strange that few came south of this into the great open country between the Tolt and the Bay de Nord River, but Indians have told me that at this time it was the rarest thing to see more than a few odd deer in this area north of Fortune Bay, which is now their principal home at this season. To-day a certain number of deer never migrate at all, and live in the woods of the interior and the peninsulas, which are their summer home. There are always some to be found at all seasons in the Northern Peninsula, and many other isolated tongues of land, such as are found south of St. John's and Placentia; and on the east coast many too remain throughout the year in the forests about Red Indian Lake, Victoria Lake, St. George's Lake, the Gander, the La Poile, Round Lake, and the Western Maelpeg —in fact, over the whole island.

The building of the railway, which cuts the island in two in the north centre, proved what had already been known for years, that a vast body of deer commenced its migration from the Northern Peninsula early in September. In cold seasons this movement commenced early in the month with the advent of does and calves with a few young stags. These crossed the track at various points between the Gaff

[1] A good instance of this has occurred recently in East and North-Eastern Ontario. Previous to the year 1897, all the country from Mattawa to Abatibi was caribou ground. About that year the caribou began to desert it for Northern Quebec, and in their place entered moose in great numbers.

Topsails and Bay of Islands, the main body pursuing lines
across the White Hill plains, Howley, Goose Brook, and
Patrick's Marsh.   In mid-September came more does and
half-grown stags, and at the end of the month the breeding
deer, consisting of adult does and stags.   Throughout October
more and more stags, influenced according to the weather,
continued to pass southwards, and in the first week in
November the last of the big deer and the "main jamb"
of small deer brought up the rearguard—the migration being
over about the 20th of that month.   Of the subsequent
movements of the animals but little was known, except that
during the late winter great numbers made their appearance
between White Bear River and La Poile, on the south-west
coast, and were killed by the men of this district.

During the first few years of the railway every man who
had a rifle or gun repaired in the autumn to various crossing-
places of the deer, and in a couple of days killed all he desired.
At first good heads were not considered, but soon it became
known to the fishermen that a fine stag's horns were worth
money, so the slaughter of the adult stags became as much
a matter of importance as a saleable article as a fat doe
meant to themselves.   Without any restrictions the slaughter
of stags commenced, and it was not unusual for one man who
was a good shot and knew the trails to kill as many as twenty
heads in a fortnight.   This went on for several years, until
the slaughter became so reckless[1] that the Government took
notice of it, and enforced a law by which only five deer

---

[1] A man armed with a Winchester rifle seated in the railway line near Howley, in
October 1897, killed the leading doe of a herd of twenty-eight deer.   As she fell
the others were thrown into helpless confusion, and stood about offering easy targets.
The ruffian then killed the whole herd, of which only one carcase was removed.
This dastardly act was reported in St. John's, and was the chief cause of the
Game Act.

THE END OF THE SEASON—QUITE GOOD FRIENDS AGAIN, BUT VERY THIN

FOX PLAYING WITH A STAG

might be killed by a single hunter. As the adult stags continued to decrease, this was further reduced to three, at which it now remains. But during these years the stags, and no doubt many of the does, had been learning a lesson by which they have now profited. Instead of crossing the line on their northern migration in spring, the majority go no farther than the chain of impenetrable forest which stretches from Glenwood to Round Pond, and again at intervals from Pipestone to the headwaters of the La Poile. In this area quite two-thirds of the caribou live in peace and security, and are scarcely molested at all until they move south to the open country, north of Fortune and Hermitage Bays, in the winter. Consequently the adult stags are now hardly touched, because the winter shooters invariably choose fat does in preference to lean stags.

A great number of deer, nearly all does and young animals with a few mature stags, still traverse the line at their old crossing-places, and the great open country north of Grand Lake, and on as far as George IV. Lake, and come south as they always did, but during the past few years very few good heads have fallen to the guns of the "pot-hunters," who bewail the absence of the crowned monarchs, and think that they have gone for ever. At the present day there are probably more adult stags in Newfoundland than ever there were, but they take better care of themselves ; this is the opinion of the Indians, and I believe the correct one, and as long as the great central sanctuary is not invaded in summer, when the females are bringing forth their young, and no other railway is built to pierce their autumn trails to the south of the forest belt, Newfoundland will always keep her deer, one of her most valuable assets.

From the central forests the migration commences early in

September by the does coming out to the open places. About the 15th of this month the first stags also begin to show up, at first timidly and then with greater confidence. The sign of the approaching rut is seen by their peculiar behaviour. The stag stands looking about in strange fashion. He ceases to feed except to suck up mud and water, and in the evening and early morning is seen rushing in and out of the forest in silent passion. As yet he does not grunt, but when he stops will stand and gaze for long periods at some object that may develop into a possible mistress. If the does have gone on, for at this season they make curious little migrations in any direction, he "noses" along, following on their tracks, and stopping now and again to lick and snuff up their delicious scent. Soon he finds the object of his desire, and captures one or two wives, with whom he may stop for a short period in the little open marshes that adjoin his forest home. I am no believer in the fidelity of the caribou or of the moose. He rapidly tires of his wives or they of him, and though he may even "trek" south for a short distance with the first females he has picked up, he soon leaves them and looks for fresh charmers. When in full "rut," which we may place at 11th October, he will, if a big and strong beast, gather as many as fifteen or eighteen does into his harem, but this is unusual, ten or twelve being the usual limit. At this season one constantly sees wandering troubadours, full of noise and passion, rushing madly along the hillside and simply "spoiling" for a fight. These are large adult stags, which are much "run," and have just left their harem and are looking for fresh conquests. If they meet another like themselves or a master-stag with does, a fight is certain to ensue. No deer fights oftener or with greater savagery than the reindeer, and they are often drowned in the bogs in their reckless

INTERLOCKED ANTLERS PICKED UP BY T. P. MILLER NEAR MILLAIS'S LAKE,
SEPTEMBER 1905

passion. Hardly an adult stag is free from traces of combat at the end of October. It is common to see them scarcely able to crawl from the blows they have received, and with horns knocked to pieces. In 1904 Joe Jeddore walked up to two large stags that were fighting and put a charge of buckshot into one of them at a distance of fifteen paces. The stag thinking his opponent had inflicted the blow, made one mighty rush at him and fell dead. The other deer then ran forward and pounded the carcase of the fallen one, when the Indian fired his other barrel and killed the second stag on the top of the first. Even young stags fight most savagely. I watched two on the hills one day in 1906 going at each other for over an hour, until in fact they were both so exhausted that their blows had no power and they could only reel about.

At this season the smell of the stag is very pungent. The mucus of the nostrils is so impregnated with a musky odour that if any of it gets on your fingers it is most difficult to remove. The flesh is so charged with the taint that adult stags are uneatable from 3rd October to 20th November.

Caribou do not make "wallows" like other species of deer. In late September the stags often stand on little mounds and scrape away shallow pits with their feet, generally in spots where some doe has been and left traces of her presence. This habit is very similar to that of the bull moose, but I have never seen the pits so deep as those made by the larger deer.

On the 25th of October the rutting season may be said to be at an end, and the main migration begins. The first sign of the general movement is the joining of parties and the presence of one or two old stags moving together. They still eye one another, and one stag will not permit another to approach too closely. They also commence to feed again and to travel. If cold weather in the shape of a heavy snowstorm with the wind in the north-east sets in, the whole stock of deer in the island may be set in motion on a single day. The reader must not, however, imagine that the Newfoundland caribou migrate in a great mass like "la foule" of the Barren-lands. On the contrary they travel singly or in small parties of from two or three individuals to twenty or at the most thirty. They are to be seen running or walking swiftly along their main "fall trails," and are generally led by an old and experienced doe, with the stag or stags bringing up the rear. In this way they will go forty or fifty miles in a single night, and soon reach the desired open ground, where they stop a few days until they are moved on by successive waves of deer. In the late fall it is common to find an area of country swarming with deer one day and deserted the next. Two days afterwards the same ground may be again covered with the animals, and so this southward movement goes on until the end of November, when the whole body of deer that intends to migrate have reached their southern limit and their winter quarters. Here they remain until March, when the north-ward migration sets in and they return to their summer homes.

The Millicete Indian name "Megaleep" (the wanderer) is the most applicable one for the caribou; for a more fidgety, wandering, and dissatisfied creature does not exist on the face of the globe. It is always thinking that the other place is the best and trying to prove its theories. Its whole character is one of restlessness and curiosity. Except in summer, when it lies down in the woods at midday, and in the autumn, when the rutting parties may be seen sleeping at midday on the lake edges, it is rare to see the caribou rest like other creatures, and so the man who goes to find it must have long and strong legs. It is more than a fool when it comes running back again and again to stare at you or to take the wind, and more than cunning when it makes its summer bed in some dense thicket full of dry sticks where not one hunter in a thousand can creep in or out without giving the alarm. In fact its whole nature is one of complication and a mixture of qualities alternately wise and idiotic.

The complex character of the reindeer is noticed in its extreme shyness of certain things that other animals will hardly notice, and its total absence of fear at the sound of the rifle or the avalanche. I have seen many instances of their nervousness. One day in 1906 I was watching five does and a large stag, when a cock willow grouse ran out of a small depression and stood upon a rock about half-way between myself and the deer. The caribou actually heard the scratching noise made by the grouse as it ran up the rock, and all dipped their bodies suddenly and started to run. Then seeing that it was only a grouse they commenced feeding again. A moment later the bird rose and flew over their heads uttering its merry cry, whereupon the company without warning took to their heels with all speed, and galloped away over the sky-line. On another occasion I saw a small herd stampeded by a pair of ravens which were simply "diving" through the air at each other. The deer appeared to be much frightened and ran out of sight. Wild geese rising also puts them on the move,[1]

---

[1] G. L., writing in the *Field*, April 21, 1906, says that Greenland reindeer will even take alarm at a snow-bunting flying by.

and stones falling down a hill create a state of "jumps."
Red deer, however, will take little notice of falling stones;
but I have had more than one stalk spoilt in Norway by
dislodging a few pebbles which came within the hearing of
reindeer. This is the more curious, because stones are falling
all day in the high fjelds of Norway when the snow is melting.
On the other hand I have fired at and killed a stag in the
midst of a herd of caribou, when the deer, after merely turning
their heads, have continued to feed. In fact, if a strong wind
is blowing, and the fallen deer does not roll and kick, and
the hunter lies hidden, it is unusual for caribou to take much
notice of a shot.

The female call is a low grunt which she utters either
when travelling or to attract her calf. She uses it at all
times, and the watch doe often makes this signal of alarm
before she raises her tail and bristles out the hair of the
rump. Females and males also make a loud puffing snort
or hiss as they spring into the air. In the rutting season
the stag makes use of two calls. It depresses the neck and
raises the nose, giving vent to three loud grunts. If much
excited it makes a second call, which is produced in the
throat by means of the breath being inhaled and exhaled
quickly. Mr. Thompson Seton, in an excellent article[1] on
caribou, says, "In several parts of the country I find traditions
that formerly the Indians used to call the caribou as they
do the moose, but the art has been forgotten." The Indians
of Newfoundland invariably call the caribou stag in the
rutting season, and I have called many myself. The art
is quite easy, and can be learnt in a few days. The only
skill required is to know when to give the call. Travelling
stags come to the cry more easily than herd stags, and

[1] *Scribner*, 1906.

THE FORTY-FIVE POINTER

PORTAGING HEADS ON THE LONG HARBOR RIVER

of this I have given several instances in the preceding pages.

Caribou make a curious crackling sound as they walk which has been explained in various ways. The Micmacs say that it is produced by the hoofs overlapping on the ground and springing back to the proper position as the leg is raised. But this cannot be correct, as the sound is made when the foot rests on the ground and the weight of the body is thrown upon it. Sometimes it crackles twice as the weight descends, and again as it lifts, and it is probably made, as Mr. Thompson Seton suggests, by the tendons slipping over the adjoining bones. The sound is not produced at every step, but is generally heard when the leg is placed in some strained position, as for instance when the deer grazes forward, leaving a hind leg at full tension. A herd passing close to the observer make a rattling sound like a band of castanets, and can be heard at a distance of fifty feet or more on a still day.

Between the front of all the hoofs there is a large gland,[1] from two to four inches deep, and with the entrance covered with bristly hairs, which secretes a musky yellow fluid. It is almost the diameter of a pencil. It has been stated that when the deer cross a human trail they put their noses to their feet and then rush off at full speed. I have never seen them do this. They put their noses to the ground and carefully smell all the human tracks, and then gazing at each other show unmistakable signs of fear, such as sudden starts, springing into the air, and bristling out the stern. I have never seen them actually smell at their own feet, and think the gland is used for some occult purpose which at present

---

[1] The Greenland Esquimaux call this gland *klookirtal;* the Micmacs have no especial name for it.

we do not understand. Even the purpose of the human glands are not yet understood.

The feet of the caribou are better adapted for running on bogs, snow, and ice than anything that the brain of man could devise. In a morass a 200-lb. man sinks in much deeper than a 400-lb. caribou, whilst the former on snow-shoes or "ski" has no chance whatever with the sure-footed reindeer. I remember once pursuing some reindeer along the side of a steep mountain in Norway when we came to a "snow-brae" going up and over the mountain. It was so steep that it was quite impossible to follow the deer in their ascent without the help of an ice-axe to cut steps. Until then I had no idea that these deer possessed such activity on snow and ice, for their movements could only have been equalled by mountain sheep, ibex, or markhor.

The hair of the caribou is very light and porous. It is not thought that the deer possess wool, but the shoulders of the adult Newfoundland caribou male are covered with a soft, silky brown wool, which rises above the ordinary coat of hair in October. The hair is so light that it causes this deer to swim higher in the water than any other species. It is so buoyant that it has been used to stuff life-belts, whilst Dr. Wintz has invented a cloth of reindeer hair which when made into clothes prevents the human body from sinking. In consequence of the natural advantages of its covering the caribou takes to the water with readiness and can swim long distances at a considerable speed. It makes two men put forth all their power as paddlers to overtake them in the water, through which they can pass at five miles an hour. When unmolested they go much slower, say three miles an hour, and are very careful to take the wind of any spot they have selected as a landing-place.

A caribou will as soon swim as walk. I once saw two does enter the extreme end of a long narrow lake about one mile long and two hundred yards broad, and swim the whole length, when they could easily have walked along the side.

The Newfoundland caribou are plagued throughout the greater part of the year by flies and their maggots. Two kinds of gad-fly infest them, and a large species squirts its maggots, furnished with small hooks, into the channels of the nostrils, where they feed on the mucus, and grow to a large size by July, when they are ejected by the deer and finish their final stage in the ground. The other, a small one, whose maggot is laid in the skin of the back and flanks, must give the deer endless torture. These commence to grow in October, and are not got rid of until the end of July, when the skin is riddled as if by swan-shot. The irritation caused by these pests must be intense, for the deer are often to be seen rubbing their flanks on the rocks and stones in spring-time. In the summer, too, hosts of mosquitoes, sand flies, and black flies attack them, and drive them to the highest points of land away from the rivers.

It is very difficult to figure out the number of caribou in Newfoundland, and all estimates must be mere guesses. Mr. Moulton of Burgeo, judging by the numbers wintering in the barrens north of that place and White Bear Bay, puts it at 250,000, and thinks they are increasing at the rate of 10,000 annually. Mr. Howley, on the other hand, places the figures at 100,000, and I think that double this number is a very fair estimate. In spite of the enormous slaughter which takes place annually, and which is every year greatly on the increase,[1]

---

[1] I have the best authority for stating that over a thousand guns were sold by one firm in St. John's in 1905. "Personally conducted" parties, numbering fifty men in each party, are now coming from America every year, and who knows to what this number may reach.

Newfoundland will keep her deer for many centuries to come if all shooters are licensed, and the number of deer shot by each person does not exceed three. Thus putting the death-rate at the highest estimate of three animals each to 4000 shooters, 12,000 would be killed out of 200,000, that is a depreciation of 6 per cent. Now this is a much smaller rate of killing than takes place amongst the stags of Scotland, and they are undoubtedly on the increase. Ninety-nine per cent. of the interior of Newfoundland is only fit for a caribou preserve, and the authorities now recognise this.

It is a great pity that so little has been done in the way of domesticating the Newfoundland caribou, and that for causes easily explained only a few have been caught and tamed. From their greater size,[1] strength, and ferocity during the breeding season the stags are too unsafe to keep, but something might be done with the does on a small scale, the stags being killed when they reached the age of three years.[2]

The Governor of Newfoundland, Sir William MacGregor, is much interested in the importation of Norwegian reindeer into Labrador, where he believes they will be of much advantage to the natives. Owing to the generosity of Lord Strathcona, a ship-load of these animals will shortly be sent to Labrador, and it is intended that the Esquimaux of the north coast will be put in charge of them as herdsmen. Personally I think that it will be a mistake if these careless little sea-rovers are assigned to this task, and that the deer

---

[1] Peter John had a stag for three years. It was perfectly tame and could be handled until the third year, when it became so dangerous to all persons that he was obliged to shoot it.

[2] It is a common theory that two-year-old stags cannot beget good stock. This is quite erroneous. A large percentage of calves of all deer are sired by these youngsters, and are as good and strong as those begot by adult animals.

will suffer in consequence. Their whole natures are different from those of the Lapps or the Indians, and they may neglect their charges for the excitement of the chase. But that the deer will thrive and breed if properly looked after there is not a shadow of doubt. In Alaska a similar experiment has met with great success, and all well-wishers of the poor Labrador "Liveres" will rejoice if this unselfish experiment on the part of Sir William MacGregor and Lord Strathcona turns out well, for it is as yet too soon to criticise it.[1]

In 1905 several moose were imported, but were in such an enfeebled state when they were turned out that it is doubtful if they survived, although various reports of their being seen at points so widely apart as Black River, the Upper Humber, and Bay of Islands, were current in 1906. It is a matter of the highest importance that more of these fine mammals should be introduced annually for a period of five or six years, and that their care should be entrusted to a competent keeper of wild animals both during transport and after arrival. Every one who is acquainted with the nature and habits of wild beasts is aware that during journeys by sea and train most large animals are terribly upset and will not feed, and that to turn them out in a new country immediately on arrival is generally fatal. A stockade of say two hundred yards square should be built somewhere near the railway on a good site, say in the woods on the Gander Lake, where the food of moose is abundant. There they should be tended by their keeper for two or three weeks, and fed with artificial food until they take to the natural

---

[1] As this work goes to press I am informed by Sir William MacGregor that "Dr. Grenfell has ordered three hundred reindeer, and that they will be kept for the first year at Anse Sablon." It is probable that these deer will be looked after by Lapps or Norwegians who have spent their lives amongst reindeer.

browsing and have partially recovered their condition. Then they could be liberated. All this would be rather more expensive, but the extra money would not be wasted, and I feel certain that if such methods were adopted moose would be a great success in Newfoundland from every point of view. They do no harm to timber trees, as they live principally on rowan and birch, and in summer on water-lily roots, so that the wood companies could have no objection to them. The few hundreds of pounds which the Government would have to spend would be worth thousands in years to come.

One important point in connection with the introduction of these animals is that it is necessary that all inhabitants of Newfoundland should know of the experiment, otherwise the animals are certain to be shot. I found in 1906 that the Indians knew nothing of the moose that had been imported, and if they had come across them the deer would have been killed. It is therefore necessary that the Government should inform the chief, Reuben Lewis, that they are anxious to establish the moose, and that the Indians must not touch them. In this case they would not be molested.

APPENDIX

SOME men will always be successful in a new country, whilst others will be unsuccessful. I have therefore never *advised* any man to go to Newfoundland in search of sport, nor do I do so now, unless he is personally known to me ; for there are a variety of reasons why certain people should not go where disappointment may await them.

In September heads are very difficult to obtain, and the hunter must go far afield and work hard for his game. Besides this, many who would like to visit the island are deterred by the fact that they will only be allowed to shoot three stags. In late October, however, it is not difficult to get three good specimens. Be that as it may, I am continually receiving letters from strangers who are anxious to hunt in Newfoundland, and so in self-defence I have appended the following list, which comprises the whole outfit and its cost for one sportsman for a month and ten days :—

Outfit for Forty Days' Travel

One waterproof sailor-bag, containing all personal necessaries, including fishing-tackle, cartridges, photographic materials, clothes, &c.

One reindeer sleeping-bag (can be obtained from Mr. Brandt, furrier, Bergen, Norway, for £2, 10s.) ; in this package place a light sou'wester.

Two rifles in waterproof covers, with cleaning rod.

One trout-rod and landing-net.

One 20-foot basswood canoe and paddles, which can be obtained from Mr. Blair, St. John's ; price, with landing dues, &c., £12.

(If a long trip is projected, an additional 16-foot canoe to carry extra provisions should be taken.)

Two guides, at 2 dollars a day each.

One box of provisions, which can be obtained from Mr. Blair, Water Street, St. John's, containing the following :—2 Premier axes, 1 hatchet, 6 fathoms cod line, 3 bottles rum, 1 bottle brandy, 1 large kettle, 2 small kettles, 1 steel frying-pan, 3 tin boxes for holding tea, sugar, &c., 2 pepper and salt tins, 2 lbs. powdered alum, 1 iron bake-pot, 20 lbs. bacon, 5 stone American flour, 7 lbs. tea, 2 dozen boxes matches, 20 lbs. best sugar, 3 lbs. candles, 2 lbs. baking-powder, 12 tins Swiss milk, 3 lb. tins of jam, 9 lbs. of best butter, 6 calico bags, 3 sets knives and forks, 3 teaspoons, 1 can-opener, 6 sail-needles, 1 ball twine, 6 cakes of soap, ¼ lb. pepper, 4 lbs. dried apples, 1 tin lard, 4 lbs. tobacco, 2 bags of hard bread, 1 bag onions, 3 cups and saucers. To this list may be added anything the traveller fancies.

Cost of whole outfit, including fares from England and return, about £100.

MICMAC INDIAN NAMES FOR ANIMALS, TREES, PLACES, &C.

Animals.

Bear . . .	Mouin.
Fox . . .	Wauk-wis.
Marten . .	A-bis-tan-ouch.
Ermine . .	Skource.
Otter . . .	Ku-nik.
Beaver . .	Cub-it.
Musk-rat . .	Kee-wa-su.
Lynx . . .	A-buk-sigan.
Wolf . . .	Pak-tissum.
Whales . .	Pudup.

Trees.

Birch . . .	Masqui.
Var . . .	Stogan.
Spruce . . .	Kowat.
Poplar . . .	Mid-di.
White Pine .	Ku-wow.
Rowan . . .	Sem-o-se.
Cherry . . .	Wig-was-mose.
Witch-hazel .	Nim-mogan.
Alder . . .	Tup-si.
Reindeer Moss .	Wab-im-whol.
Maldow . .	Hal-net
	(Old man's beard moss).

Birds.

White - headed Eagle . .	Kit-pu.
Osprey . .	Wisk-ma-guaso.
Horned Owl .	De-digle.
Jay . . .	Mik-ja-go-guch.
Woodpeckers (three-toed) .	A-bodich.
Greater Yellow-shanks . .	Geg-wig-a-dich.
Canada Goose .	Sinnunk.
Dusky Duck .	Hap-soi-smimuch.
Red - breasted Merganser .	To-makon-e.
Great Northern Diver . .	Quimuk.

Fish.

Ouananiche . .	Towanow.
Salmon . .	Plamu.
Trout . . .	Had-a-wasu.
Stickleback . .	Cum-gila-gwitch.
Herring . .	Halunch.
Cod . . .	Pa-chu.

Lakes, Rivers, &c.

Bay Despair	Lub-despe.
Long Pond	Waleje.
Soulis Ann Pond . . .	Souli-an-ek.
Brazil Pond . . .	Brazil-ek.
Little Burnt Pond . . .	Bad-e-wis-gek.
Round Pond . . .	Mem-kus-cowpe.
Pipestone Lake . . .	To-mag-on-apse-wagodie.
Sit Down Lake . . .	Eneuchabeech Cospen.
Gander River . . .	Ha-glacea-waag.
Millais's Lake . . .	Haliboo-waygodie.
St. John's Lake . . .	Sambadista.
Long Harbor River . .	Sibook.
Mount Sylvester . . .	Minacktu.
Bond's Lake . . .	N'Mooch-waygodie.
Prowse's Lake . . .	Podopsk.

SOME NEWFOUNDLAND COLLOQUIALISMS

The most of these are old English expressions of the days of the Tudors and the Stuarts. The local population came mainly from the west of England, Devon, and Somerset. Old colonial customs and words all had their origin in Devon, &c. All lakes are *ponds*, and grouse are *partridge*, simply because there were no lakes or grouse in Devon.

Breaching, fish rising on the top of the water.
Brews, a dish made of soaked biscuit, fish, &c.; very good mess (cp. Beaumont and Fletcher, "What an ocean of *brews* shall I swim in").
Cruising, paying visits. A lady sent her servant to a friend, asking her would she like to pay some calls with her in the afternoon. *Servant man*—"The Missus wants to know if you will go *cruising* with her this afternoon."
Curry, the fish offal.
Douse, to put out a light. ("Douse the glib," put out the lantern—Hamlet.)
Dout the fire, to put out (see Shakespeare).
Droke, a wooded narrow valley (probably same as the old English word *drock*).
Drung, a narrow lane.
Flankers, sparks from a wood fire coming out of the chimney.
Frore and *froke*, for frozen. ("The parching air burns frore"—Milton.)
Heft, to feel the weight of anything. *Heft it*, that is, see how heavy it is.
Linhay, a lean-to attached to the main building; pronounced by the natives *linney*. Well-known English word used in "Lorna Doone."
Logy, heavy, dull. Thus, a *logy* day.
Moidered, muddled, bothered. An old English expression.
Mouch, to play the truant from school.
Scat of snow, just a light fall.
"Scattered fish" means a small catch.
Seal: an old seal is a Doter; a two-year-old one, a Bedlamer.
Spurt, a run of fish.
Starrigans, small decayed sticks of trees; boughs of burnt fir-trees; a word of contempt. A mean building of the Reformed Church of England in one out-harbour was always known as the *Starrigan* Church.
Stog: to *stog* a house is to stuff moss, &c., between the posts.
Strouters, piling for a wharf.
Swoil is a seal. The seal fishery is always spoken of as the *Spring* of such a year.
Yaffle, an armful of fish.
Yary, pronounced *yarry*; means a careful, early-rising man. From the old English. (Shakespeare, "Twelfth Night"—"Be yare in thy preparations.")

THE GAME LAWS OF NEWFOUNDLAND

Provide that—

No person . . . shall pursue with intent to kill any caribou from the 1st day of February to the 31st day of July, or from the 1st day of October to the 20th October, in any year. And no person shall . . . kill or take more than two stag and one doe caribou in any one year.

No person is allowed to hunt or kill caribou within specified limits of either side of the railway track from Grand Lake to Goose Brook, these limits being defined by gazetted proclamation.

No non-resident may hunt or kill deer (three stag) without previously having purchased (50 dollars) and procured a licence therefor. Licences to non-resident guides are issued, costing 50 dollars.

No person may kill, or pursue with intent to kill, any caribou with dogs or with hatchet . . . or any weapon other than firearms loaded with ball or bullet, or while crossing any pond, stream, or water-course.

Tinning or canning of caribou is absolutely prohibited.

No person may purchase, or receive in barter or exchange, any flesh of caribou between 1st January and 31st July in any year.

Penalties for violation of these laws, a fine not exceeding 200 dollars, or, in default, imprisonment not exceeding two months.

No person shall hunt or kill partridges before the first day of October in any year. Penalty, not exceeding 100 dollars or imprisonment.

Any person who shall hunt beaver or export beaver skins before 1st October 1907 shall be liable to confiscation of skins and fine or imprisonment.

No person shall use any appliances other than rod, hook, and line to catch any salmon, trout, or inland-water fishes within fifty fathoms from either bank on the strand, sea, stream, pond, lake, or estuary debouching into the sea.

Close season for salmon- and trout-fishing, 15th day of September to 11th day of January following.

NEWFOUNDLAND CARIBOU.

Tarandus rangifer terrae-novae.

"Man'll goa fer swoile where gold won't drag 'un."

Newfoundland Proverb.

ROLLING FALLS.

IN THE PLACE WHERE NO MAN COMES.

DOG LAKE.

THE NEWFOUNDLAND WILLOW GROUSE.

Lagopus lagopus alleni.